THE LEGACY OF BRUCE YANDLE

ADVANCED STUDIES IN POLITICAL ECONOMY

Series Editors: Virgil Henry Storr and Stefanie Haeffele

The Advanced Studies in Political Economy series consists of republished as well as newly commissioned work that seeks to understand the underpinnings of a free society through the foundations of the Austrian, Virginia, and Bloomington schools of political economy. Through this series, the Mercatus Center at George Mason University aims to further the exploration of and discussion on the dynamics of social change by making this research available to students and scholars.

Nona Martin Storr, Emily Chamlee-Wright, and Virgil Henry Storr, *How We Came Back: Voices from Post-Katrina New Orleans*

Don Lavoie, *Rivalry and Central Planning: The Socialist Calculation Debate Reconsidered*

Don Lavoie, *National Economic Planning: What Is Left?*

Peter J. Boettke, Stefanie Haeffele, and Virgil Henry Storr, eds., *Mainline Economics: Six Nobel Lectures in the Tradition of Adam Smith*

Matthew D. Mitchell and Peter J. Boettke, *Applied Mainline Economics: Bridging the Gap between Theory and Public Policy*

Jack High, ed., *Humane Economics: Essays in Honor of Don Lavoie*

Edward Stringham, ed., *Anarchy, State and Public Choice*

Peter J. Boettke and David L. Prychitko, eds., *The Market Process: Essays in Contemporary Austrian Economics*

Richard E. Wagner, *To Promote the General Welfare: Market Processes vs. Political Transfers*

Ludwig M. Lachmann, *The Market as an Economic Process*

Donald J. Boudreaux and Roger Meiners, eds., *The Legacy of Bruce Yandle*

THE LEGACY OF BRUCE YANDLE

EDITED BY DONALD J. BOUDREAUX AND ROGER MEINERS

Arlington, Virginia

ABOUT THE MERCATUS CENTER AT GEORGE MASON UNIVERSITY

The Mercatus Center at George Mason University is the world's premier university source for market-oriented ideas—bridging the gap between academic ideas and real-world problems.

A university-based research center, the Mercatus Center advances knowledge about how markets work to improve people's lives, training graduate students, conducting research, and applying economics to offer solutions to society's most pressing problems.

Our mission is to generate knowledge and understanding of the institutions that affect the freedom to prosper, and to find sustainable solutions that overcome the barriers preventing individuals from living free, prosperous, and peaceful lives.

Founded in 1980, the Mercatus Center is located on George Mason University's Arlington and Fairfax campuses.

Printed in the United States of America.

The Mercatus Center at George Mason University
3434 Washington Blvd., 4th Floor
Arlington, Virginia 22201
www.mercatus.org
703-993-4930

This volume was made possible thanks to the generous support of the Searle Freedom Trust.

Cover design by Jessica Hogenson
Cover illustration by Travis Pietsch
Editing and composition by Westchester Publishing Services
Index by Harry David

ISBN 978-1-942951-90-2 (hardcover)
ISBN 978-1-942951-91-9 (paperback)
ISBN 978-1-942951-92-6 (e-book)

Library of Congress Cataloging-in-Publication Data are available for this publication.

CONTENTS

ABOUT BRUCE YANDLE

Bruce Yandle is a teacher, writer, speaker, and consultant on economics and political economy. He is Distinguished Adjunct Fellow at the Mercatus Center at George Mason University where he releases a quarterly report, "The Economic Situation"; frequently briefs Capitol Hill policymakers on economic issues; and lectures regularly in Mercatus programs for House and Senate staffers.

Yandle is cofounder of the Clemson Institute for the Study of Capitalism, dean emeritus of Clemson University's College of Business, and Alumni Distinguished Professor Emeritus in the Department of Economics at Clemson University. While at Clemson, Yandle served as the dean of the College of Business from 2004 to 2007 and taught in graduate programs in France, Italy, Germany, and the Czech Republic. He is also Senior Fellow Emeritus at the Property & Environment Research Center (PERC).

Yandle served in the federal government on two occasions, first as a senior economist on the president's Council on Wage and Price Stability during the Ford administration and later as executive director of the Federal Trade Commission during the Reagan administration. He was a member and chairman of the South Carolina State Board of Economic Advisors, member and chairman of the Spartanburg Methodist College board of trustees, and member of the board of trustees of the Foundation of Economic Education. Before entering an academic career, Yandle was in the industrial machinery business for 15 years.

He has authored or edited 17 books, including *Bootleggers & Baptists: How Economics Forces and Moral Persuasion Interact to Shape Regulatory Politics*, coauthored with economist Adam Smith and published by the Cato Institute in 2014. In 2012, he received the Adam Smith Award from the Association of Private Enterprise Education for his career-long leadership in promoting the free market economy.

PROFESSOR BRUCE YANDLE, A TRIBUTE

RICHARD B. McKENZIE

Many people are treated to "celebrations of life," but only after they can no longer enjoy the reflections on their marks in the world, the levity of the festivities, and the warmth and good feelings of those whose lives have been impacted. Those who gathered at the Festschrift symposium did so to make sure that the celebrated hears and *feels* what we have to say both about his scholarship and his life in our midst.

And what a life of distinguished scholarship and great comradery it has been for Professor Bruce Yandle—and for those of us who can now pass on our abiding respect, affection, and immense admiration to a younger generation of economists, several of whom joined us in the celebration.

Professor Yandle, I speak for everyone who attended the celebration, and for your many former students and colleagues who have scattered to all points in academe and beyond, to thank you for the careers and lives we have had because of the life you have led as a scholar, teacher, and friend over these many years. Personally, I *know* deep down that my career and life would have been diminished had I not passed through yours. All here at this Festschrift event would likely say the same.

Professor Yandle, in this setting among friends in your eighty-fifth year, I hope you will politely accede to my calling you "Bruce." That is how we all have come to know you, despite the reference of the event that would have us think of you on a pedestal above, our esteemed "professor," even when we have remained disguised as colleagues.

Everyone here knows at least a portion of Bruce's scholarly work, especially his articles in regulatory economics, but mainly those on "Bootlegger and Baptist coalitions," which economists now agree helped animate George Stigler's work on regulatory markets directed by the intense supply and demand forces of

Richard McKenzie is indebted to Karen McKenzie, Roger Meiners, Dwight Lee, and Donald Boudreaux for editorial improvements.

politics. We heard much about bootleggers and Baptists during the short conference that is reported in this volume of Festschrift papers, but our discussions were always bounded, undergirded, and guided by a central attribute of Bruce that has been far more powerful for those of us who have known him—his *character*, which enveloped him as he walked with us through our halls of ivy.

Few of our colleagues ever considered character to have third-party effects, but those who attended the Festschrift symposium beg to differ and to insist that we felt the surrounding glow, the warmth, and the goodness that can, and has, radiated from Bruce's presence when he has been among us. As Terry Anderson, an environmental economist and Bruce's colleague at a distance, noted during a session, seconding the comments of others, "When Bruce speaks, people listen because he is a good person."

What is so remarkable about Bruce is that he steadfastly built his scholarly career organized around people's self-interested motives and, at the same time, has never strayed in his collegial life from acting on anything other than the good of the whole. Bruce has an abiding concern for the policies that are likely to emerge from interactive politics, but no one thinks of Bruce as being political in his dealings with others, even in highly politicized and sometimes politically brutal academic settings.

Henry Kissinger is renowned for having observed that "University politics are so vicious precisely because the stakes are so small." Bruce steadfastly avoided the fray because he understood what many do not: the stakes for our students are too high.

We joined to celebrate Bruce's charity, mainly his willingness to talk at length with us and to read our papers with a single focus, that of helping us without delay to improve them and, by extension, our careers. In following his calling to be a *colleague* in the best sense of that word, we learned and prospered. I am confident that the attendees at this event have thought at some point, "By the grace of Bruce, I have been able to do what I have."

Roger Meiners, one of Bruce's many long-term colleagues and coauthors, poignantly noted that:

> Everyone knows Bruce is kind, but he is also the adult in the room called upon when there are problems. He is the person you know you could trust for sound advice and assistance. When our dear colleague at Clemson, Bob Staaf, died unexpectedly of a heart attack, Bruce was the one who stepped in to guide the suffering family in dealing

> with the funeral and the many other problems that arise in such situations. Bruce is a self-interested economist, who believes people are self-interested, but the most unselfish person I know in giving to others.

No one will ever accuse Bruce of having shaded the truth or gone back on his word. Instead, we have always been able to count on his word, as well as his support. He has helped us all be better economists and people. In that regard, he has been underpaid by the amount that we have been overpaid for his work with us, and we know we have benefited in other ways from his generosity of time and good humor.

With Bruce's close-up demonstration of how to live and treat others, might we economists have exaggerated the importance of self-interest, with some denying other motivations? After all, Adam Smith believed that people were driven by a constellation of interests, not the least of which were "beneficence," "pity," "compassion," "pride," and "vanity."[1] He seemed to have anticipated the late nineteenth-century economist Alfred Marshall's point that the drive of self-interest was primarily dominant in commercial affairs. Smith seemed also to have been trying to make the point that even under what many might consider the worst of conditions in people's market affairs—when people are driven exclusively by their narrow self-interest—societal gains could be expected from the free flow of trade.

Perhaps economists today could learn not only from Bruce's way of living economics, but also from Philip Wicksteed, who, in his *Common Sense of Political Economy*, a widely read text in the early 20th century, made an obvious point now long lost to the dictates of modern economic modeling: markets are agnostic toward buyers' and sellers' motivations. Markets do not care whether buyers in the market seek to buy sweaters for themselves or to pass them out to the homeless on the back streets of cities. Neither does it matter if people produce electric cars to make a profit or to save the planet. Variously held values can be accommodated within market supply-and-demand forces without discrimination.[2] However, as Bruce has shown, non-self-interest motives can be crucially important in nonmarket settings, such as university departments.

Adam Smith (the original, not the grandson—sorry Adam!) wrote eloquently about people having imagined "Impartial Spectators," who, as I read Smith, found perches on their shoulders and to whom ordinary and exalted people alike deferred on the multitude of daily matters of right and wrong. Few understand that Smith based his free-market arguments in *The Wealth of Nations* on the presumption that, as covered in his earlier treatise *The Theory of Moral Sentiments*, most people's Impartial Spectators are on sentry duty for much of their daily lives. That has to be. Without the Impartial Spectators (or without people's personal behaviors being constrained and guided by principles other than those economic principles we teach our students), it is hard to believe that Smith could have thought that markets could work as well as he argued. Only belatedly have economists recognized the critical role of trust, and other large and small virtues, in the smooth functioning of the institutional settings we study. Those virtues are the "dark energy" of cohesive and synergetic groups and successful economies, as neuroeconomist Paul Zak and others have demonstrated and as Bruce has shown.[3]

Many of us have had the good fortune of having had Bruce perched on our shoulders, always available for the imagined question, "What would Bruce do?"

At Clemson University, when I was there starting in 1977, we all walked taller and with longer strides, feigning more confidence than our age and experience warranted—because Bruce *showed* us an academic life to emulate. You cannot teach what Bruce has taught us, and I am at a loss for words to explain what I mean to the few of you who did not walk with him daily. I do not need to explain myself to those who were there. Simply put, he was a force among us.

Dwight Lee found the words I have been struggling to convey, first by characterizing Bruce as "Mister Rogers for adults" and then adding:

> I never benefited from taking one of Bruce's classes, but I have been fortunate over the years to have experienced his ability to communicate ideas in a way that captivates both the head and heart. I vividly remember one example. It was at a Liberty Fund conference at least 20 years ago in Jackson Hole, Wyoming, and the general topic was creativity and entrepreneurship. Bruce brought up the example of Alexander Graham Bell and the telephone in a way that left an imprint on my memory and emotions that will last as long as I do. Simply stated, Bruce said that Bell was motivated to improve his understanding of how sound was transmitted because he wanted to develop a more effective hearing aid for the sake of his mother, who was deaf. But what I just wrote lacks Bruce's words, his voice, his inflections, and his pleasing presence. I should point out that

> my response was not because Bruce made me think of my hearing difficulty, which was not very noticeable at the time. It was because he made me think of Bell's achievement in terms of how much I loved my mother. What most of Bruce's students and friends have learned from him is surely the result of the mysterious and wonderful way his narratives stir them both intellectually and emotionally.

I still remember fondly my early years at Clemson, from the late 1970s to the mid-1980s, for the unexpected treats they provided. By "treats" I mean the midmorning coffees at the Canteen in the student center and the combative but wonderful discussions we had practically every morning over the policy mistakes of the day coming out of Washington, all led and guided by Bruce—and, I must add, the venerable Hugh Macaulay. Some might see coffee breaks as downtime. Most of us there saw them as our most productive hour of the day.

Anyone in Sirrine Hall can remember how most mornings, at 10:00 A.M. sharp, Hugh would come clanking with a limp down the hall (Hugh had been shot in the butt during World War II, which required him to walk with a full-length leg brace for the rest of his life). He would tap on people's doors as he walked, saying, "Want to have coffee?" We would fall in and immediately be challenged by Hugh as we walked the 200 yards to the Canteen over whatever crazy thing the government had done in economic policy the day before. A debate inevitably flared as we walked, with Hugh always insisting that any anti-market argument had to be wrong on the face of it. Markets were, and had to be, efficient; Hugh would insist: "Give me an objection!"

On arriving at the Canteen, we surrounded two or three tables pulled together to continue the discussion, with our comments becoming ever more energized. Bruce would settle in, pipe in hand, obviously contemplating the best time to interject a studied point. What is remarkable is how often our debates, peppered with hearty laughter, became so intense that nearby students would move to distant tables, or the manager would come over and say with a grin something to the effect of "I have heard what you have been saying, and you really should consider the third-party effects you are imposing on others. If not, I will impose a tax on your use of these tables. So there!" We quieted down, but only temporarily.

Those conversations were extraordinarily productive for me—and, I am sure, for so many of you—because they were so civil, conducted in good humor and good spirits, frequently ending with one of Bruce's chin-to-Adam's-apple drawn-out deep laughs.

Throughout, Bruce set the tone. I have never been in another setting with colleagues who wanted so badly to combine the impulse to win arguments with the desire to hear a new counterintuitive twist on an old argument. Because of those coffees, all of us reached higher in our careers than we otherwise could have. We could venture putting forth new—often crazy—thoughts that in a less congenial environment we would have held in reserve.

"Bootleggers and Baptists" had to be one of those crazy thoughts that were entertained at more than one coffee and then chewed on by all. I say that only because when I went back to read Bruce's original article on the topic, I felt short-changed, surprised at his making only a passing reference to its history and meaning. I thought the details of the original coalition would have been fleshed out. I must have absorbed the details from those coffee discussions. I knew what was left unsaid in Bruce's article, and felt privileged that I was there at its inception, but I have also felt a compulsion to ask what so many asked at those coffees. "What is wrong with this argument? It's too neat and settled."

Nevertheless, the Bootlegger-and-Baptist expression is pregnant with an important insight: the regulatory process is fraught with odd bedfellows, some with diametrically opposite political and economic objectives. Few economists have been able to have their names tied to such a notable theoretical construct as solidly as Bruce has.

In his original treatment of bootleggers and Baptists, Bruce drew on discussions from his youth spent in Georgia, where people commonly talked about how the bootleggers in the woods of Georgia would support the Baptist churches' campaigns to restrict legal alcohol sales, at least on Sundays, if not to make their counties "dry" altogether. On returning from the Festschrift symposium, I learned again the wisdom of another of Bruce comments: "Bootleggers and Baptists are like termites. They come out of the woodwork everywhere."

The New York Times recently reported that this year New Zealand celebrates the centennial of women getting the right to vote, in spite of opposition from the country's alcohol industry. Apparently, the men of the country had a serious problem with alcoholism, which was making family life difficult. The alcohol industry opposed giving women the vote for fear that they would pursue restrictions on alcohol sales in the name of improving the lives of women and children. The US alcohol industry was similarly opposed to women's suffrage, especially since Susan B. Anthony, the leader of the suffrage movement, had previously been an organizer for Daughters for Temperance.[4]

I have never felt more pride in my academic career than I felt at a coffee in 1979. In those salad days, I had begun to doubt the wisdom of the traditional case against hiking the minimum wage, which was then, as it remains today, a litmus test for market economists. "Thou shalt believe conventional minimum-wage wisdom: minimum wage hikes are bad. End of story," Hugh would insist in one way or another.

At the time, the accumulating empirical work showed that minimum wage hikes had precious little to almost no negative effect on employment opportunities, even among the most vulnerable worker group, teenagers (often significantly less than 1 percent of covered jobs for a 10 percent wage hike). The debate, to me, seemed to be much ado about nothing. But why?

The traditional dismissal of the data amounted to nothing short of a restatement of the findings: "The demand for menial labor is inelastic." That did not make sense. There are plenty of substitutes for menial jobs. So I proposed an alternative argument, that employers could largely offset the labor-cost effects of minimum wage hikes by cuts in fringe benefits and increases in work demands. I then only intuitively understood what I was saying, which is to say, I had no convincing model.

Hugh went ballistic, in his inimitable way. "That can't be! Have you lost your mind?" I had to believe that minimum wages were bad. Others joined Hugh. "Heresy!" My seat at the table was put in doubt. By way of contrast, Bruce drew back, took puffs on his pipe, and gave a number of objections, but he said what he often said to me as we left: "I think you could be on to something, Richard. Work on it," his way of adding a pat on the back for someone under collegial siege.

I returned to the subject daily, and each time I was trashed, humbled. I was wrong—no, dead wrong! After six weeks, I came back with a graphical model that laid out my points. I showed it to each person around the table. Employers could offset a wage hike of $1 with, say, $0.90 in costs from fewer fringes, which had to be worth more than the $1 money-wage hike to the affected workers (or else they would not be provided in the first place). Those covered workers who kept their jobs were worse off than without the money-wage increase and were even likely worse off than workers who left the covered market for better employment venues. Economists had long understated how many workers were harmed by narrowly focusing on the count of jobs lost (a conclusion that resurrected my credibility with Hugh!).[5] The model was conclusive! They agreed. Hooray!

After being humbled for so long, I could not resist going around the table, asking each person there, "Do you agree I'm right? Do you agree?" . . . and so on. I have never felt more triumphant in my career. I got Hugh to bend. I got a thumbs up from Bruce. The feeling has never been duplicated. Even though the predicted effects have been confirmed by at least a dozen empirical studies over the intervening years, people still miss the lesson, maybe because there are too damn many bootleggers and Baptists on both sides of the perennial minimum wage debate!

But everyone there has a similar tale to tell to this day, that of having a triumphant moment in a search for improvement in argument. Those were the days when we all pushed each other to go beyond what we could imagine we were capable of reaching.

I have had the good fortune of having sat before the throne of academic greatness. First, at Virginia Tech, when James Buchanan and Gordon Tullock were holding court. Second, when I happened to fall within the orbit of Bruce and Hugh at Clemson. Hugh was important for reasons that most people who have known him understand—his dogged conviction that markets were (almost) always right. Doggedness is underappreciated. But Bruce filled an equally important role, that of the reserved sage who held back and seemed to question, by how he drew puffs on his pipe, the claims being made. I felt proud when Bruce would concede, "Richard, that's a good point, *but*. . . ." I cherished his reviews of my papers, which he returned, in the predawn of the high-tech era, before, seemingly, the next sunrise.

Several years ago, I returned to Clemson for a visit. I took the opportunity to sit with Bruce on his second-floor front porch, where he and Dot now live by the train track that runs through town. I began by lamenting how I had never recovered in the universities where I have landed the good spirit and camaraderie of those Canteen coffees. I gave up on developing coffee groups in the last years of my academic career position (even though I provided the coffee). Few colleagues saw coffee breaks as productive, and in the few times I joined colleagues from the several disciplines in my business school, the topics discussed were often not interesting to me or the discussion didn't measure up to the vibrancy of those at the Canteen. However, I must share some of the blame. As so many professors did in the 1990s, I progressively sought to substitute bidirectional email exchanges for multidirectional personal interactions, not fully realizing that in the former, only kilobytes of information were exchanged. In the latter, terabytes were involved, given that all senses were tapped.

I expressed to Bruce some distress about what we—Bruce and I—had lost in academia over the intervening forty years. I lamented with Bruce, "Young economists don't know what they are missing." I saw the glass as half empty. In his fatherly way, Bruce reminded me that there was always another perspective. I remember his wise counsel to this day: "Richard, you know, what we have to remember is that we *had it*. It's not so much what they are missing, but what has been our good fortune. We are fortunate to know what so many others have missed. But maybe they are finding what we had in other ways."

NOTES

1. On non-self-interest motives, Smith observed:

> How selfish soever man may be supposed, there are evidently some principles in his nature, which interest him in the fortune of others, and render their happiness necessary to him, though he derives nothing from it except the pleasure of seeing it. Of this kind is pity or compassion, the emotion which we feel for the misery of others, when we either see it, or are made to conceive it in a very lively manner. That we often derive sorrow from the sorrow of others, is a matter of fact too obvious to require any instances to prove it; for this sentiment, like all the other original passions of human nature, is by no means confined to the virtuous and humane, though they perhaps may feel it with the most exquisite sensibility. The greatest ruffian, the most hardened violator of the laws of society, is not altogether without it. (1982, I.I.1)

See also Smith ([1759] 1982, I.I.14).

2. Wicksteed stressed early in his book,

> Economic *relations* constitute a complex machine by which we seek to accomplish our purposes, whatever they may be. They do not in any direct or conclusive sense either dictate our *purposes* or supply our *motives*. We shall therefore have to consider what constitutes an economic relation rather than what constitutes an economic motive. And this does away at a stroke with the hypothetically simplified psychology of the Economic Man which figured so largely in the older books of Political Economy, and which recent writers take so much trouble to evade or qualify. We are not to begin by imagining man to be actuated by only a few simple motives, but we are to take him as we find him, and are to examine the nature of those relations into which he enters, under the stress of all his complicated impulses and desires—whether *selfish* or *unselfish*, material or spiritual,—in order to accomplish indirectly through the action of others what he cannot accomplish directly through his own. (Wicksteed 1910, 4)

See also Wicksteed (1910, 171).

3. See Zak (2012) and Zak and Knack (2001).
4. See Perry (2018) and Weiss (2018).
5. Economist Walter Wessels at North Carolina State University had independently developed the themes in my argument during the same period, but he was first to publication. Wessels's first article on the negative effects of minimum wage hikes on fringe benefits was published in April 1980 and mine in June 1980. I have revised and extended my arguments, with citations to the empirical work, in my textbook with Dwight Lee, *Microeconomics for MBAs* (2017, chap. 4).

REFERENCES

McKenzie, R. B. 1980. "The Labor Market Effects of Minimum Wage Laws: A New Perspective." *Journal of Labor Research* 1, no. 2: 255–64.

McKenzie, R. B., and D. R. Lee. 2017. *Microeconomics for MBAs: The Economic Way of Thinking for Managers*, 3rd ed. Cambridge: Cambridge University Press.

Perry, N. 2018. "New Zealand Celebrates 125 Years of Women Having the Right to Vote." Associated Press, September 19. https://apnews.com/437161a5587c416e8a8f03ec67a5e872/New-Zealand-celebrates-125-years-of-women-having-the-vote.

Smith, A. [1759] 1982. *The Theory of Moral Sentiments*. Indianapolis, IN: Liberty Fund.

Weiss, E. 2018. "Women, Booze and the Vote." *New York Times*, March 5. https://www.nytimes.com/2018/03/05/opinion/women-votes-feminism-alcohol.html.

Wessels, W. J. 1980. "The Effect of Minimum Wages in the Presence of Fringe Benefits: An Expanded Model." *Economic Inquiry* 18, no. 2: 293–313.

Wicksteed, P. H. 1910. *The Commonsense of Political Economy, Including a Study of the Human Basis of Economic Law*. London: Macmillan.

Zak, P. 2012. *The Moral Molecule: The Source of Love and Prosperity*. Boston: Dutton.

Zak, P., and S. Knack. 2001. "Trust and Growth." *Economic Journal* 111, no. 470: 295–321.

Introduction

DONALD J. BOUDREAUX AND ROGER MEINERS

Bruce Yandle worked in industry when he decided to change careers and earn a PhD. He became a professor of economics at Clemson University in the 1960s and was based there for his career, helping the department and business school rise in stature. He took leaves from Clemson to be a staff economist on the president's Council on Wage and Price Stability in the 1970s and to be executive director of the Federal Trade Commission in the 1980s.

His experience in industry, academia, and government brought him to realize that much of what we observe in policy making is complex. It is not just the result of high-minded reformers seeking to do good, or just the pernicious influence of those seeking to exploit the power of government (that is, the special interests at work at all levels of government). Rather, he realized, we see an odd, often unintentional, combination of the two. In the early 1980s, he named his new theory of regulation "Bootleggers and Baptists"—the joining of seemingly opposing forces who support similar government policies. Most academics would have used a more ponderous name for the concept, such as Diverse Asymmetrical Forces Achieving Equilibrium in the Policy Spectrum, but Yandle knew that important ideas can be communicated to broader audiences without needless academic puffery, and that doing so would help spread knowledge.

Over the years Yandle served many roles. He authored dozens of journal articles, reports, editorials, and books. He served as dean of Clemson's business school and took concrete steps to have students play a meaningful and constructive role in raising the quality of the school. Besides his service in Washington, DC, he had long affiliations with other organizations, including the Mercatus Center at George Mason University, where he contributes scholarly research and is a frequent speaker at programs for congressional staffers and others. His talks are always well crafted and his voice a well-modulated southern drawl, capturing the attention and curiosity of his audience.

Yandle's work focuses on regulation, especially environmental regulation, but he wrote about macroeconomic policy and other topics as well, gracing many coauthors with his guidance and collaboration. In the academic and policy world, however, his singular most important work is the Bootleggers and Baptists theory, which, according to Google Scholar, has been referenced more than 5,000 times.

All academics want their ideas to have impact. Yandle is one of the rare individuals who has achieved recognition and success but is not afflicted by the gravity of his academic "greatness." He is a truly gentle and gracious, but purposeful man.

In honor of Bruce Yandle's 85th birthday in 2018, a gathering of colleagues and students convened for a Festschrift symposium to honor his productive career and to advance research inspired by his work. The original essays and reflections in this volume, drafted for and discussed at the symposium, pay tribute to Bruce Yandle, a scholar of unusual ability as a teacher and researcher.

OVERVIEW OF THE VOLUME

Peter J. Boettke and J. R. Clark explain, in chapter 1, that Bruce Yandle's Bootleggers and Baptists insight helps eliminate a tension between pure interest-group theories of government regulation and theories that propound that government policies are steered by ideology. Yandle's unique manner of connecting the role of self-interest with that of ideology and ideas saves analysts from having to make an either-or choice between one or the other as the principal driver of government regulation. The result is a richer and more realistic understanding of regulation.

Much of Bruce Yandle's work is on environmental economics and policy. The standard approach of many environmental economists is to declare anything someone does not like to be an externality that requires statutory or regulatory intervention. Typically, a tax on the offending activity is called for, as we have seen for some years now with respect to carbon emissions, or emission caps, perhaps employing a trading scheme involving the limited emissions that will be recommended. In all such instances the presumption is that economists can divine the "correct" tax or emission cap so as to enhance economic efficiency through central planning. Yandle always searched for market mechanisms to resolve problems rather than assuming that economists could know what was best.

In chapter 2, Donald J. Boudreaux and Roger Meiners, both former colleagues of Yandle at Clemson, cite Yandle for calling into question the efficacy of standard externality analysis. They build on that to detail the history of the evolution of externality in economics. That primarily leads to A. C. Pigou, who advocated regulatory solutions for things he decried as ills in the market. They review the scholarly literature on externality theory in detail and show that by 1970, James M. Buchanan and others had shown, in terms of pure economic theory, that there was little to justify externality as an analytic concept.

Economists and others do not want to abandon the convenient straw man. They plow ahead, seeing externalities under every rock and asserting that highly skilled analysts can guide society to higher levels of wealth and quality of life as they search for "bliss points" through regulations. Boudreaux and Meiners work through numerous scenarios of situations in which people face real costs due to situations they do not like and show the concept of externality to be empty, with few trivial exceptions.

In chapter 3, Terry L. Anderson, a longtime colleague of Yandle at the Property and Environment Research Center (PERC) in Montana, continues the tradition of Yandle in searching for market resolution of alleged externalities that should be controlled by planners. Anderson takes on the poster-boy environmental villain in wealthy nations—carbon emissions. Anderson, like Yandle, explains that property rights are at the core of analyzing the impact of something such as carbon emissions. Even if we accept the assertion that emissions cause climate change, there is little reason to think public policy will resolve the matter.

Like Yandle, Anderson returns to Ronald Coase for insights about the reciprocal nature of costs and the ability of markets to internalize changes in values and circumstances that require adjustments. Anderson explains the fallacy of "the balance of nature" that is often at the core of discussions of carbon and other matters—any deviation from today is environmentally destructive and must be prevented. But nature has never been "in balance," as it is dynamic, like markets. Even Pigou recognized that a problem with asking for the state to provide solutions to problems is that special interests will intervene to distort policies (subsidized Teslas, anyone?). Anderson traces the current discussions about taxes and caps on emissions and explains how voluntary adaptation to change over time will be more economically beneficial. Regardless of the source of changes in conditions, humans are amazingly entrepreneurial in responding to evolving circumstances. Tomorrow will not, and should not, look like today.

In chapter 4, Todd J. Zywicki, once a student of Yandle's at Clemson, notes how Yandle in his lectures and writing, whether for students, members of the professoriate, or the public, consistently converses in appealing terms. Yandle weaves parables and narratives into economic stories, making analysis more accessible. He understands that few people comprehend fancy math or graphs that economists are wont to employ to dazzle the public with their genius. And, unlike most economists who would disdain the notion, Yandle knows that people are attracted by arguments that are, at base, moral. People should be appealed to in terms they can comprehend, so they can absorb the lesson. That unusual ability to converse affected Zywicki and many other students and colleagues of Bruce Yandle.

Zywicki's paper builds on Yandle's comprehension of people's vision of the world. That was best explained by Thomas Sowell in his book *A Conflict of Visions*. It undergirds arguments that we fancy to be based only on high economic analysis. Zywicki explains how Yandle employs the constrained vision of human behavior. It recognizes that self-interest at all levels affects not just private ordering but public policy decisions. Presumptions that unbiased scientific prescriptions can or will be employed to resolve public policy issues are based on an unsound understanding of human nature and policy making. Zywicki takes the analysis further by noting its relationship to work that emerges from psychology about underlying personality typing that affects all of us in how we view the world. He cites evidence that those who think scientific planning can solve social ills may be rooted in personality biases that direct one's vision of how the world works.

In chapter 5, Randy T. Simmons, a longtime colleague of Yandle at PERC, despite being a political scientist, explains that one of Yandle's papers helped him understand Ronald Coase's work on what is commonly called externalities, a term Coase avoided. Simmons applies that to the case of water, a scarce commodity in his home state of Utah and the rest of the West.

Whereas the eastern states, with generally plentiful water, used the common-law doctrine of riparian water rights, western states adopted the prior appropriation doctrine, which provides strong property rights to water. Mormon pioneers in Utah, some of the first settlers in the West, adopted that rule. Simmons explains how strong rules of property, under which trade can occur, encouraged investments in canals and other capital-intensive developments that encouraged trading in water to allow homesteaders' agriculture to flourish. While water is often considered to be a public good where it is common, in the West, where it is precious, parties freely devised efficient, voluntary devices, such as irrigation districts, to protect water for beneficial uses with little need for formal government interference.

While about half the papers in the volume apply Bruce Yandle's work related to environmental issues, focusing on property rights and the evolution of market mechanisms to resolve conflicts in that sensitive area, the remaining papers extend Yandle's work to other areas of policy analysis. Much of this relates to his most famous notion of bootleggers and Baptists—which now provides us much of the backbone for the political economy analysis of the regulatory process.

A former student of Yandle's, Sean E. Mulholland, explains, in chapter 6, the long regulatory history of something we have all noted in the past decade—the little light on the dashboard that indicates low tire pressure in at least one tire. Like many things we now take for granted, that device has a regulatory history that involves its own Baptists and bootleggers.

Worry about the consequences of improperly inflated tires goes back at least a half century, to when Ralph Nader wrote about the evils of the Chevrolet Corvair. Improper tire inflation on that vehicle exacerbated instability when cornering, especially at higher speed. Nader pressed for adoption of tire pressure monitoring systems (TPMS) decades before they were required. Nader was the leading Baptist in this episode, although his religion encompassed many other concerns, including nuclear reactors.

The bootleggers are those who see opportunity in demands for regulatory controls. By the late 1970s, the Society of Automotive Engineers, those who make their fortune by devising equipment for vehicles, noted that low-pressure warning devices were possibilities. Reliable tire pressure devices came to be available on the market for voluntary buyers, but the makers of such devices would have much larger sales if they were mandatory. Mulholland relates the history of the evolution of TPMS and the federal regulatory requirement that they be standard equipment via the TREAD Act of 2000. He then explains the cost of the mandatory TPMS. They impose a multibillion dollar a year expense and may have negative safety consequences. And, the costs of such safety requirements are born disproportionally by low-income earners.

Chapter 7 comes from one who has sat at the top of the federal regulatory pyramid. Susan E. Dudley, after time at the Environmental Protection Agency, served as director of the Office of Information and Regulatory Affairs (OIRA). She explains that her admiration for Yandle goes back to when he first espoused the Bootleggers and Baptists theory. Dudley explains that it was an important addition to George Stigler's earlier economic theory of regulation. Like Yandle, who served in the bureaucracy twice, going to Washington, DC, opened her eyes to the gritty reality of the regulatory process as she saw firsthand the environmental Baptists working to further the financial interests of certain industrial interests. The stakes are huge. In Dudley's time at OIRA, more than 60 proposed regulations annually were estimated to have costs exceeding more than $100 million a year.

Dudley relates examples of Baptists and bootleggers at work. Zealots opposed to the marketing of genetically engineered animals worked to further the interests of some firms producing such products because the stringent regulatory standard proposed would increase the difficulty for new competitors to enter the market. Similarly, tobacco companies, much despised by assorted health Baptists, work to limit entrance of new competitors into the tobacco market by supporting stringent regulatory standards. While costly new regulations increased in the Obama years, the Trump administration has seen a dramatic decline in the promulgation (a favorite word of the regulators) of such costly new regulations, which Dudley reviews.

Former Yandle student and longtime coauthor Jody W. Lipford, in chapter 8, contributes to the research on the widespread cost of regulations. Like most economists, Yandle expresses concerns about regulations that deliver more costs than benefits. In a world of special interests, where Baptists care little about the costs imposed by regulations and bootleggers welcome such costs, it is no surprise that many regulations are, in net, costly to society and a burden on the economy.

Lipford looks at the hypothesis that regulation increases income inequality. He finds empirical support for that notion. It should not be a surprise; well-heeled, organized special interests will normally triumph in Washington. They seek rules that help to feather their nests and limit competition from would-be entrepreneurs who divine new, better, and often less costly ways to deliver goods and services. Rising income inequality does not come about from "unfair" capitalism per se, but from vested interests that encourage legislators to rig the game in favor of established interests. Among the key culprits are financial regulations, occupational regulations, and land use rules. The regulatory regimes in all instances, whether federal, state, or local, are purported to protect the public against bad things, but the consequence is to protect established parties in industries, occupations, and homes.

A longtime coauthor with Bruce Yandle is Andrew P. Morriss. In chapter 9, concerning bootleggers and Baptists, Morriss recounts their work on tobacco regulation, in which the industry fared very well financially from the anti-smokers' assault on that industry. Similarly, later work on e-cigarette regulations sees the same anti-smoking crusaders helping to produce regulations that further the financial interests of the tobacco industry they presumably loathe. These are not explicit, happy alliances; the Baptists truly dislike the bootleggers, but they inadvertently help produce regulations that redound to their benefit.

Morriss also references some of their joint work on regulation of diesel engines. From the early days of automobile exhaust regulation, much desired by environmental Baptists, the industry worked to slant regulations in favor of established interests. Later regulations imposed on large diesel engine makers favored special interests and retarded innovation, the standard result of regulations often hailed by Baptists. Part of driving support for regulation is successful control of the language used. Morriss and Yandle added the word televangelist to the influence groups that may help drive public support for new regulation—those skilled at spreading a message of goodness to cloak reality. Complex rules, not well understood by the public, or even by the Baptists, are hailed as bringing new, virtuous controls on polluting actors.

Chapter 10, also on bootleggers and Baptists, comes from Yandle's grandson and coauthor, the economist Adam C. Smith. The chapter extends the model to what is popularly called Obamacare, the Affordable Care Act. That massive piece of legislation was partly the result of a large Baptist effort over many years to fulfill the desire that affordable medical care be made available to more people. Seeing the political engine moving rapidly down the track controlled by a one-party Congress under President Obama, industry forces jumped in to help craft the resulting legislation. Smith documents how, as is often the case in major regulation, there are economic winners and losers. Major hospital chains or networks emerge as the winners as firms in the industry struggle to make the best of what industry members understand to be an ever more politicized market.

In chapter 11, a longtime friend of Bruce Yandle, Dwight R. Lee, extends the Bootleggers and Baptists theory to a novel area, corporate social responsibility (CSR). Lee notes that a half century ago Milton Friedman received notoriety for his position that leadership of publicly held firms had an obligation to shareholders to maximize the value of the firm over time. It was not their duty, or even desirable, that they distribute company funds for assorted social purposes. Executives and shareholders may donate their personal earnings as they wish to favored projects, but the business of business is business. At times firms have to pay homage to certain activities as part of doing business, but corporate funds should be extended no further than necessary to assorted activities that fall under the umbrella of CSR.

Lee explains that corporations receive far more in welfare from governments than they distribute in CSR donations. Executives have learned that playing the political game is often necessary and profitable. It becomes part of their self-interest to engage in CSR activities that are hailed as virtuous. It helps to provide cover for firms that also engage in lobbying activity to receive benefits via legislation and regulation. The costs of the benefits received by the firms are widespread, the benefits are concentrated—including benefits to the shareholders of the firms who share in the largesse. Lee notes that firms ranging from ADM to Enron and organizations such as the NFL have been highly regarded for their generous contributions to assorted social activities.

Economists may fail to understand this to be a rational policy to bring various Baptists to view the firm as a wonderful entity deserving of special public treatment. However, just as the relationship between Baptists and bootleggers is often subtle and uncoordinated in the legislative process, so may it be in the case of what are classified as CSR expenditures.

Finally, we asked Bruce Yandle to wrap up the volume by including his reflections about the changes in the economics profession he has observed over many years. In chapter 12, he explains what economic education was like when he started in the early 1950s. Then he notes some of the big divisions that have existed over time—some extant, others extinct. He places his work, modestly, within the large movements in the economics discipline. Those who know Bruce understand that he is exceptionally tolerant of other views, not dismissing them out of hand. It is one reason his work affected many—we are less likely to dismiss the work of others if we respect them personally.

These chapters illustrate the impact Yandle had on students, colleagues, and professional acquaintances, as their analysis of the political economy we live in was much affected. Few men affect so many as positively as has Bruce Yandle. We and many others honor him.

CHAPTER 1
Ideas and Interest in the Economic Analysis of Regulation

PETER J. BOETTKE AND J. R. CLARK

Efforts to regulate economic and social life go back to antiquity. Just price doctrine, prohibitions on interest, restrictions on what could be bought and sold, as well as what human beings could do with their property (if they could in fact own property) and even their person have been constants across history. These stymie innovation, curtail progress, and degrade people. Despite such oppression, resourceful and creative individuals have found ways around restrictions and prohibitions to expand opportunities for mutually beneficial exchange and social interactions. Sometimes these efforts to subvert the regulatory environment were clandestine. Other times, the rulers simply looked the other way. But the arbitrary nature of such arrangements always impacts the environment of social intercourse. Regulation of economic and social life is never neutral, and is largely detrimental to human flourishing.

That last clause is controversial. One of the primary explanations for why regulations are there in the first place is because of a harm (real or imagined) that is supposedly in need of correction (Kirzner 1985, 134). In the face of harm, the state is entrusted to enact regulations of economic and social life to either prevent the harm, or to compensate those who suffer and penalize those who perpetrate. The state is supposed to enact regulation in *the public interest*. Public interest explanations for the prevalence of regulation are the most common reason offered in law, political science, and history.

The Pure Food and Drug Act of 1906 was enacted to protect the consumer from abuse at the hands of unscrupulous sellers who foisted upon them adulterated and mislabeled products. These products could harm consumers and the sellers could confiscate their money for goods that could not live up to promises made. The Food and Drug Administration (FDA) was founded in June of 1906. In the past century, the FDA was joined by a host of economic regulatory bodies, such as the Federal Trade Commission, and by social regulatory bodies, such as the Environmental Protection Agency. Despite the omnipresence of state regulation in history, the 20th century saw an explosion in the scale and *scope* of regulation (see Fishback 2007).

By the 1970s, the expansion of regulation started to have a rising deleterious impact on economic performance in the economy. The public interest explanation was running into an interpretative paradox. Policies that were supposed to improve the human condition were producing unintended and undesirable consequences in terms of human welfare. Building on the emerging field of public choice economics, the 1970s saw the development of the theory of regulation grounded in private interest group logic. Who benefits at whose expense became the question that drove inquiry. Gordon Tullock, George Stigler, and Sam Peltzman all developed variations of this interest group theory of public policy in the 1960s and 1970s (Tullock 1967; Stigler 1971; Peltzman 1976). It was the material self-interest of the parties involved that would both explain the initiation of regulatory action and ensure its capture by the interested parties once enacted. Self-interest could explain it all.

But this private interest group analysis had its own set of interpretative paradoxes. In the pursuit of regulation, resources were expended in moral crusades, and in the legislative history there were strange alliances forged to build a minimum winning coalition. It was at this juncture that Bruce Yandle (1983) introduced his Bootleggers and Baptists theory of social regulation to address the interpretative paradoxes. Yandle's theoretical framework focuses attention on the alignment of ideas and interests, and demonstrates with historical analysis how public interest explanations are recruited to ease the pursuit of public policy actions that benefit private interests.

Yandle is able to overcome the either/or thinking that dominated the previous generations, and in many ways brings back the classical economists' understanding. This was summed up by J. S. Mill:

> Ideas, unless outward circumstances conspire with them, have in general no very rapid or immediate efficacy in human affairs; and the most favourable outward circumstances may pass by, or remain inoperative, for want of ideas suitable to the conjuncture. But when the right circumstances and the right ideas meet, the effect is seldom slow in manifesting itself. (1845, 503)

The logic of politics, as developed in public choice, is to concentrate benefits on the well-organized and well-informed in the short run, and disperse the costs onto the unorganized and ill-informed in the long run. But the climate of public opinion during any era provides the background against which this logic of politics is played out.

James Buchanan's contributions to public choice theory, and especially his development of constitutional political economy, recognized these two levels of analysis—the rule level and the strategic behavior given the rules adopted. That is, the Baptists are working at the rule level to obtain prohibition, while the bootleggers are working at the strategic level to profit from prohibition. Ironically, if the Baptists are successful, the bootleggers find it easier to achieve their goals. This leads to their unintended and unrecognized alliance in the political process of enacting and enforcing prohibition. This example of the theory developed by Yandle is widely applicable to the rise of social regulation in the second half of the 20th century.

Yandle's innovative work relates to the recent effort by Dani Rodrik to incorporate ideas back into an economic theory of politics. As Rodrik puts it: "Ideas are strangely absent from modern models of political economy" (2014, 189). The dominant models stress "vested interests." While any model that did not account for special interests would be vacuous, it does not follow that interest is the sole determining factor in politics and that ideas play no role in robust explanations of policy choice. Ideas must find a role in the analysis, if only for the simple reason that, as Ludwig von Mises put it in *Theory and History* (1957, 138), "Ideas tell a man what his interests are."

In a broader sense, we can postulate a linear relationship that runs from ideas to institutions to performance, where good ideas lower the costs of both implementing and enforcing good institutions, resulting in high levels of performance, whereas bad ideas have the opposite impact. Part of the reason the interest group theory of regulation came to dominate in modern political economy is the empirical record that revealed that policies introduced in the name of the public interest produced persistently frustrating results. Yandle's work highlights the deleterious impact of the growth of social regulation not only on economic growth, but also in many instances on the intended improvement in the targeted social goal. As a consequence, the economist is left with the task of answering not only who benefits and at whose expense, but why these costly policies that frustrate persist through time.

That persistent question, however, can only be answered once we have a clear understanding of the status quo benefits and costs. That means we have to study the origins and legislative history of the regulations under investigation. In developing the implications of his Bootlegger/Baptist theory, Yandle explores the strategic alliances that can be forged in the effort to build a minimum winning coalition for the passage of the regulation. Of course, the role of vested interests must always be remembered. As Adam Smith warned in *The Wealth of Nations*:

> The proposal of any new law or regulation of commerce which comes from this order, ought always to be listened to with great precaution, and ought never to be adopted till after having been long and carefully examined, not only with the most scrupulous, but with the most suspicious attention. It comes from an order of men, whose interest is never exactly the same with that of the public, who have generally an interest to deceive and even to oppress the public, and who accordingly have, upon many occasions, both deceived and oppressed it. (1981, 267)

Such naked self-interest regulation, though, has difficulties in passing through the democratic process of policy deliberation. That does not mean it isn't always present; it just means that it rarely is starkly presented. In the most cynical presentation of the Bootlegger/Baptist theory, naked self-interest is merely cloaked in public interest rhetoric. In this rendition of the theory, there simply are no real Baptists; they are, when unmasked, actually bootleggers themselves. This version may be predictive, but in many ways it is uninteresting.

What appears to be the more intriguing phenomenon to explain is how politics makes for strange bedfellows in the effort to build a minimum winning coalition for the passage of desired legislation. The sincere Baptist is led in the effort to pass the desired legislation to unknowingly align with the cynical bootlegger, not just to provide cover for the naked self-interest, but to get legislation that they believe will improve the general welfare. The bootlegger's resources are recruited to aid the Baptist in building the minimum winning coalition for the legislation.

Yandle's theory of social regulation is a useful way to meet Rodrik's challenge to a considerable extent and to integrate ideas back into modern political economy. The Yandle theory does not focus analytical and empirical attention on the critical point where ideas trump interests, which is Rodrik's contribution, as much as it highlights how ideas and interests work together along the lines suggested in the Mill quote provided above.

Make no mistake, ideas are incorporated into political economy. And when you pivot from the origins of regulation to reversal during periods of deregulation, ideas may play an even more pivotal role. There are pivotal moments, what have been called "Overton windows" (see Russell 2006), and there are pivotal actors, known as public entrepreneurs. But ideas rarely trump special interests unless coalitions are formed that can help command the resources and votes to pass legislation. The cynic may say it is bootleggers (interests) all the way down, while the romantic may claim it is the Baptists (ideas) that light "the fire in the minds of men." But realism in political economy must work through the interaction of ideas and interests.

Yandle provides an important antidote to one-sided explanations in economics and political economy. It is one that should be most welcome to modern political economists, especially those influenced by James Buchanan and Vincent Ostrom. In addition to the intellectual contribution that Yandle has made to the enrichment of public choice and the political economy analysis of economic and social regulation; he also contributed greatly to our analytical apparatus for incorporating the role of ideas into our understanding of political transformations. The Bootlegger and Baptist theory is an essential component in the tool kit of the modern political economist.

REFERENCES

Fishback, P., ed. 2007. *Government and the American Economy: A New History*. Chicago: University of Chicago Press.

Kirzner, I. 1985. *Discovery and the Capitalist Process*. Chicago: University of Chicago Press.

Mill, J. S. 1845. "The Claim of Labor." *Edinburgh Review* 81, no. 164: 498–525.

Mises, L. 1957. *Theory and History: An Interpretation of Social and Economic Evolution*. New Rochelle, NY: Arlington House.

Peltzman, S. 1976. "Toward a More General Theory of Regulation." *Journal of Law & Economics* 19, no. 2: 211–40.

Rodrik, D. 2014. "When Ideas Trump Interests: Preferences, Worldviews, and Policy Innovations." *Journal of Economic Perspectives* 28, no. 1: 189–208.

Russell, N. J. 2006. "An Introduction to the Overton Window of Political Possibilities." Mackinac Center for Public Policy, January 4. https://www.mackinac.org/7504.

Smith, A. [1776] 1982. *An Inquiry into the Nature and Causes of the Wealth of Nations*. Indianapolis, IN: Liberty Fund.

Smith, A., and B. Yandle. 2014. *Bootleggers and Baptists: How Economic Forces and Moral Persuasion Interact to Shape Regulatory Politics*. Washington, DC: Cato Institute.

Stigler, G. J. 1971. "The Theory of Economic Regulation." *Bell Journal of Economics and Management Science* 2, no. 1: 3–21.

Tullock, G. 1967. "The Welfare Costs of Tariffs, Monopolies, and Theft." *Western Economic Journal* 5, no. 3: 224–32.

Yandle, B. 1983. "Bootleggers and Baptists: The Education of a Regulatory Economist." *Regulation* 7, no. 3: 12–16.

CHAPTER 2
Externality
The Biggest Straw Man of Our Time

DONALD J. BOUDREAUX AND ROGER MEINERS

As a list of his publications shows, Bruce Yandle has written many articles and books addressing many issues about the environment. It is a topic he drew us into that we otherwise may have ignored, but Bruce, as a generous colleague, gets one to work on topics he demonstrates to be of interest. Here we address a slice of the giant topic of environmental economics and policy, to which Bruce contributed much. We focus on the now de rigueur use of the term "externality" when discussing the environment.

Externalities are ubiquitous in academic writing and, by definition, in the life of everyone. Conscious decisions by people and facts of nature affect us physically and mentally in positive and negative ways in all aspects of existence. People born with good looks earn a beauty premium that is largely

We would like to thank the participants at a workshop at Case Western Reserve University Law School, sponsored by the Property and Environment Research Center of Bozeman, Montana, and the Searle Freedom Foundation, for unusually beneficial comments on an earlier version. More than 25 years ago the two of us overlapped with Bruce Yandle at Clemson. The hours we spent together, congratulating each other on the profundity of our insights, were among the happiest days we enjoyed in academia. Bruce was unfailingly kind to us—more than we deserved. Few people have meant more to us personally and professionally over the years than Bruce, who it is our privilege to help honor at this Festschrift symposium.

independent of occupation (Hamermesh and Biddle 1994).[1] In the competition for jobs (and mates), it is not just looks that matter—clothes may make the man. The job candidate who shows up in a custom-made suit has an advantage over those in drearier garb. To prevent such disadvantages, people may "over-invest" in fancy duds to improve perception at interviews. The nice clothes create "positional externalities"—that is, individual candidates suffer, as does society, from the competition to buy clothes some deem to be needlessly fancy. Due to such behavior, some argue that public policies should be considered to deal with such things.[2]

Economists have also worried about consumption externalities: "keeping up with the Joneses." People feel bad about the nifty things their neighbors buy, so they make purchases to compensate for self-perceived deficiencies. This leads to a "misallocation" of resources that might be corrected by taxes (Eckerstorfer and Wendner 2013). Going further, we may compare ourselves to people in other countries (global positional externalities), which could be solved by a "Pareto-efficient tax policy in a cooperative framework" (i.e., transnational) that will produce "large welfare gains" (Aronsson and Johansson-Stenman 2015).[3]

Public policy interventions in most aspects of existence are then "justified" on the grounds that externalities impose alleged harms on society that can be reduced, or create benefits that can be increased, by edicts that address the issues.

Steven N. Cheung explained years ago that externality is an example of ad hoc theorizing. People make observations and then link that to a plausible theory, and soon, if others join in, a whole body of analysis arises that sits on less bedrock than is commonly presumed (Cheung 1970). Bruce Yandle is one of the few who took Cheung's observation to heart and expounded upon it. Yandle and Andy Barnett wrote a hopefully titled piece, "The End of the Externality Revolution" (Barnett and Yandle 2009). They noted that economists assert externalities to posit problems in search of solutions that are graciously offered, usually a tax or a subsidy. But, as Barnett and Yandle explain, the analysts often ignore institutional underpinnings or special interests that undergird observed things that are branded as externalities.[4]

To understand the pervasive role of externalities in the academic literature, we review the century-long development of the concept in economics. As the examples above indicate, application of the notion of externality has become generic, although its most common use in recent decades is its application to environmental matters. Merely invoking the term provides a straw man to allow one to argue for policy innovation (usually taxes) to help resolve perceived problems. After reviewing the literature, we discuss a more principled way to employ the concept of externalities.

ORIGINS: MARSHALL AND PIGOU

The authors of a leading environmental economics text assert that "Marshall and Pigou, in particular, developed the concepts of external economies and diseconomies, which are crucial in understanding environmental problems" (Mills and Graves 1986). They are referring to Alfred Marshall, a major economist who wrote the leading text in economics from 1890 to 1920, and Arthur Cecil Pigou, one of his students—and the successor to his chair at Cambridge—a major figure in the profession in the first half of the 20th century.[5]

Marshall, in the oft-cited eighth edition of his *Principles of Economics*, explained that external economies were factors relevant to a firm from the outside, such as better technology that could be adopted. Internal economies were factors under the control of those running a firm—for example, a clever manager figuring out how to use existing assets so as to run a company better.

"External economies" are discussed in terms of scale of production; they are "those dependent on the general development of the industry," whereas "internal economies" are "those dependent on the resources of the individual houses of businesses engaged in it [a particular kind of production]" (Marshall 1920, 266). External economies grew as technology improved and large-scale production came to dominate. This included valuable knowledge "beyond the reach of anyone who could not afford to have well-paid agents in many distant places" (Marshall 1920, 284–85). That is, small producers had access to valuable information that allowed them the possibility of more efficient, larger-scale production. This knowledge enhanced the "efficiency of capital and labour" (Marshall 1920, 314).[6]

Improved knowledge allows greater efficiencies in production, so supply can be expanded at lower per unit cost. There is a downside to such productivity. Marshall worried that large-scale efficiency could result in a monopoly—a so-called natural monopoly—when one firm can serve the market at lower cost than would two or more smaller firms. Natural monopolies require government intervention so as to maximize social welfare (Marshall 1920, 503). However, Marshall opposed "collective ownership of the means of production" as it would "deaden the energies of mankind, and arrest economic progress" (Marshall 1920, 713).[7]

Marshall did not discuss pollution; he noted that "waste"—things thrown away in the production process—is reduced by large-scale producers who make more efficient use of inputs. "No doubt many of the most important advances of recent years have been due to the utilizing of what had been a waste product" (Marshall 1920, 279). Fifty years later, the Marshallian view of external economies still held sway. In a leading microeconomic theory text, external economies were still discussed in terms of greater industrial efficiency resulting from technical improvements that force competitors to operate more cost-effectively. Diseconomies are external effects that *raise* firms' costs. Pollution is not mentioned in Marshall's textbook (Henderson and Quant 1971, 111).

While Marshall mentioned the notion of external impacts on production, the expansive use of externality begins with Pigou (Pigou 1920). He acknowledged that private property–based free markets can work well. However, "even Adam Smith had not realised fully the extent to which the System of Natural Liberty needs to be qualified and guarded by special laws, before it will promote the most productive employment of a country's resources" (Pigou 1920, 128).

According to Pigou, the price system and legal and social institutions fail to cause all to act in ways that maximize *social* welfare. This failure justifies government intervention to correct the imperfections. Widespread market failures "prevent a community's resources from being distributed among different uses or occupations in the most effective way. The study [of this problem] . . . seeks to bring into clearer light some of the ways in which it now is, or eventually may become, feasible for governments to control the play of economic forces in such wise as to promote the economic welfare, and, through that, the total welfare of their citizens as a whole" (Pigou 1920, 129–30).

How should economists deal with this problem? Pigou explains:

> [W]e have next to distinguish precisely between the two varieties of marginal net product which I have named respectively *social* and *private*. The marginal social net product is the total net product of physical things or objective services due to the marginal increment of resources in any given use or place, no matter to whom any part of this product may accrue. It might happen, for example, as will be explained more fully in a later chapter, that costs are thrown upon people not directly concerned, through, say, uncompensated damage done to surrounding woods by sparks from railway engines. All such effects must be included—some of them will be positive, others negative elements—in reckoning up the social net product of the

> marginal increment of any volume of resources turned into any use or place. (Pigou 1920, 134)[8]

Pigou explains further:

> [I]f private and social net products everywhere coincide, the free play of self-interest, so far as it is not hampered by ignorance, will tend to bring about such a distribution of resources among different uses and places as will raise the national dividend and, with it, the sum of economic welfare to a maximum. . . . The essential point for our present purpose is that, when marginal private net products and marginal social net products coincide, any obstacles that obstruct the free play of self-interest will, in general, damage the national dividend [income]. In real life, of course, marginal private and marginal social net products frequently do not coincide. (Pigou 1920, 143)

Much of the market's failure to produce maximum national income arises from "imperfect knowledge on the part of those in whose hands the power to direct the various branches of the stream [of resources] resides" (Pigou 1920, 149).[9] Pigou argues that private resource owners will not maximize social value:

> In general industrialists are interested, not in the social, but only in the private, net product of their operations. . . . [S]elf-interest will not tend to bring about equality in the values of the marginal social net products except when marginal private net product and marginal social net product are identical. When there is a divergence between these two sorts of marginal net products, self-interest will not, therefore, tend to make the national dividend a maximum; and, consequently, certain specific acts of interference with normal economic processes may be expected, not to diminish, but to increase the dividend. (Pigou 1920, 172)[10]

While Pigou does not call the divergence between social and private costs an externality, he explains its essence as now employed. He saw the problem as being nearly universal. Pigou gave numerous examples of what we would call negative and positive externalities, all of which are explained to be forms of market failure that warrant consideration of state intervention to close the gap between private and social costs. For example, lighthouses provide benefits for ships that do not pay for their services.[11] Public roads may produce higher real estate values for adjoining landowners. Inventors generate valuable knowledge that can be exploited by others for personal and social gain. On the other side, factory smoke dims sunlight and inflicts filth on buildings and laundries, and intoxicating beverages lead to the need for more prisons and policemen (Pigou 1920, 183–86).[12] In all such situations, social and private costs and benefits diverge—and are not easy to resolve due to the "technical difficulty of enforcing compensation for incidental disservices" (Pigou 1920, 185). (Later, Coase encouraged us to think of these as transaction costs.)

There is much in the world not to like, today and in Pigou's time. He explained what he saw as the single worst social cost:

> [T]he crowning illustration of this order of excess of private over social net product is afforded by the work done by women in factories, particularly during the periods immediately preceding and succeeding confinement; for there can be no doubt that this work often carries with it, besides the earnings of the women themselves, grave injury to the health of their children. The reality of this evil. . . . (Pigou 1920, 187)

Such evil necessitates legislation and regulation:

> It is plain that divergences between private and social net product . . . cannot . . . be mitigated by a modification of the contractual relation between any two contracting parties, because the divergence arises out of a service or disservice rendered to persons other than the contracting parties. It is, however, possible for the State, if it so chooses, to remove the divergence in any field by "extraordinary encouragements" or "extraordinary restraints" upon investments in that field. The most obvious forms which these encouragements and restraints may assume are, of course, those of bounties and taxes. (Pigou 1920, 192)

Pigou's call for subsidies and taxes to reduce the gaps between social and private costs is a bedrock in modern externality analysis.

THE 1950S AND 1960S

Building on Pigou, in a 1954 article, Professor Tibor Scitovsky of Stanford explained that "external economies are a cause for divergence between private profit and social benefit and thus for the failure of perfect competition to lead to an optimum situation" (Scitovsky 1954). He identified "four types of direct interdependence": (1) when one's satisfaction is related to the satisfaction of another person; (2) when one's satisfaction is affected by inconveniences, such as smoke from production; (3) when producers learn to offer goods and services at lower cost, so as to offer more satisfaction at lower cost; and (4) when the output of a producer depends on the activities of other firms (Scitovsky 1954, 144).[13]

Scitovsky explained that economists generally have little to say about the first kind of externality, even though they know it is hugely important. Economists are not good at understanding interpersonal utility or satisfaction, so we generally set aside that huge set of issues. He notes that this kind of externality is related to arguments for governmental provision of social services.

As an indication of how times change (most pollution levels were much higher in the 1950s than they are today[14]), Scitovsky thought the second kind of externality, such as emissions from production, were "unimportant" as they could be handled by zoning rules (move producers to industrial areas) or regulations for public health and safety.

Similarly, Scitovsky regarded the third kind of externality—the one that occurs as more efficient methods of production cascade through to other production processes, as noted by Marshall and Pigou—were unimportant in a policy sense because patents allow innovators to capture gains from innovations and so encourage such productive activities. Innovators sell their output to buyers who benefit by using the new technology in their production. Other innovations result from research sponsored by the public, such as in agriculture, where the research results are made available to all.

The fourth kind of externality—interdependence among producers—seemed to Scitovsky to be "few," so of little import (Scitovsky 1954, 145).[15] Such an externality can involve unpaid factors of production. Scitovsky recalled an earlier paper by James E. Meade, in which Meade gave the example of apple orchards benefiting from bees, which allowed beekeepers to benefit from apple blossoms, even though the two may not contract with each other (Meade 1952). If one or both of these parties fails to take adequate account of the effects of his actions on the output of the other party, there will be a suboptimal production of apples and of honey. This divergence from optimality could justify a subsidy paid by apple growers to the beekeepers to encourage beekeepers to produce more honey (Meade 1952, 61).[16]

Similarly, the relationship among outputs as one firm's knowledge or product spills over to others (as noted by Marshall) played a role in the literature on network externalities. The benefit one receives from a good, such as the telephone or the internet, depends on how many other users there are. Without a network of other users who rely on the products of others, phones or the internet have little or no value (Liebowitz and Margolis 1994).[17]

Economists have long distinguished "technical" from "pecuniary" externalities. According to Scitovsky, this distinction originated with Jacob Viner in 1931. Within a firm, "technological internal economies would be savings in the labor, materials, or equipment requirements per unit of output resulting from improved organization or methods of production," whereas pecuniary internal economies "consist of advantages in buying, such as 'quantity discounts'" (Viner 1931, 3).

While distinctions are made between technical and pecuniary economies, their form does not matter to the firm or the individual decision maker because both represent financial benefits or losses. A gain is a gain and a loss is a loss. Economists, however, now distinguish technical from pecuniary diseconomies, contending that the former matter to society while the latter do not. The reason is that technical externalities are believed to reduce social welfare while pecuniary externalities do not. Put differently, technical externalities result in physical production that is either too much or too little, whereas pecuniary externalities merely redistribute wealth among economic actors without diminishing it.[18]

Following Scitovsky, who found externalities not to be something to worry about too much, F. M. Bator of MIT published an influential article (Bator 1958). Bator's article forms the more formal basis for the now-common notion of externality. Bator uses the notion of Paretian efficiency. If Pareto optimality[19] is achieved in a society, no improvement in utility or efficiency is possible—no one can be made better off without making someone else worse off—society has achieved its "bliss point" (Bator 1958, 351).[20]

Bator was concerned primarily with income redistribution via taxation to achieve social bliss, but his analysis applies to all economic matters. He notes that bliss is impossible due to "imperfect information, inertia and resistance to change, the infeasibility of costless lump-sum taxes, businessmen's desire for a 'quiet life,' uncertainty and inconsistent expectations, the vagaries of aggregate demand, etc." (Bator 1958, 352).

Bator discusses multiple sources of market failure (Bator 1958, 353–54): *failure of existence* (due to lack of perfect marginal rates of substitution as related to input-output points or production needed to generate optimal prices); *failure by signal* (concerning proper levels of profit for each producer; having too much profit leads to over-allocation of resources in some areas), and, on the converse side, *failure by incentive* (inadequate profits for some producers who should have higher levels to stimulate investment in their output); *failure by structure* (in the absence of perfect information and pure competition, prices and output will deviate from optimality, as we observe in many markets where a few firms dominate); and *failure by enforcement* (legal and organizational imperfections). Bator explains that the Lange-Lerner model of socialist direction (scientific planning of an economy) faces many difficulties and that the literature on these issues is complex and convoluted.

As explained by Marshall and Pigou, the existence of market imperfections requires that industries and individuals be taxed or subsidized to bring society closer to bliss (Bator 1958, 357). Bator noted that economists who wrote soon after Marshall and Pigou—including Dennis Robertson, Piero Sraffa, Frank Knight, and Jacob Viner—demonstrated that the conclusion that such taxes and subsidies are necessary is mistaken. Changes in ownership arrangements can internalize many technological economies, while pecuniary external economies in competitive markets are simply the evidence for and consequences of competition (Bator 1958, 357). Bator explains that this conclusion leaves as problems only those technological external economies ("externalities") that cannot be handled by a change in ownership arrangements. Those markets (and this description applies generally) "will be efficient if, and only if, this *private* marginal cost ratio reflects the true marginal cost to society of an extra apple in terms of foregone honey." This class of externalities, however, is huge. In them, market prices "diverge from true, *social* marginal cost" (Bator 1958, 360). Bator's explanation of social marginal cost in case of external technological economies is what economists have worried about ever since.

Bator gives examples of bridges and radio (Bator 1958, 361–62). Bridges face lumpiness in use not resolved by pricing, and we have limited options in what we hear on the radio—including advertisements. Many functioning markets are afflicted with externalities that justify consideration of state-imposed improvements. Externality, therefore, should mean "any situation where some Paretian costs and benefits remain *external to* decentralized cost-revenue calculation in terms of prices" (Bator 1958, 362). That is, we are not at bliss points due to "uncompensated services" and "incidental uncharged disservices"—the essence of market failure.

Bator then argues that there are three, sometimes overlapping, categories of externalities. First are *ownership externalities*. Even if markets work perfectly ("an Adam Smith dream world"), because of "circumstances of institutions, laws, customs, or feasibility, competitive markets would not be Pareto-efficient" (Bator 1958, 362). This problem exists in private venues, such as beekeepers' interactions with orchardists, and in the public sector, such as in public-domain fishing waters. Second are *technical externalities*. These arise from lumpiness or indivisibility in many goods, such as bridges. These would benefit from "a set of shadow-prices which, if centrally quoted, would efficiently ration among consumers the associated (fixed) total of goods" (Bator 1958, 368). Third are *public good externalities*. A pure public good is one where consumption by one person does not affect consumption by another (e.g., the benefits I receive from national defense against Russian missiles do not affect your ability to "consume" or to enjoy the same benefits) (Bator 1958, 370).[21] As the price mechanism cannot work for demanders and suppliers, administered prices are required (Bator 1958, 372). He cites lighthouses, schools, and open-air concerts among many examples, but not pollution.[22]

About the time Bator's article was published, Ronald Coase argued that the radio spectrum could be privatized to improve its efficiency (Coase 1959). At that time, the Federal Communications Commission (FCC) granted licenses to use bits of the spectrum. It was asserted that regulation was the only way to prevent one spectrum user from disturbing the use by another spectrum user—broadcasts would spill over into each other. Scientific control by the FCC was needed to prevent chaos and cutthroat competition, and allow for the orderly development of radio and then television. Private enterprise could not work (Coase 1959, 13). Coase testified before the FCC in 1959, arguing that the spectrum could be efficiently privatized. Apparently, commissioners were scandalized by this strange notion from a professor with a British accent, one asking him if the proposal was a "big joke" (Bohn 2013).

The broadcast spectrum fits Bator's definition of technical limitations that require government intervention. Coase noted that, among other things, because the government controlled the licensing, valuable licenses were not handed out randomly; they went to favored interests, allowing them to obtain "extraordinary" gains (Coase 1959, 23). Coase explained the then-revolutionary idea that spectrum can be made private property just as land is owned by private parties. The fact that there is a fixed quantity of land does not mean it must be in public hands to ensure its efficient use. "The advantage of establishing exclusive rights to use a resource when that use does not harm others (apart from the fact that they are excluded from using it) is easily understood" (Coase 1959, 26). Once private rights exist, parties may bargain over how the property is used, with the party who values a piece of property most highly being the one who ends up owning it.

Coase explained, in his FCC paper, what has come to be called the Coase Theorem, although his more famous paper of the following year is more commonly cited as the source. Coase used an 1879 case, *Sturges v. Bridgman* (11 Ch.D. 852) to illustrate. A confectioner used his property for years for business. A doctor later came to occupy the adjoining property. There were no problems until eight years later when the doctor built a consulting room that abutted the confectioner's premises. Noise and vibration from the confectioner's machinery disturbed the doctor's consulting room. The doctor sued and obtained an injunction against the machinery.[23]

Coase did not address Bator's concerns about market imperfections from lumpiness, dominant firms, and other external effects; rather, Coase focused on the importance of property rights and the ability to exchange these rights or have them enforced. He followed the FCC paper soon with his famous "Social Cost" paper (Coase 1960). This paper is, for most readers, difficult to comprehend as a whole. It is cited to support many different propositions, and is said to be the most cited publication in law and economics.[24]

In his work, Coase did not use the terms externality or external costs, although many economists directly associate his work with those concepts. His nonuse of the terms was intentional. He explained:

> [A]s employed today, the term carries with it the connotation that when "externalities" are found, steps should be taken by the government to eliminate them. As already indicated, the only reason individuals and private organizations do not eliminate them is that the gain from doing so would be offset by what would be lost (including the costs of making the arrangements necessary to bring about this result). If with government intervention the losses also exceed the gains from eliminating the "externality," it is obviously desirable that it should remain. To prevent being thought that I shared the common view, I never used the word "externality" in "The Problem of Social Cost" but spoke of "harmful effects" without specifying whether decision-makers took them into account or not. (Coase 2012, 27)[25]

Coase directly addressed Pigou's welfare economics and its concern with the divergence of social and private costs (Coase 1959). Coase used Pigou's example of sparks from a railroad causing fires to adjoining farmland (Coase

1959, 29–31). Pigou saw the cost of fire as a social cost—that is, uncompensated damage that injured the social optimum. But, as Coase explained, statutory law in Britain often exempted railroads from liability for fires caused by sparks from engines. Pigou was apparently ignorant of the law but, more importantly, viewed the matter as a cost imposed unilaterally by railroads on adjacent property owners. The divergence between social and private cost could, in Pigou's reckoning, be reduced if railroads were forced to pay compensation and, thus, were forced to "internalize" the cost imposed on landowners.

Coase's celebrated insight is that it does not matter who has the liability so long as a property-rights assignment exists, is enforceable, and the parties can bargain (Coase 1959, 34). Another key insight is that costs are reciprocal; each party's action (or inaction) contributes to a problem. If bargaining is possible, the parties can be expected to choose to minimize the costs of their interactions regardless of who is initially assigned the right (Coase 1960).

Suppose, for example, the expected value of the damage from fires is greater than the cost of limiting sparks by investing in spark arresters. If the railroads have the right to emit fire-causing sparks, sparks will be emitted despite the fact that the damage caused by the sparks is greater than the cost of preventing the damage. After all, the cost of fire damage is borne by landowners and not by the railroads. Coase's insight is that the ability to bargain is sufficient to internalize this cost. Landowners will offer to pay railroads to prevent sparks from flying. The landowners will offer an amount greater than the railroads' costs of preventing the sparks. If the railroads foolishly refuse the landowners' offer, the cost of the resulting fire damage would be internalized on the railroads in the form of forgone payments from landowners.[26] Seeking to avoid this cost, the railroads' self-interest will prompt them to accept the offered payments and install spark arresters.

The outcome would be no different if the landowners owned the right to be free of fire from railroad sparks. Then the railroads would have to compensate landowners for fire damage caused by sparks. Using the lower-cost option, the railroads would install spark arresters rather than pay landowners the higher-cost damages for fires caused by sparks.

On a separate matter from the exposition of what is now called the Coase Theorem, Coase criticized Pigou for not bothering to investigate the law regarding railroad liability before decrying what he concluded was the obvious injustice of the rule. Pigou, like modern welfare economists, seemed to presume that enlightened government leaders would get the rules right if economists pointed out to them defects in the rules that cause social waste. Parliament knew very well what it was doing when it passed the Railway (Fires)

Act of 1905, which was amended various times, likely at the behest of affected parties (Coase 1960, 30).[27]

Coase acknowledged that Pigou admitted that government agencies might not always perform as well as their champions wished (Coase 1962, 20). But Coase dismissed Pigou's warning of poorly performing government agencies as formulaic and unreflective of his generally great confidence in such agencies. For evidence, Coase cites Pigou's optimism that improvements in democracy and in public administration—especially the advent of the independent regulatory commission—are sufficient to ensure that government (at least in the United Kingdom and the United States) will generally execute market-correcting tasks in the apolitical and scientific manner prescribed by economists (such as Pigou) (Coase 1962, 21–22).[28] The bottom line, for Coase, of Pigou's optimism about government's capacity to correct market "imperfections" is that neither economists nor government officials take seriously enough the alternatives to regulatory intervention, including the choice of what Coase described as "inaction" (Coase 1962, 24).

Besides having a naïve view that politicians and other government officials will devise "optimal" solutions to "correct" the divergence of private from social cost, those who adopt the Pigovian stance also fail to consider the social costs of *government* actions. Discussions of externalities are overwhelmingly about private actors who allegedly need to be set straight. But state-imposed rules create costs that are unnecessary when judged by an inappropriate ideal, which, for Coase, is an ideal that fails to account for the reality of transaction costs. Coase uses the example of a red light installed at an intersection. Drivers stop at red lights even when no crossing traffic or pedestrians are visible because the cost of running a red light—a combination of the risk of getting a traffic ticket and of getting into an automobile accident—is too high.

We follow state-imposed rules that are inefficient when judged by the same standard of perfection against which private rules are typically judged—and some rules that are inefficient even when judged by appropriately realistic standards. The social costs imposed by such imperfect state controls are largely ignored (Coase 1960, 34).[29] When welfare economists and others prescribe "fixes" to social cost problems, they should, at a minimum, investigate the practicality of the consequences—including those of the proposed remedies—rather than *assuming* that social planners, legislatures, and agencies know best how to improve social efficiency.

Government agencies engage in cost-benefit analysis all the time to assure us of the high value of rules that are imposed, but the analyses are often suspect.[30] For example, estimates by excellent economists about the costs of economic events and government programs can vary wildly. The 2010 BP oil spill in the Gulf of Mexico caused many people to change their vacation plans, such as going to Hilton Head instead of Panama City. One estimate of loss incurred by recreationalists from the oil spill was $661 million. Another group estimated the same loss to be 26 times greater.[31] Imaginary numbers (or wild assumptions employed in devising numbers) are routinely made to bolster alleged values in seeking the social optimum (Boudreaux, Meiners, and Zywicki 1999).

Pigou and Bator were among the many economists who believed that corrective taxes could align social and private costs so as to reduce undesirable behavior and compensate aggrieved parties. That is, those suffering from smoke or railroad sparks would be compensated by the party that "caused" the externality. The notion of ownership, exchange, and liability apparently escaped attention. In the case of the railroad sparks, Pigou simply divined the rule he favored would be efficient and equitable. Presumably, if Pigou understood that railroads often had legislation in their favor, so a liability rule did exist, he would have objected and proposed reversing the rule. But any such imagined response by Pigou misses the point that the result, and costs, would be much the same regardless of the rule *if bargaining is allowed*. Terry Anderson makes this point in his paper in this volume, as applied to the issue of climate change.

Welfare economists argue that actual compensation of "victims" is not needed because accurately set corrective taxes are sufficient to adjust the behavior of the party engaged in the disfavored act to improve social productivity. The tax revenues go to the general treasury.[32] This "solution" ignores the social costs *created* by government use of resources. As noted by Meckling and Alchian: "The problem is identical with the familiar problem of divergence between private and social costs. Once tax receipts reach the Treasury, they are owned by no one. To the individuals entrusted with their expenditure, the costs of using these funds is not equal to their value. They are not required as a condition of survival to see that value of output exceeds the value of inputs" (Meckling and Alchian 1960). The use of resources moved to political control compounds the problem by charging imperfect government officials with the task of correcting "imbalances" among endless social and private cost imbalances. Real resources are always at stake and are entrusted to the tender mercies of politicians for distribution.

To return to the evolution of economic thinking on externalities, next came two papers by James Buchanan. In the first paper, Buchanan begins by putting aside the notion that welfare economists can make meaningful policy prescriptions to solve the problems of market failure (Buchanan 1962). He acknowledged that competitive markets do not satisfy the conditions for optimality.

That is, bliss points are constructs not related in any operational way to the real world. Economists cannot explain how to get society to nirvana; however, they talk as if economic engineering is possible "to justify their own professional existence" (Buchanan 1962, 18). When Buchanan was writing (1962), economists had devised the many prescriptions we hear today—"tax-subsidy schemes," "multipart pricing," "collective stimulation of ideal market processes," and other notions alleged to enhance economic efficiency.

Buchanan asked: If economists think their prescriptions are not, in fact, policy relevant, why should they bother to advance such notions? (Buchanan 1962, 18–19). To argue that the existing order is imperfect, and then to advance "solutions" that are recognized as unattainable, is not as useful as focusing on what is likely to emerge in a majoritarian democracy (Buchanan 1962, 21).[33] Each decision maker, including the politician and the polluter, balances social and private costs against social and private benefits as they understand the world. Cost margins in a world of private and political decision makers are very different from those in the Pigovian world of universal benevolence.

Buchanan said to think of a world in which all activity is organized privately except for things involving genuine public goods (where consumption by one person does not affect use by another person). Assume further that taxes for public goods are based on marginal benefits, so each person pays a tax proportional to his own marginal rate of substitution between the collective good and all other goods. Different people would pay different taxes, as the marginal utilities of these public goods varies across people. Such a world is filled with externalities as each citizen "buys" public goods based on her evaluation of it. She considers her marginal benefit in her decision-making, which includes whatever value she might assign to benefits others receive (Buchanan 1962, 25–26).[34]

That paper was quickly followed by another in which Buchanan and Craig Stubblebine worked through the mechanics (math and graphs) of the notion of externalities and social equilibrium. They note that discussions of Pareto-relevant externalities are common but vague; they dispose of pecuniary externalities, focusing on technical externalities where the actions of an actor—an individual or a firm—impact others (Buchanan and Stubblebine 1962). The discussion in the paper is precise, concerning equilibrium conditions, but it adds little relevant to our discussion here.

Several years later, Buchanan added to the growing discussion in the 1960s about how externalities could be internalized (resolved) by the use of corrective taxes and subsidies (Buchanan 1969).[35] He demonstrates that imposing corrective taxes to deal with, say, pollution emitted by a firm in a less than purely competitive industry will reduce consumer welfare. The trend in welfare economics to divine proper taxes and subsidies is not beneficial. "Even if we disregard all problems of measurement, making the marginal private cost as faced by the decision-taking unit equal to marginal social cost does not provide the Aladdin's Lamp for the applied welfare theorist" (Buchanan 1969, 177).[36]

The "Pigovian tradition" soon replied. William Baumol led the charge, contending that Coase, Buchanan, and others cast aspersions on Pigovian prescriptions "that might prove effective in practice" (Baumol 1972). While one-on-one bargaining cases need not be addressed as they are "relatively unimportant cases" (Baumol 1972, 308),[37] in large-number cases, such as air pollution or traffic congestion, "taxes upon the generator of the externality are all that is required" (Baumol 1972, 307). The fact that the resulting allocation of resources is not optimal does not matter. Taxes and subsidies improve upon what exists even if they do not achieve bliss points.

Baumol used the classic example of the smoky factory that damages a neighbor's laundry. Forget party-to-party bargaining, Baumol explained. The smoke is a public bad that should be taxed (Baumol 1972, 311–14). When it is taxed, the smoke will be reduced and the laundry business will be in a better position (as will everyone else in society) due to the reduction in smoke. There need be no compensation to the laundry owner via the tax scheme; social benefits arise from the tax because the smoke is reduced to a reasonable level. If we want more output from a smoky factory, keep the tax low and there will be more factory output and laundries will not locate nearby, thereby producing a superior allocation of resources.

While Baumol assumed the tax/subsidy scheme would work, he admitted that discovering the exact correct level of, say, smoke emissions is difficult. After all, "a very substantial proportion of the cost of pollution is psychic," and differs across people, so the measurement problems are immense (Baumol 1972, 316). A process of trial and error involving different tax rates might need to be worked through to grope toward the socially optimal level of output.

As optimal tax rates are unknowable a priori, Baumol recommended setting satisfactory levels of emissions, such as for sulfur. There needs to be a balance of emissions and production. He likened the matter to macroeconomic stabilization policy, "where it is decided that an employment rate exceeding *w* percent and a rate of inflation exceeding *v* percent per year are simply unacceptable, and fiscal and monetary are then designed accordingly" (Baumol 1972, 318). Such policy avoids heavy administrative costs and does not use the police or the courts much. It is a system of direct controls "to achieve decreases in pollution . . . at minimum cost to society" (Baumol 1972, 319). Policymakers should not be "paralyzed by councils of perfection" (Baumol 1972, 320) in an effort to achieve optimality, so we should have flexible rules that point us in the right direction.

Baumol set the stage for how much environmental economics has progressed since that time. Social costs, which may include "psychic" costs, must be considered. Economists can help craft "solutions" to assorted problems, including pollution. On the other side, Coase spawned a literature that focuses on property law and other institutional arrangements, formal and informal, that serve to resolve disputes over the use of resources without the need for top-down edicts.[38]

Harold Demsetz explained the divide (Demsetz 1996). He noted that Marshall's primary concern about external impacts on industry efficiency is no longer of much interest. The externalities that matter are those in which one party inflicts costs on another party. These cases can be divided into two categories: the first is where bargaining between the parties is possible; the second is where such bargaining is too costly.

The first of these two categories is illustrated by a tenant–landlord situation. The tenant has a short time horizon, so little incentive to make long-term investments that the landlord would like. Pigou thought legislation could help correct this situation; he ignored the ability of landlords and tenants to solve problems through the contracts that they strike with one another. It is now generally understood that Coasean bargains will resolve such problems. Of greater relevance are situations in which bargaining is too costly to resolve differences between parties. That leaves a gap between private and social costs, and hence leaves open the possibility that taxes or subsidies are the best means for achieving optimal outcomes (Demsetz 1996, 569–70).

Demsetz explained that Pigou and others presumed too much when they asserted that bargaining will not resolve problems. Beekeepers and lighthouses were common examples used to show that the market was limited in application, but those examples have been shown not to be descriptive of reality: private parties learned to strike mutually beneficial deals or to otherwise devise efficiency-enhancing institutional arrangements.[39]

Just as being transported from one place to another involves transportation costs, transactions entail transaction costs. Economists often assert that the Coasean world means zero transaction costs—when parties will surely reach a bargain. But Coase never meant a world of zero transaction costs to be the center of analytic (or policy) attention. Zero transaction cost is much like a frictionless world or one with zero transportation costs: it is practically irrelevant.

What is instructive is to understand how parties achieve resolution of problems in the real world of positive transaction costs. Transaction costs are why firms exist and why bargains are struck all the time, everywhere. The fact that transaction costs are pervasive is taken by the advocates of regulatory intervention as justification for "an expanded government role in resource allocation" (Demsetz 1996, 573). Coase's acceptance of transaction costs, and the focus of study of these costs, is what can help us challenge the presumption that the mythical state interested in perfecting the world (under the wise direction of learned economists) is required to resolve problems (Demsetz 1996, 576).

WHAT WE HAVE COME TO

By the 1970s, the notion of externalities was pervasive. The notion now, at root, is normative. Carl Dahlman put the matter well (original emphasis):

> [T]he concept of externalities—insofar as the word is intended to convey, as Buchanan and Stubblebine would have it, the existence of an analytically proven market failure—is void of any positive content but, on the contrary, simply constitutes a normative judgment about the role of government and the ability of markets to establish mutually beneficial exchanges. That is to say, it cannot be shown with purely conceptual analysis that markets do not handle externalities; any such assertion necessitates an *assumption* that the government can do better. That this assumption is valid cannot be proved analytically, and it follows that market failure is an essentially normative judgment. (Dahlman 1979)

The argument can be summarized. Market failure implies that there exists a reallocation of resources—some change in the structure of market activities—that will enrich society. In more formal economic terms, market failure exists whenever the existing resource allocation is declared to be Pareto-inefficient. As noted above, Pareto-efficient allocation of resources exists when no person can be made better off without making at least one other person worse off. Any Pareto-*in*efficient allocation of resources, therefore, implies the possibility of changing resource allocation in a way that improves the well-being of at least one person without making anyone else worse off. Whenever a Pareto-inefficient allocation of resources persists, the market is said to fail, for it leaves potential social gains on the table.

Any failing market necessarily contains the opportunity for profit—that is, the possibility of converting unexploited "social gains" into exploited private gains. Whoever works successfully to improve the allocation of resources (say an "entrepreneur") can profit from their efforts: the person or persons who gain from the improved allocation will be willing to pay the entrepreneur for the results of his effort. The amount paid will be large enough to allow the entrepreneur not only to cover his costs (which might include compensating people who are harmed by his resource-reallocation efforts) but also to reap profit for his successful effort to improve the structure of resource allocation.

The entrepreneur undertakes such efforts only if his expected cost of doing so is less than his expected gain. Suppose, if we ignore whatever costs the entrepreneur must bear to change the pattern of resource allocation, the gain to society of changing the resource-allocation pattern is $100. If the cost to the entrepreneur is greater than $100, efforts to change the resource-allocation pattern are not worthwhile. If the entrepreneur who successfully changes the allocation pattern discovers that it costs $101 to do so, not only does he suffer a loss, so too does society. It is wasteful from society's perspective to use $101 worth of resources to generate $100 of benefit. Put differently, if the cost of improving the resource-allocation pattern is greater than the benefit from doing so, the unimproved pattern is optimal. The unimproved structure of resource allocation, it turns out, was Pareto-efficient. The existing pattern did not reflect market failure.

This logic prompts three different sorts of responses: responses from analysts we call Stiglerians, Hayekians, and Stiglitzians.[40] When Stiglerians[41] are confronted by an observer (one who makes value-neutral observations about the state of the economy) with allegations of a market failure, Stiglerians reject the allegations. They argue that whatever exists is optimal; otherwise some profit-seeking party would already have acted to improve the situation. Therefore, say the Stiglerians, the current situation only *appears* to the observer to be suboptimal because the observer fails to see and to account for some of the costs that must be incurred to rearrange the resource-allocation pattern. Because such costs cannot legitimately be ignored when assessing the propriety of rearranging the resource-allocation pattern—and because any worthwhile change will be brought about by economic agents—assertions of market failure reflect myths.

When Hayekians[42] are confronted by an observer with assertions of some market failure, they acknowledge that the market may be failing. But Hayekians have confidence that the profit motive prompts people to discover ways to earn a profit by improving the pattern of resource allocation. Profit-seeking entrepreneurs can be relied upon to improve the matter. Like Stiglerians, Hayekians reject the notion that government officials (economists or not) are better than entrepreneurs and other economic actors at assessing the costs and benefits of resource allocation. Unlike Stiglerians, Hayekians believe that human error is real. Time is required to discover suboptimal patterns of resource allocation so that economic actors can work toward improvements.

Although the details of their analyses differ, Stiglerians and Hayekians reach identical policy conclusions when confronted with claims that some putative market failure must be corrected by the state. That conclusion usually is "no it does not." The claim is dismissed as being false (Stiglerians), or as one that fails to appreciate the superiority of the entrepreneurial market process over the political process to discover and correct market failures (Hayekians).

When Stiglitzians[43] are confronted by an observer with allegations of some market failure, they are generally sympathetic. Stiglitzians have little confidence in the ability of private parties to correctly assess the state of the market or to competently act in pursuit of profit to improve resource allocation. They have confidence in the ability of government officials (especially economists) to assess the state of the market and to competently design and execute effective interventions that generate improved resource allocation. Stiglitzians' policy conclusions are very different from those of Stiglerians and Hayekians.

We need to explore the strengths and weaknesses of these three dispositions. Our point is that all of these positions (and any others that might exist or be imagined) are just that: *dispositions*. None can be proven analytically to be correct or even to be better than the others. Where any particular person comes down—as a Stiglerian, a Hayekian, or a Stiglitzian—is determined by that person's *judgment*, or even by his or her *priors*, about the competence of people acting privately compared to that of people acting politically.

Despite the differences that separate Stiglerians from Hayekians, and both of these tribes from Stiglitzians, all three accept the reality of externalities. Stiglerians insist that almost all externalities are what Buchanan and Stubblebine labeled "Pareto-irrelevant externalities"—that is, externalities that, while real, are not worth the cost of internalizing. Hayekians agree with Stiglerians that many externalities about which politicians, professors, and pundits complain are Pareto-irrelevant, but Hayekians disagree with Stiglerians' insistence that *all* externalities are such. Hayekians concede the reality of Pareto-relevant externalities, but argue that these will reliably and cost-effectively be corrected, sooner or later, by private market forces. Stiglitzians, of course, agree with the Hayekians that Pareto-relevant externalities exist in the real world, but disagree that many alleged externalities are Pareto-irrelevant. Stiglitzians insist also, contrary to Hayekians, that few, if any, Pareto-relevant externalities can be corrected adequately by market forces. Unlike the Hayekians, Stiglitzians believe that government action can correct Pareto-relevant externalities in cost-effective ways.

We agree more with the Hayekians than with either the Stiglerians or the Stiglitzians. We part company with all three in our understanding of the *nature* of externalities and offer a different conception of externalities, one based upon expectations. We argue that nearly all discussions of externalities proceed from a flawed understanding of third-party effects, be they negative or positive. We conclude that externalities are far less common than is commonly asserted.

A standard description of an externality is to say that it is an unbargained-for "third-party" effect. That is, it is a "spillover" effect that arises whenever an actor fails to take account of the cost or the benefit that an instance of her action has on a third party.

Our objection is to the typical (Pigovian) manner of reckoning social costs. The common assertion of externalities fails to take adequate account of expectations. Assertions of externalities—of "market failure"—pay insufficient attention to the fact that real-world economic actors form reasonable expectations about the likelihood that they or their properties will encounter spillover effects from other people's actions. When people expect certain consequences (either physically or to their own properties' market values) from other people's actions, they adjust their own actions to minimize the costs they bear (or to maximize the benefits they receive) from the expected actions of others. These expectations, and the adjustments they spark, "internalize" the consequences of spillover effects that appear as externalities in standard market-failure analyses. The internalized reasonable expectations of spillover effects are reflected in—incorporated into—property rights and the value placed on them. Once incorporated, these expectations render many spillover effects that appear on casual observation to be externalities but are, in fact, part of the structure of property rights.

A common example: Because someone who buys land located near a busy airport expects (or reasonably should expect) to regularly hear noise from airplanes, that person's property right to her land does not include the right to be free of airport noise. (In the language of the common law, the person "comes to the nuisance.") The price that she pays for this land is discounted to reflect the absence of this particular "stick" in the bundle of rights received when she purchases the land. This price discount reflects the internalization on this landowner of airport spillover effects.

SORTING OUT CLASSES OF EXTERNALITIES

Given that expectations constantly adjust to the changing state of the world, property rights—and the prices attached to them—constantly adjust in an ongoing process of internalization. In a world in which people can and do change activities to reflect their evolving expectations, externalities exist only when spillover effects are unexpected. Some examples will be helpful.

(1a) Smith owns a piece of land. Jones offers Smith $10,000 for an easement allowing Jones lawfully to drive his truck to and fro across Smith's unpaved land for the next ten years. Smith accepts. Jones then drives across Smith's land according to the agreement. Although Jones's truck leaves tire marks on Smith's land—marks that are unsightly to Smith—there is no externality. Why isn't Jones's crossing Smith's land an externality? One answer is "because Jones bought the right to drive his truck across Smith's land." While true, this answer doesn't reveal the essence of the situation.

Once Smith sold the easement to Jones, Smith *expected* Jones to drive across his land and leave tire marks. The price Smith received for the easement reflects his expectations of such negative spillovers. Smith internalized Jones's infliction of damage to Smith's land when he reasonably came to expect such damage. There is no externality despite one person (Jones) physically damaging property belonging to another person (Smith).

(1b) Changing the example only slightly yields a different outcome. If Jones owns no easement over Smith's land but drives his truck across the land and leaves unsightly tire marks, then Smith may suffer a negative externality. More to the point, his expectation of not having his property invaded by another has been violated. His property is damaged. A court would be expected to grant Smith's request to enjoin Jones's damaging actions, as well as hold Jones liable for damages inflicted on Smith. The parties could resolve the problem by bargaining or litigation.

(2a) Johnson's residence is 10 miles from downtown, where she works. She drives to and from her office on open-access roads. Her route, driven at 3:00 A.M., would take 15 minutes. But during rush hour the drive often takes an hour. The standard assessment of this situation is that it is rife with negative externalities.[44] The economist reasons that, when deciding to drive on particular roads, each driver considers the costs and benefits she experiences. Drivers do not account for the costs their driving imposes on other drivers.

There is no externality. Each day as she sets out to drive during rush hour, she is aware of the likely traffic conditions. Although Johnson is unhappy with those conditions, she chooses to drive on the traffic-jammed roads. She *expects* to encounter heavy traffic during rush hour. She internalizes the effects of the actions of the many other drivers who share the roads with her. They *owe* her nothing.

Moreover, her internalization of traffic congestion causes Johnson to alter her behavior. Where she chooses to live might be closer to her place of work than it would be if she didn't expect to encounter congestion. The price of her abode reflects expectations of congestion. *Ceteris paribus*, the prices of homes any given distance from a city center will be lower the greater the expected amount of traffic from that location. Suppose that Johnson would have paid $200,000 for a home 10 miles from the city if she expected little traffic during rush hour. If she expects heavy traffic, however, the value of that home to her falls. The *market* value of the home also falls because most people share Johnson's expectations of heavy traffic. So Johnson purchases the home for, say, $180,000 rather than the $200,000 that she would have paid in the absence of traffic congestion. The lower price of her home compensates her for the commute she expects to endure.

(2b) Suppose instead that Johnson bought a home that, although 10 miles from where she works, is next to a privately owned highway on which tolls are charged at market rates. Tolls are designed to ensure that traffic volumes are always socially "optimal." Given that traffic congestion on an identical open-access road imposes high costs on drivers—that is, given that the cost to each driver of the congestion is asserted to be inefficiently high—the cost to Johnson of paying tolls to drive on the uncongested restricted-access highway is lower than is the cost to Johnson of enduring the congestion that regularly slows her commute on an identical open-access highway. Johnson's cost to her of using the tolled, restricted-access highway is lower than is the cost to her of using the open-access highway, justifying to her the $200,000 price she paid for her home just off the restricted-access highway.

Unexpectedly, a year after Johnson bought her home, the government uses eminent domain to seize the restricted-access highway and convert it into a public, open-access highway. Johnson's commute suddenly becomes much longer. We might say that the conversion of the highway from restricted to open access imposes an externality on Johnson. Not only does she find herself confronting a longer commute than she reasonably expected when she bought the home, but the market value of her home will fall to reflect the increased inefficiency of the commute.[45] Because the government's action was unexpected, Johnson could not reasonably have adjusted to that action to shield herself from these losses. As in example (1b), a party here suffers an *unexpected* loss, or cost, because another party acted in a way not reasonably expected.

(3a) Williams has worked since she was 18 years old in a factory making furniture. Williams loses her job at age 50 because consumers' preference for lower-priced furniture imports causes her employer to go bankrupt. Williams suffers a loss. Economists generally classify Williams's loss as a "negative pecuniary externality." That is, she incurs a real loss, but its value is more than offset by positive pecuniary externalities (gains) to consumers from the lower prices paid for furniture. Because there is no net *social* loss with pecuniary externalities, economists conclude that corrective action by government is neither necessary nor appropriate.

That is, with pecuniary externalities there is no market failure. The failure of consumers, when buying furniture, to account for the consequences of their decisions on Williams and other domestic furniture producers is not a failure of consumers to take adequate account of the marginal social costs of their decisions. With pecuniary externalities there is no divergence between the marginal private cost and the marginal social cost of a decision. Although consumers do not account for the cost that purchases of imports impose on workers in domestic furniture factories, the consumer *does* account for gains from lower prices. Because the gains to consumers from competition-driven economic change can be shown to be at least as large as the losses the changes cause producers, there is no net *social* cost of competition-driven economic change.

We agree with standard economic analysis that in this example there is neither economic inefficiency nor any need for corrective intervention by government. But we disagree with those who contend the furniture worker suffers an externality so that some action, such as taxpayer-sponsored training programs, may be justified. In a market economy, particularly one in which employment contracts are at-will, no worker reasonably expects that she will keep her job for as long as she wants. Put differently, Williams expects, or should expect, that she might lose her job for any number of regularly occurring reasons, including changes in market conditions.

Williams reasonably *expected* the prospect of job loss and, therefore, internalized the prospect. She adjusted to it, or reasonably should have adjusted to it. For example, she and other furniture workers likely earned wages higher than for work at similar jobs in industries less likely to be subject to increased import competition. When the job loss occurs, Williams suffers no *externality*, no spillover effects from other people's actions that are not already internalized. She suffers nothing that "ought" to be compensated or that other people ought to be taxed for or prevented from imposing on her.

(3b) Williams at age 18 is unusually forward-looking and unusually economically risk-averse. She seeks the most secure employment possible.[46] She avoids employment in "tradable-goods" industries. She seeks employment in an occupation unlikely to be destroyed by imports. Williams moves to Nevada and works as a prostitute. After 20 years of work, the state of Nevada unexpectedly outlaws prostitution statewide. Williams might be said to suffer an externality. Having no good reason to expect that her occupation would be outlawed, Williams loses the opportunity to earn a living in that particular occupation, but, more to our point, she had no opportunity to adjust her actions to protect against this unexpected change.

Each of these examples features a person who experiences negative consequences, spillover effects, as a result of the actions of others. Yet in examples (1a), (2a), and (3a) the person *expects or should expect* to experience these consequences. Expectations lead one to adjust his or her actions to compensate for the expected negative effects. These expectations and the adjustments they spark internalize the spillover effects. In contrast, in examples (1b), (2b), and (3b), none of the individuals expects, or has reason to expect, the negative spillovers. The spillover effects in these cases can sensibly be called "externalities."

Example (1a) describes an obvious case of a spillover effect not being an externality on the person suffering that effect. Landowner Smith gave Jones permission to take the actions that generate some negative effect on Smith.[47] The absence of an externality in (2a) is less obvious. Nevertheless, no externality exists in (2a) because commuter and homeowner Johnson, expecting long commutes, takes other drivers' actions into account and changes her behavior accordingly. Given the existing property-rights structure of the roads (open access), Johnson has no property or other legal interest that is damaged, obstructed, or taken from her by other drivers. In (3a), Williams has no legal right to continued employment at any particular job and, thus, when she loses her job making furniture, she has no legal interest that is upended.

Matters differ in each of the "b" parts of the examples. In (1b) Smith suffers a violation of a legal right long recognized and enforced at common law. The violations in (2b) and (3b) are less straightforward but real. The expectations of Johnson in (2b) and Williams in (3b) were grounded in the existing structure of law and legislation. There was no reason to expect the changes. Unlike in (1b), neither of the individuals in (2b) and (3b) suffers an infringement of a right recognized at common law; each of the individuals in (2b) and (3b) suffers as a result of a legal change that no reasonable person had cause to expect.

To repeat: In a world in which people adjust activities[48] to reflect their expectations, externalities exist only when spillover effects are unexpected. When expected, spillover effects are incorporated into the structure of property rights. Transactions such as the purchase and sale of property, and the creation of contracts and protection of those interests from tortious interference, result in market prices for those rights that reflect expected spillover effects. When Jones buys an easement across Smith's land, Smith knows his enjoyment of his property will be affected. If after six years, Smith sells his land to Wilson, the property right that Wilson acquires does not allow him to unilaterally prevent Jones from crossing the land, according to the terms of the easement. When the easement was created, the nature of the property changed.

When Johnson drives on open-access roads, she has no reasonable expectation of enjoying exclusive use of the roads. If Johnson sues to reduce the number of drivers, and she proves that when she began to use the roads they were not as clogged with traffic, the court would deny her claim to possess a right to less traffic on those roads. Johnson should have expected the possibility that open-access roads could become clogged with traffic. If, in contrast, she had built and operated the roads privately, reserving to herself the right to decide who uses the roads and on what terms, matters would differ. Use of the roads by drivers who drive on them without Johnson's permission, even if she was not using the road, violates her property right.

In the case of Williams, who works in a furniture factory, her agreeing to work at-will means that she should reasonably expect the possibility that one day she will lose her job. She has no property right in her job. If Williams's employer contractually agreed never to fire her for as long as the employer remained in business, then Williams would have, by contract, certain property rights in her job.

A WORLD FILLED WITH SPILLOVERS

Prices, wages, and other market values adjust to reflect expectations of spillover effects. Obvious when stated, this conclusion is more substantive than it first appears. Most discussions of externalities begin midstream. Landowners are assumed to exist, and are assumed to use their land in certain ways. Factories are assumed to exist and are assumed to produce certain outputs using certain production methods. Drivers are assumed to exist, driving wherever they happen to drive. Residential areas are assumed to exist in locations particular distances from factories. The analyst then identifies spillovers across parties.

In a common example, a factory emits pollutants that dirty the air used by a nearby laundry to clean the clothes of customers, thereby inflicting a spillover on the laundry. A Pigovian (or Stiglitzian) draws a graph showing that the marginal private cost confronted by the factory owner is less than the marginal social cost of the factory's production activities. The Pigovian concludes that the factory produces too much output that results in too much pollution. Corrective taxes or regulations are necessary. The Coasean agrees with the Pigovian that a spillover exists, but disagrees on the solution. The Coasean notes that if rights to air quality exist, the parties can bargain or litigate to enforce rights. The "optimal" result will arise because the party who values the property right the most will buy it from (or not sell it to) the other party.

Factories and laundries do not simply pop into existence. Each sets up at a particular time and place, with a set of expectations about what it may and may not do. The decision by the party coming to the scene after the first party arrived determines the second party's expectations about the state of the world. If the laundry arrived on the scene after the factory, decisions by the laundry owner must incorporate legitimate expectations of the operation of the factory, including whatever spillover effects are likely to occur. The price the laundry owner paid for the site reflects these expectations, as do the supplies the laundry owner buys to operate his laundry.

The physical spillover effects the factory has on the laundry are indisputable, but are not externalities. The laundry owner's expectation of the effects must be presumed to be internalized in his decisions. Put differently, these spillover effects are part of the definition of both the laundry owner's property rights and the factory owner's property rights: to wit, the factory owns the right to emit certain pollutants, while the laundry owner owns no right to be free of such pollutants.

Externalities exist *only* when another party's actions create unexpected spillover effects.[49] Put differently, for there to be no externality, all that is necessary is that the party encountering spillover effects expects (or reasonably should expect) to encounter them. This expectation prompts the party to adjust to the expected effects.[50] To the extent that adjustments to the spillover effects do not occur because the benefits of adjusting do not justify the costs of doing so, the market value of affected properties adjusts to reflect the "unavoided" spillover effects.

When a spillover is expected, it is internalized on the parties to the effects, which eliminates the externality. Internalizing the externality does not require the party who might conventionally be identified as "causing" the spillover effect to take account of the effect either consciously or by responding appropriately to prices, taxes, or subsidies that include the value of the effect on the "victim" of the spillover. For example, for there to be no externality, it is not necessary (although it would be sufficient) for a railroad to take account of the effects that sparks from its locomotives have on the owners of lands adjoining the railroad's tracks. If the landowners expect their lands will be damaged by the sparks from locomotives, the landowners internalize such costs, say by moving their crops farther from the tracks or by growing crops less likely to burn easily. Further, the market value of the land incorporates the landowners' success or failure at avoiding the ill effects of the sparks.

When a pattern of effects is expected, the details of those expectations define the specific contours and contents of property rights. If owners of land adjoining railroad tracks expect routine damage to the land from locomotive sparks, the landowner does not own the right to be free of railroad sparks. That right is not one of the sticks in the landowners' bundle of rights. That stick is owned by the railroad.

PROPERTY RIGHTS LAW, NOT SOCIAL ENGINEERING

Unlike in the literature on externalities, nothing said here suggests that the absence of spillovers implies a Pareto-optimal allocation of resources. The problem is not externalities or spillover effects (anticipated or not). The problem, if one asserts there is a problem, is in the structure of property rights. It is necessary to have a set of institutions that allows parties to make deals under a set of enforceable and protected rights.

This approach describes traditional common-law courts. In *Sturges v. Bridgman*, the court was not called upon to make an economic assessment of which of the two parties was the least-cost avoider. The court was asked to determine which party had the property right to the noise and vibration environment of the building: the confectioner or the physician. When courts make such determinations, they ask which party acted consistently within prevailing expectations (rights structure).

The process of determining, in any legal case, which party is the least-cost avoider is not a rational calculation by the court but evolves from human behavior leading up to the dispute that gave rise to the case. The determinative factor, in short, is prevailing custom. The courts have long looked to community expectations, broadly defined, to discover as best as they can which party acted in a way most consistent with expectations. That party is the one declared to have "the right." Property rights are a bundle of *expectations* about how others (including the state) will act in different circumstances. Expectations may originally give rise to de facto property rights which, if courts rule in ways consistent with these expectations when disputes arise, become de jure property rights.

The prevailing pattern of expectations—and, hence, the particular arrangement of property rights in which expectations are embedded—is not necessarily economically optimal. The point is that no *externality* occurs when spillover effects are expected, or reasonably should be expected. In some instances, altering existing property rights might improve economic efficiency even if doing so violates prevailing expectations.[51]

The challenge is not for external observers, such as wise economists, to design and implement government policies that "internalize externalities" given transitory circumstances. There are few instances when someone experiences a consequence that he did not expect or had no good reason to expect (and, hence, to which he has not already adjusted his actions in a Pareto-optimal way). The challenge is to allow the evolution of a system of property rights that encourages productive social cooperation. Framing the problem as one centered on external effects deflects attention from the core issue and gives rise to the notion that planners can respond to issues and help construct statutory or administrative rules to enhance economic efficiency. To believe that can succeed requires omniscience by observers who generate policies divorced from politics. Both assumptions are absurd (Buchanan 1959).

CONCLUSION

Recall the origins of the concept of externality. Some economists asserted that by pulling the right levers, higher levels of wealth (all the way up to "bliss points") could be achieved. That tradition traces back at least to Marshall, as he worried that unregulated economies would underperform and, thus, that optimal performance required knowledgeable guidance. For years, development economists touted that line—backward countries could be pulled into modernization and wealth by assorted planning tools—investment in select infrastructure, import substitution policies, and more. Such ideas are not outmoded; they still abound, especially in the environmental area.

At the end of his paper with Barnett, Yandle explained that "a great deal of public policy is inappropriately based on the externality rationale. Neoclassical welfare economists let this genie out of the conceptual bottle. It is time to do what we can to put it back" (Barnett and Yandle 2009, 150). Perhaps it is slowly being pushed back in the bottle—a look at Ngram counts of "negative externality" indicates about a 10 percent decline following its peak in about 2003. Some of Bruce Yandle's thoughtful analysis of institutions and the environment may have contributed to this deserved decline.

NOTES

1. This is true of men and women.
2. We are not making light of the matter. Sex bias in orchestra auditions appears to be reduced by having the candidates behind a curtain when they perform (Goldin and Rouse 2000).
3. Keeping up with the Joneses can mean overconsumption, which could lead to obesity, which is an externality. See Mann (2017).
4. For an overview of the need to study institutions and special interests when considering environmental issues, see Yandle (1999).
5. We must note Bruce Yandle's synopsis of the much-misattributed Pigou in Yandle (2010).
6. This would be branded a positive externality in today's terminology.
7. That is the closing statement in his text, likely in opposition to Marxist thought much in vogue at the time.
8. Pigou recognized that transportation costs played a role in determining where resources would be allocated. He took such costs as a fact that prevented what might otherwise be a superior allocation of resources (Pigou 1920, 138–39). He did not discuss other transaction costs that "limit" the "best" distribution of resources. It fell largely to Ronald Coase later to note the prevalence of transaction costs and their effects on resource allocation. Part of the genius of successful organizations is to reduce such costs. See Coase (1937). See also Williamson (1985).
9. That is, the fact of imperfect knowledge causes wealth production to be lower than it could be. This conclusion is much like saying engines would work better if friction did not exist.
10. Pigou understood incentives. He noted (Pigou 1920, 183) that tenants would treat property differently than would property owners.
11. The scholar credited with first introducing lighthouses as supplying a good that cannot be adequately supplied in free markets is the British economist Henry Sidgwick. See Sidgwick (1883).
12. Pigou did not mention the health injuries that might be inflicted by pollution; the injury was to vegetables, laundries, and buildings. Perspectives change with knowledge, but the essential point is unchanged.
13. The article is called "two concepts," but the first four fit into the general notion of externality; the second concept he discussed relates to "industrialization of underdeveloped countries," where economists worry about incentives for savings tied to investment opportunities and about the desired amount of public investment in roads and such. It also mattered in a general equilibrium analysis of an economy where investment in industry A could spill over to benefit the development of industry B. One can see the impetus such work could produce for those concerned with central planning of an economy, but we will ignore this kind of externality.
14. Although the population almost tripled, SO_2 emissions in 2010 were less than half of what they were in 1950 in North America. See Hannah Ritchie and Max Roser, "Air Pollution," *Our World in Data*, https://ourworldindata.org/air-pollution/.

15. In contrast, in more recent times much has been made of "agglomeration externalities" that arise as groups of educated people benefit from each other. Acknowledging that this is obviously true does not justify government intervention. See Glaeser and Gottlieb (2009).

16. Meade later came to think subsidies and taxes may not be as justified as he thought earlier, as he expressed in a course on externalities that one of us took from him in 1974. Meade's example of beekeepers and orchardists benefiting each other but not through formal arrangements was shown to be factually incorrect (Cheung 1973).

17. Network externalities generally provide positive benefits—for example, the more people are connected to telephones or the internet, the more useful they are to others. The authors say we should think of "network effects," not "externalities" that imply something being imposed on someone against their will.

18. The economic view that pecuniary externalities are not things that should be of policy concern is consistent with the common law. There is no cause of action by an existing firm that suffers an income loss due to a new competitor. That rule goes back at least 700 years, as illustrated by the "Schoolmaster Case," *Hamlyn v. Moore*, Court of Common Pleas, 11 Henry IV 47 (1410). In that case, two schoolmasters sued a new schoolmaster who opened in competition, drawing students and their tuition away. Revenues fell by more than two-thirds at the existing school. The court rejected the claim. As Judge Hank explained: "if my neighbor built a mill and those accustomed to patron my mill went instead to his, whereby my profits were diminished: I would have no action. But if a miller disturbed the water running to my mill, or performed some other such nuisance, I would have recourse such as the law provides."

19. An allocation of resources is Pareto-optimal if it cannot be changed without making at least one person worse off. In contrast, if the current allocation of resources can be rearranged in such a way as to improve the welfare of at least one person without making anyone worse off, this allocation is not Pareto-optimal. In this case, the possibility exists for a "Pareto-superior" move—namely, reallocating resources in a way that makes at least one person better off without making anyone worse off.

20. The term "bliss point" must not be taken literally. An allocation of resources can be Pareto-optimal even though many, or even most, individuals in society are poor and miserable.

21. Bator drew on Paul Samuelson (1995, originally published 1955).

22. Bator was writing when air pollution was likely at its worst in the United States. Pollution was so bad in Los Angeles that crops were injured and many people suffered from the effects. Air pollution is now a tiny fraction of what existed in the 1950s and 1960s but, given the paucity of notice by economists, must have been considered an unavoidable part of economic progress.

23. Coase noted (Coase 1959, 27) that owning a bit of the radio spectrum would be the same. The owner could sue for interference.

24. Citation numbers are a bit dubious; nevertheless it is highly cited. In Google Scholar the paper is less cited than his earlier paper (Coase 1937). "Social Cost" may be the most cited paper in law reviews; see Shapiro and Pearse (2012). It should be noted that his 1937 paper presaged the later papers in that it made the point that transaction costs are critical to many things, including the existence of firms. In a world of zero transaction costs there would be no need for organizations such as firms.

25. Therefore, Herbert Hovenkamp, in an article critical of Coase's harsh treatment of Pigou, errs when he writes that "Coase uses the term 'externality' to signify the difference between marginal social and marginal private net product" (Hovenkamp 2009).

26. Landowners could take other action, such as keeping a barren strip along the railroad so sparks would be less likely to cause fires.

27. Coase later elaborated on this criticism of Pigou (Coase 1962):

> All this shows very clearly the bent of Pigou's mind. Notwithstanding that Pigou was, as Austin Robinson observes, "primarily concerned . . . with 'fruit' rather than 'light'; with

> writing a theory of welfare that was applicable in practices," he did not make any detailed studies of the working of economic institutions. His discussion of any particular question seems to have been based on the reading of a few books or articles and often does not rise above the level of the secondary literature on which he relied. The examples to be found in his works are really illustrative of his position rather than the basis for it. Austin Robinson tells us that in his reading Pigou was "seeking always realistic illustrations for quotation in his own work," and this indicates his manner of working. It is hardly surprising that, acquiring his illustrations in this way, Pigou often fails to realize their significance. For example, as I pointed out in "The Problem of Social Cost," the situation in which sparks from a railway locomotive could start fires which burnt woods on land adjoining the railway without the railway having to pay compensation to the owners of the woods (the legal position in England at the time Pigou was writing and one of which he had perhaps heard) had come about not because of a lack of governmental action but in consequence of it.

28. Coase (1962, 21–22):

> Pigou seems to have had no doubt that these Commissions would work in the way he describes. So, starting with a statement about the imperfections of government, Pigou discovers the perfect form of government organization and is therefore able to avoid enquiring into the circumstances in which the defects of public intervention would mean that such intervention would tend to make matters worse. Pigou's belief in the virtues of the independent regulatory commission, which seem to us laughable today, was first expressed in *Wealth and Welfare* in 1912 and repeated in all editions of *The Economics of Welfare* without change.

29. Public-sector decision makers, especially politicians, are rife with perverse incentives.
30. See Meiners and Czajkowski (2014). The Environmental Protection Agency takes credit for trillions of dollars worth of GDP.
31. The $17.2 billion estimate is at Bishop et al. (2017); the $661 million estimate is at E. English et al., "The Nationwide Loss of Recreational Ecosystem Services from the BP Gulf Oil Spill," 2017, manuscript available.
32. Again, economists are not to be concerned with personal distribution of resources, but helping achieve optimal outcome for society.
33. Buchanan was writing at the time he was working on *The Calculus of Consent* with Gordon Tullock, the primary reason he won the Nobel Prize. He was explaining something that seems obvious now, that politicians are not angels but actors who respond to special interests relevant to their self-interests. There is no reason to believe politicians will devise "optimal" policies.
34. That is, not only are politicians self-interested, but voters are too, and such interests cannot lead to imaginary bliss points, however economists imagine them to exist.
35. Buchanan noted that the discussion is what may be called the Pigovian tradition rather than what Pigou himself discussed or advocated.
36. Buchanan comes to this conclusion using the same theoretical models employed by welfare theorists.
37. Baumol (1972) ridicules Coase, noting that murder victims were in small-number situations but did not come to an acceptable bargain. He then asserts that, in the cases Coase discussed, a tax on pollution would have controlled the problem, so bargaining need not even occur (at page 309).
38. Informal arrangements often handle problems, in some instances contrary to formal rules. See Ellickson (1994). Even richer is the work of Elinor Ostrom on the evolution of ground-up institutions that resolve many resource conflicts (Ostrom 1990).
39. Beekeepers were noted previously; how lighthouses were privately provided was explained in Coase (1974).

40. These are oversimplifications but help make the point about viewpoints that often color analysis.

41. Named for George Stigler, who argued that markets are hyperefficient and, therefore, are almost never marked by Pareto-inefficient patterns of resource allocation. See Stigler (1976).

42. Named for F. A. Hayek, who argued that free markets generally *tend* toward optimal patterns of resource allocation but, because of imperfections in human knowledge and because of dynamic changes in the economy, this tendency is always a work in progress. Put differently, Hayek believed that the market is a *process* of constantly discovering and correcting error, but a process that is never complete. See Hayek (2002).

43. Named for Joseph Stiglitz, who argues that imperfect information, human weakness, and institutional imperfections generate a great deal of market failure—failure that can be reliably corrected only by government officials. See Stiglitz (1989).

44. Economists often advocate addressing the externality by pricing highway use, especially at peak hours, so as to close the gap between private costs and social costs—those imposed by a driver on other drivers. The assertion that raising the cost of driving will result in less driving is obviously correct. Harold Demsetz uses the congested roads example in Demsetz (2011).

45. Alternative parties can be said to "cause" the negative externality: one is the government, the other is the set of drivers whose actions create congestion. We can blame one or the other but not both. If the government had not converted the highway into an open-access road, the congestion would not occur. On the other hand, if each driver would altruistically and accurately take into consideration the effects that her use of the road has on other drivers, the congestion likewise would not occur. Deciding which of these two parties to "blame" likely reflects the analysts' normative position rather than any objective principle (Dahlman 1979). Nevertheless, because the government in this example actively altered an existing property-rights arrangement—and because, in doing so, it reasonably should have expected that one result would be traffic congestion—the government is the party appropriately identified as imposing the externality on Johnson (and on others similarly situated). In contrast to the government, none of the drivers on the now-congested, open-access highway took active steps to alter the property-rights arrangement. Each driver simply continues to behave consistently as a rational, utility-maximizing private actor. Given the choice of identifying one or the other of these parties as the "cause" of the externality, choosing the party that actively *and unexpectedly* altered the property-rights arrangements makes most sense. It should be noted that, under American law, Johnson would have no cause of action against the government for the losses it imposed on her, as the government was acting within its powers, regardless of the unexpected impacts.

46. The most secure employment possible, in fact, is one that we rule out here: self-sufficient existence, which necessarily involves subsistence farming. A truly self-sufficient person, one with no economic contact with others beyond his or her immediate family, will never want for work. His very survival requires constant toil and effort. The fact that almost no one today chooses such an existence implies that almost everyone today chooses to incur the risks of market variations in exchange for the benefits made available to those who participate in the market economy.

47. In the example, Smith received from Jones payment for this permission. Yet such a payment is not necessary. The essence of the example would be unchanged if Smith had given the easement to Jones free of charge.

48. These activities include the expression of valuations through decisions to buy and to sell (and to not buy and to not sell). This is a key point Terry Anderson makes in his chapter in this volume—if some people believe climate change is occurring, they incorporate that information into their decisions.

49. That is, externalities occur only when an existing property-rights arrangement is changed or violated.

50. It is possible that the expectation of some spillover effect causes no adjustment in the activities of the affected party. The absence of any such adjustment would signal that the costs of any possible adjustment outweigh the corresponding benefits.

51. In the example of open-access roads, if government restricts access to drivers who pay tolls that mimic market prices, Johnson and other drivers will be made better off. We recognize that certain activities may be deemed repugnant and so prohibited, such as restrictions on the entertainment called dwarf tossing. See Roth (2007).

REFERENCES

Aronsson, T., and O. Johansson-Stenman. 2015. "Keeping Up with the Joneses, the Smiths and the Tanakas: On International Tax Coordination and Social Comparisons." *Journal of Public Economics* 131: 71–86.

Barnett, A. H., and B. Yandle. 2009. "The End of the Externality Revolution." *Social Philosophy and Policy* 26, no. 2: 130–50.

Bator, F. M. 1958. "The Anatomy of Market Failure." *Quarterly Journal of Economics* 72, no. 3: 351–79.

Baumol, W. J. 1972. "On Taxation and the Control of Externalities." *American Economic Review* 62, no. 3: 307–22.

Bishop, R. C., K. J. Boyle, R. T. Carson, D. Chapman, W. M. Hanemann, B. Kanninen, R. J. Kopp, J. A. Krosnick, J. List, N. Meade, and R. Paterson. 2017. "Putting a Value on Injuries to Natural Assets: The BP Oil Spill." *Science* 356, no. 6335: 253–54.

Bohn, D. 2013. "Ronald Coase, the 'Father' of the Spectrum Auction, Dies at 102." *The Verge*, September 3. https://www.theverge.com/2013/9/3/4691908/ronald-coase-the-father-of-the-spectrum-auction-dies-at-102.

Boudreaux, D. J., R. E. Meiners, and T. J. Zywicki. 1999. "Talk Is Cheap: The Existence Value Fallacy." *Environmental Law* 29: 765–802.

Buchanan, J. M. 1959. "Positive Economics, Welfare Economics, and Political Economy." *Journal of Law & Economics* 2: 124–38.

——. 1962. "Politics, Policy, and the Pigovian Margins." In *Classic Papers in Natural Resource Economics*, edited by Chennat Gopalakrishnan, 204–18. London: Palgrave Macmillan.

——. 1969. "External Diseconomies, Corrective Taxes, and Market Structure." *American Economic Review* 59, no. 1: 174–77.

Buchanan, J. M., and W. C. Stubblebine. 1962. "Externality." In *Classic Papers in Natural Resource Economics*, edited by Chennat Gopalakrishnan, 138–54. London: Palgrave Macmillan.

Cheung, S. N. 1970. "The Structure of a Contract and the Theory of a Non-Exclusive Resource." *Journal of Law & Economics* 13, no. 1: 49–70.

——. 1973. "The Fable of the Bees: An Economic Investigation." *Journal of Law & Economics* 16, no. 1: 11–33.

Coase, R. H. 1937. "The Nature of the Firm." *Economica* 4, no. 16: 386–405.

——. 1959. "The Federal Communications Commission." *Journal of Law & Economics* 2: 1–40.

——. 1960. "The Problem of Social Cost." In *Classic Papers in Natural Resource Economics*, edited by Chennat Gopalakrishnan, 87–137. London: Palgrave Macmillan.

——. 1962. "The Interdepartment Radio Advisory Committee." *Journal of Law & Economics* 5: 17–47.

——. 1974. "The Lighthouse in Economics." *Journal of Law & Economics* 17, no. 2: 357–76.

——. 2012. *The Firm, the Market, and the Law*. Chicago: University of Chicago Press.

Dahlman, C. J. 1979. "The Problem of Externality." *Journal of Law & Economics* 22, no. 1: 141–62.

Demsetz, H. 1996. "The Core Disagreement between Pigou, the Profession, and Coase in the Analyses of the Externality Question." *European Journal of Political Economy* 12, no. 4: 565–79.

——. 2011. "The Problem of Social Cost: What Problem?" *Review of Law & Economics* 7: 1–13.

Eckerstorfer, P., and R. Wendner. 2013. "Asymmetric and Non-Atmospheric Consumption Externalities, and Efficient Consumption Taxation." *Journal of Public Economics* 106: 42–56.

Ellickson, R. C. 1994. *Order without Law: How Neighbors Settles Disputes*. Cambridge, MA: Harvard University Press.

Frank, R. H. 2008. "Should Public Policy Respond to Positional Externalities?" *Journal of Public Economics* 92, nos. 8–9: 1777–86.

Glaeser, E. L., and J. D. Gottlieb. 2009. "The Wealth of Cities: Agglomeration Economies and Spatial Equilibrium in the United States." *Journal of Economic Literature* 47, no. 4: 983–1028.

Goldin, C., and C. Rouse. 2000. "Orchestrating Impartiality: The Impact of 'Blind' Auditions on Female Musicians." *American Economic Review* 90, no. 4: 715–41.

Hamermesh, D. S., and J. E. Biddle. 1994. "Beauty and the Labor Market." *American Economic Review* 84, no. 5: 1174–94.

Hayek, F. A. 2002. "Competition as a Discovery Procedure." *Quarterly Journal of Austrian Economics* 5, no. 3: 9–23.

Henderson, J. M., and R. E. Quant. 1971. *Microeconomic Theory: A Mathematical Approach*, 2nd ed. New York: McGraw-Hill.

Hovenkamp, H. 2009. "The Coase Theorem and Arthur Cecil Pigou." *Arizona Law Review* 51: 633–49.

Liebowitz, S. J., and S. E. Margolis. 1994. "Network Externality: An Uncommon Tragedy." *Journal of Economic Perspectives* 8, no. 2: 133–50.

Mann, R. 2017. "Controlling the Environmental Costs of Obesity." *Environmental Law* 47, no. 3: 697–739.

Marshall, A. 1920. *Principles of Economics*, 8th ed. London: MacMillan.

Meade, J. E. 1952. "External Economies and Diseconomies in a Competitive Situation." *Economic Journal* 62, no. 245: 54–67.

Meckling, W. H., and A. A. Alchian. 1960. "Incentives in the United States." *American Economic Review* 50, no. 2: 55–61.

Meiners, R., and R. Czajkowski. 2014. "Making Cost-Benefit a Political Tool." *LSU Journal of Energy, Law, & Resources* 3: 225–57.

Mills, E. S., and P. E. Graves. 1986. *The Economics of Environmental Quality*, 2nd ed. New York: W. W. Norton.

Ostrom, E. 1990. *Governing the Commons: The Evolution of Institutions for Collective Action*. Cambridge: Cambridge University Press.

Parrish, D., and W. Stockwell. 2015. "Urbanization and Air Pollution: Then and Now." *EOS: Earth & Space Science News*, January 8. https://eos.org/features/urbanization-air-pollution-now.

Pigou, A. C. 1920. *The Economics of Welfare*. London: Macmillan.

Roth, A. E. 2007. "Repugnance as a Constraint on Markets." *Journal of Economic Perspectives* 21, no. 3: 37–58.

Samuelson, P. A. 1995. "Diagrammatic Exposition of a Theory of Public Expenditure." In *Essential Readings in Economics*, edited by Saul Estrin and Alan Marin, 159–71. London: Palgrave Macmillan.

Scitovsky, T. 1954. "Two Concepts of External Economies." *Journal of Political Economy* 62, no. 2: 143–51.

Shapiro, F. R., and M. Pearse. 2012. "The Most-Cited Law Review Articles of All Time." *Michigan Law Review* 110, no. 8: 1483–1520.

Sidgwick, H. 1883. *The Principles of Political Economy*. Cambridge: Cambridge University Press.

Stigler, G. J. 1976. "The Xistence of X-efficiency." *American Economic Review* 66, no. 1: 213–16.

Stiglitz, J. E. 1989. "Markets, Market Failures, and Development." *American Economic Review* 79, no. 2: 197–203.

Viner, J. 1931. "Cost Curves and Supply Curves." *Zeitschrift für Nationalökonomie* 3, no. 1: 23–46.

Williamson, O. E. 1985. *The Economic Institutions of Capitalism*. New York: Free Press.

Yandle, B. 1999. "Public Choice at the Intersection of Environmental Law and Economics." *European Journal of Law and Economics* 8, no. 1: 5–27.

——. 2010. "Much Ado about Pigou." *Regulation* 33, no. 2: 2–4.

CHAPTER 3
Viewing Carbon Emission through Coase-Colored Glasses

TERRY L. ANDERSON

When climate scientists noted an uptick in global temperatures and attributed it to greenhouse gas emissions, both the hypothesized cause and the measured effect were clear—CO_2 was hypothesized to cause global temperatures to rise. Drawing the analogy with a greenhouse made the hypothesized connection even more understandable. As models and measurement have become more sophisticated, however, it appears that factors other than CO_2, such as ocean currents and variations in distance from the sun, may contribute to climate change. Thus, isolating the effects of human action on climate has become all the more difficult.

Whatever the source, climate change brings consequences. Changes in crop yields, in frequency and intensity of wildfires, in habitats for living species, in water supplies, and in recreational possibilities such as skiing, all disrupt our status quo lives, especially as they are conditioned by fixed investments. Wine production might have to move to other locations, wildfires change our viewsheds to say nothing of destroying houses and killing people, species may

This paper is an adaptation of material found in Anderson and Leal (2015) and in Anderson and Libecap (2014).

have to move or even go extinct, water storage may have to be increased, and ski lifts may be without snow.

In short, climate change is about dealing with new variations and new risks, both of which are time and place specific and neither of which is easily predictable in the short run. Moreover, regulations designed to reduce greenhouse gas emissions are difficult to implement, difficult to enforce, and likely to make little difference to the climate in the short run.

Economists have not been very useful in policy debates because they have framed climate change as an externality problem, thus leading to recommendations to internalize alleged social costs. Their solutions emphasize the need for carbon taxes or cap-and-trade programs, and both generally have been nonstarters.

Though prices are not the only information through which humans might adapt to climate change, they are part of the matrix of information that stimulates decision-making. Through asset market processes, adaptation will generate prices that reflect the effect of climate change on resource values, location of production, financial services, and insurance, to mention a few areas. The important policy issue, therefore, is whether markets accurately reflect the geographic and temporal risks associated with climate change or, for that matter, reflect the basic limits and variations associated with forces other than those of human action.

If we cannot reduce greenhouse gas emissions and if mitigation is slow, expensive, and often ineffective, is there anything to be done other than throwing up our hands in despair? The answer is that we will have to adapt through human ingenuity—ingenuity in response to new information about climate that is time and place specific.

In order to shift the focus to adaptation, it is useful to refocus using the insights of Nobel laureate Ronald Coase regarding the reciprocal nature of costs, the importance of transaction costs, and the potential for adjustments other than direct bargaining. Applying these insights to environmental issues generally owes much to Bruce Yandle, who recognized more than most that property rights and transaction costs are at the heart of virtually every environmental problem (Yandle 1997). His insights emphasize that environmental problems result from competition for the use of resources.

In the case of climate change, the competition is between those who want to use the earth's atmosphere as a depository for greenhouse gas emission and those who value the atmosphere as the determining factor in climate variations. In the absence of clear property rights to use of the atmosphere, competition leads to conflicts that cannot be resolved by bargaining. Viewing climate change through Coase (or Yandle)-colored glasses provides a way to understand how market forces can and will cause human adaptation. To the extent that market processes generate prices reflecting new variation and risk associated with climate change, they signal benefits from adapting. Thus, the key policy issue is how to ensure that market prices reflect climate change reality and, if not, what policies would encourage such a reflection.

Even if bargaining is precluded due to transaction costs between parties competing for use of a scarce resource, nonetheless, one or both of the parties using that resource will see costs reflected in other asset prices. In other words, regardless of who is causing what and who has what rights, resource rents will change as the climate changes. In summary, climate change will affect resource rents—especially land prices—with those rents rising for people who benefit from carbon emissions and falling for those who bear the costs. Changes in rents, in turn, will induce human adaptation to climate change.

DYNAMIC NATURE AND DYNAMIC HUMANS

The idea of stability and equilibrium in nature is deeply rooted, but ecologists have increasingly begun to question the notion of a balance of nature. As ecologist Daniel Botkin documents in his influential book, *Discordant Harmonies: A New Ecology for the Twenty-First Century*, the conventional view of stable nature is unsupported by the evidence. In reality, Botkin argues, "nature undisturbed is not constant in form, structure, or proportion, but changes at every scale of time and space" (Botkin 1990, 62).

Despite increasing recognition that nature is neither static nor balanced, environmental policies remain rooted in outdated views of equilibria in nature. Daniel Botkin summed up the extent to which equilibrium views are entrenched in the way ecologists think about environmental policy: "If you ask an ecologist if nature never changes, he will almost always say no. But if you ask that same ecologist to design a policy, it is almost always a balance of nature policy" (as cited in Marris 2011, 30).

Such policy prescriptions abound for the global climate. Regulations on energy technology, caps on greenhouse gas emissions, and carbon taxes are examples of static policies that assume we can know some optimal level of emissions, an optimal level of rainfall, and even an optimal level of variation in temperature. Most policies suggest there is a level of greenhouse gas emissions that will lead to a global climate balance. Unlike a resource such as a fishery, for which we can conceive of a sustainable yield dependent on the reproductive capacity of the fish and their habitat, there is no equivalent biological or climatological capacity for the atmosphere.

Just as ecologists often focus on static views of nature, economists traditionally view markets like a Kodachrome still-life image. The standard blackboard assumptions of perfect information, costless market transactions, and perfect competition focus economists' attention on points of equilibrium in which the forces of supply and demand are perfectly balanced. This view distracts economists from the market processes, entrepreneurial activities, and institutions that guide human action such as adaptation. To paraphrase ecologist Botkin, "If you ask an economist if markets never change, he will almost always say no. But if you ask that same economist to design a policy, it is almost always a market equilibrium policy" (as cited in Marris 2011, 30).

Although equilibrium concepts are useful for developing hypotheses and gaining insights into basic market responses, the Kodachrome snapshot obscures the IMAX show of the market process. Much like the interaction of organisms in nature, markets are processes of interaction among individuals, each of whom acts on time- and place-specific information. Just as individual species fill niches in ecosystems, human entrepreneurship fills niches in markets that are constantly evolving in a Darwinian sense.

In both ecosystems and markets, individual action promotes a Hayekian spontaneous order that emerges in a bottom-up evolutionary manner. The process of Darwinian evolution is akin to Adam Smith's view of human economies. As Matt Ridley explains, both are "spontaneously self-ordered through the actions of individuals, rather than ordained by a monarch or a parliament" (Ridley 2009). Market processes and evolution occur spontaneously at the individual level and aggregate through multiple evolving collectives. Indeed, the invisible hand is just as evident in ecosystems as it is in markets.

In the case of market processes, prices are the signal that incorporates information about nature's bounty (or lack thereof), technology, and human preferences. As Hayek (1945) pointed out, prices communicate decentralized knowledge of the relative scarcity of resources that cannot be easily comprehended entirely by any individual or group of central planners. They reflect dispersed knowledge that is "not given to anyone in its totality" (Hayek 1945, 520). As prices adjust to the special circumstances of time and place, people adapt their behavior to the price information.

CLIMATE CHANGE THROUGH A PIGOVIAN LENS

Given that humans and nature are inextricably connected and always in flux, the challenge is to develop institutions that encourage the generation of information and incentives that reflect the value of competing uses for resources—in the case of climate change, the atmosphere as a medium for the release of gases (e.g., CO_2) and for affecting climate. With so many different parties competing for these uses—beer producers releasing CO_2 and ski areas wanting stable and predictable snow levels—it is difficult to imagine how they could bargain with one another to resolve the competition. Unlike Coase's example of the confectioner and the doctor who share a common wall between their offices, those competing for use of the atmosphere cross time, space, cultures, and governments, making the costs of negotiation for atmospheric use astronomical.

Because property rights to the use of the global atmosphere are not defined and because negotiation costs are high, most economists conclude that markets fail without a price on the use of the atmosphere. The Pigovian argument is that treating the atmosphere as a commons results in decentralized market processes in which prices do not reflect all the costs of using the global atmosphere as a carbon sink. As A. C. Pigou explained the problem, there is a divergence between private and social costs, "owing to the technical difficulty of enforcing compensation for incidental disservices" (Pigou 1920, 185). He called the resulting efficiency loss a reduction in the "national dividend." With billions of people competing for the use of the atmosphere, affecting climate change, and billions of people emitting gases that may be responsible for the effect, it is technically impossible to enforce compensation for incidental disservices. The absence of property rights and high transaction costs preclude contracts governing the use of the global atmosphere. In other words, "technical difficulties" prevent a market from producing an optimal amount of emissions.

Through a Pigovian lens, the policy challenge is to price or regulate the use of the atmosphere for greenhouse gas emissions, and the common answer for this challenge is a carbon tax. As Pigou understood, however, establishing the right price or the right level of emissions through a political process is difficult. As he put it:

> It is not sufficient to contrast the imperfect adjustments of unfettered private enterprise with the best adjustment that economists in their studies can imagine. For we cannot expect that any State authority will attain, or will even whole-heartedly seek, that ideal. Such authorities are liable

> alike to ignorance, to sectional pressure and to personal corruption by private interest. (Pigou 1920, 296)

Thus, in addition to the knowledge problem identified by Hayek (1945), political pressures also distort the actions of decision makers in the political process. "Every public official is a potential opportunity for some form of self-interest arrayed against the common interest," Pigou warned (1920, 296–97). That is, because regulation and taxation will be conditioned by political pressures, a carbon tax is less likely to bring social and private costs into balance than it is to benefit the politically powerful.

WHY NOT REGULATION

If the problems Pigou recognized are difficult to overcome when they involve only one government—local, state, or federal—they are exponentially greater when they require collective action by many sovereign nations. Even if multiple governments can reach agreement on the level of greenhouse gas emissions or on the price for carbon, there remains the task of enforcing those agreements.

The 1997 Montreal Protocol on Substances that Deplete the Ozone Layer is heralded as a success story to be emulated as an international treaty that regulated and reduced the use of chlorofluorocarbons (CFCs). CFCs were a major propellant used in aerosols and refrigerants. Because they contribute to ozone depletion in the stratosphere, which could increase surface radiation, nations came together in an effort to agree on how to reduce CFC use.

Because poor countries were just beginning to enjoy the benefits of CFCs in consumer goods and could not easily afford alternative refrigerants if a ban was implemented, there were vast differences among countries in their willingness to cut back on CFC use. As the Associated Press (1989) reported, "China, India, and other populous developing nations embarking on mass production of consumer goods containing chlorofluorocarbons reason that since the West invented and produces most of the ozone-destroying chemicals, the West should pay to replace them."

Despite the initial disagreements and the global problems of enforcement, there has been a remarkable reduction in CFC production and use. A major lubricant for agreement was a Multilateral Fund for the Implementation of the Montreal Protocol, to which richer nations contributed and from which poorer nations could obtain funds to pay for compliance. Moreover, because richer countries contributed a disproportionate amount of CFCs, large reductions in those countries led to important changes in total levels of CFCs in the atmosphere, which, in turn, had a direct impact on reducing the ozone hole. According to the Environmental Protection Agency (2010), "U.S. production of ozone-depleting gases has declined significantly since 1988, and has now reached levels (measured by their ozone depletion potential) comparable to those of 30 years ago." Reductions have been aided by technological developments that produced cheaper substitutes, thus reducing the use of CFCs as refrigerants, aerosol propellants, and solvents. Compliance was made somewhat simpler by the fact that the protocol focuses on only one form of emissions, CFCs, which makes it easier to enforce. Finally, rapidly rising global incomes allowed even poorer countries the luxury of using alternative propellants and refrigerants, especially as they fell in price.

Although the success of the Montreal Protocol offers hope for international agreements, optimism for their success in curbing greenhouse gases is guarded (see Molina and Zaelke 2012). First, unilateral action by any individual nation or even a small group of nations will have no meaningful effect on the earth's future climate, which is in sharp contrast to the effect of US reductions in CFCs. Nonetheless, there have been limited jurisdictional efforts such as the Regional Greenhouse Gas Initiative (RGGI). This initiative is a cap-and-trade program agreed to by nine eastern states—Connecticut, Delaware, Maine, Massachusetts, New Hampshire, New Jersey, New York, Rhode Island, and Vermont—to reduce CO_2 emissions by 10 percent between 2009 and 2018. The first three years of the RGGI were successful at reducing annual emissions by 23 percent, but part of the reason for the reductions was the 2008 recession. Again, it is important to recognize that such reductions are meaningless in terms of their effect on the overall global climate.

Second, compared to controlling greenhouse gas emissions, managing CFCs is easy. The Montreal Protocol focused on a single category of gases, the production of which is relatively easily monitored, in part due to a limited number of producers; it included a mechanism to help poor countries comply; and it had relatively immediate effects on the ozone layer once reduction occurred. All of these made it easier to agree on the limits and enforce them. It is virtually impossible to identify sources of greenhouse gas emissions because they involve everyone on earth, from us breathing out CO_2 to stationary fossil fuel–burning power plants to mobile vehicle sources. Measuring and monitoring greenhouse gas emissions from diverse sources is costly, to say the least, and enforcing limits on emissions is virtually impossible.

Third, there are vastly divergent values of trading off present economic growth for predictions of future global warming. Initially, the Stern report in 2006 estimated that the rate of growth in global income would be reduced by

5 percent "per year, now and forever" owing to climate change (Stern 2006). That estimate of immediate catastrophe was reduced tremendously in 2014 by the Intergovernmental Panel on Climate Change (IPCC), which projected just a 2.5 percent reduction in the global income growth rate by the end of the 21st century. Until lower-income countries experience some of the growth that has been enjoyed by wealthier countries that have made the greatest contributions to greenhouse gases, they are likely to limit their consumption of fossil fuels.

Finally, even if cap-and-trade regulations or carbon taxes can be implemented, political meddling with the terms of trade or tax levels will undermine such efforts. Despite some successes in fisheries management and SO_2 emissions, so-called market-like approaches for greenhouse gas emissions face three important hurdles:

- First, to be effective, the cap would have to be adhered to by enough nations to make a meaningful difference in total greenhouse gas emissions. Such agreement has been elusive because developing nations such as China and India do not want to jeopardize their growth prospects by limiting the use of fossil fuels.
- Second, even if a cap can be agreed on, the distribution of the cap matters greatly because it determines who will bear the costs of greenhouse gas emission reductions. In particular, poorer nations make a legitimate case that richer nations that have already contributed to existing stores of greenhouse gases in the atmosphere should reduce more, a case that is easy to accept on principle, but more difficult to accept in practice.
- Third, enforcing adherence to a greenhouse gas cap is impossible without a global enforcement mechanism. Enforcement among the states within a sovereign nation is possible, as with the Colorado River Compact, but agreements between national sovereigns, like the migratory bird and halibut treaties, are more easily enforced because they are between nations with mutual interests and other commonalities. Enforcing greenhouse gas limits around the globe is an entirely different matter.

To see how difficult it is to apply cap-and-trade to greenhouse gases, consider the European Union Emission Trading System (EU ETS), the largest such trading scheme, covering 15 countries. Despite the fact that it involves countries with economies that are bound together by the EU and have similar economic conditions, the effectiveness of the EU ETS has been limited, not so much because of enforcement problems under the EU umbrella, but because of political manipulations of the market.

In particular, there has been a continual increase in the emission permits issued under the scheme. Just as rapid increases in the money supply reduce the value of currency, increases in the number of permits reduce their value in the trading market. Hence, between 2008 and 2011, the price of permits fell from $43 to $14.30, and has continued to decline. The economic downturn in 2008 and the increased use of natural gas (a fuel with a lower greenhouse gas footprint) for electricity production explain part of the decline, but not all of it. Anderson and Libecap (2014, 187) conclude that:

> This is indicative of a potentially insecure cap-and-trade market, subject to political and bureaucratic interventions that can undermine its effectiveness. . . . Adjusting the cap requires negotiations among EU members, and high emitters, such as Poland, resist further cap reductions. These political moves probably cannot be avoided, suggesting that the cap will be set higher than would be the case if firms were more homogeneous and located in a single political jurisdiction.

CLIMATE CHANGE THROUGH COASE-COLORED GLASSES

Ronald Coase's famous article on "The Problem of Social Cost" provides an alternative way to think about climate change (Coase 1960), one that has not received much attention but provides the basis for thinking about the incentives to human adaptation to climate change, whatever its cause or magnitude.[1] To start thinking about climate change through Coasean glasses, assume that it is not caused by anthropogenic greenhouse gas emissions, but rather is the result of some force of nature beyond the human hand. Hence, climate change is not the result of technical difficulties of enforcing compensation for incidental disservices because there is no party producing the disservices. There is no externality crutch on which to stand, but only "natural" changes that affect human productivity.

Such natural climate changes would be reflected in property values to the extent that those property values are affected by climate. Beachfront properties subject to rising sea levels would be less valuable. Agricultural land with more precipitation would be more valuable. Rather than market failure, markets would reflect resource values, and people would adjust—adapt—accordingly.

Now assume there is a connection between anthropogenic greenhouse gas emissions and global warming. Seen through Coase-colored glasses, those owning assets whose rents would decline as a result of climate change point the finger at emitters of greenhouse gases, accusing them of creating "incidental disservices." People earning rents from disposing of carbon into the atmosphere point fingers at receptors of climate change, saying that reducing carbon emissions creates an "incidental service" for which emitters are not compensated. Hence, as Coase pointed out, these costs are reciprocal. Therein lies the reason finding political solutions is difficult.

Coase showed that the direction of the reciprocal costs depends on the assignment of property rights and that the potential for compensation, that is, a market transaction, would depend on the transaction costs of trading property rights. In the case of greenhouse gas emissions and climate change, the transaction costs are, for all intents and purposes, infinite.

If we accept the point made by Harold Demsetz (2003) that transaction costs are simply costs, logically and economically no different from transportation costs, then solving the problem of climate change becomes a matter of understanding how rents change, who captures the different rents, and who adapts in what ways to the changes. It comes as no surprise that people owning beachfront property would rather continue receiving their rents without climate change and that coal-burning power plant owners would prefer to continue receiving rents from disposing of carbon into the atmosphere. If neither party can attain a political solution allowing them to capture their rents, which means establishing property rights, the status quo will prevail, with the atmosphere being a carbon dump and rents accruing to owners of carbon assets.

Putting aside the equity and distributional considerations of this conclusion, prices of assets that reflect differential rents should induce people to adapt. This is no different than if climate change were the result of some natural force where fingers could not be pointed by one party or another. Whether we conclude that adaptation generates an efficient response to climate change subject to transaction costs, as Demsetz might, is not important. What is important is that rents are the key to adaptation.

ADAPT, ADAPT, AND BECOME ADEPT

By focusing on market prices that reflect differential rents, we begin to see how adaptation to climate change might occur. Standard static models evaluate externalities by focusing on achieving "optimality" by presuming we can measure social cost and thereby force a move to a static equilibrium that now includes asserted social costs. If, instead, we recognize that people respond to changing environmental conditions (e.g., experiencing rising sea levels) and resource prices that reflect those conditions (e.g., falling beachfront property values), the prospects of gloom, predicted by the IPCC reports or by the *National Climate Assessment* for the United States, become less likely. This is because human actions through market processes, entrepreneurial activities, and institutional evolution allow us to adapt to the dynamic environment, including climate change, especially when changes are incremental and slow to occur.

When humans experience changes in their environment and are not prevented from adapting to the changes, they have shown a remarkable ability to do so. Rising sea level is one of the major concerns about global warming. As the *National Climate Assessment* puts it:

> Sea level is projected to rise by another 1 to 4 feet in this century. A wider range of scenarios, ranging from 8 inches to 6.6 feet of rise by 2100, has been suggested for use in risk-based analyses. In general, higher emissions scenarios that lead to more warming would be expected to lead to sea level rise toward the upper end of the projected range. The stakes are high, as nearly five million Americans live within four feet of the local high-tide level. (National Climate Assessment and Development Advisory Committee 2013, 4)

Comparing today to a century hence ignores the fact that sea levels rise very slowly, giving people time to move. In fact, according to the US census, between 1990 and 2008, "the growth in coastline counties fell below the growth for the nation and its noncoastline counties" (Wilson and Fischetti 2010, 3), suggesting that the geographic distribution of the population is dynamic, perhaps even already responding to global warming concerns, and certainly responding to catastrophes such as Hurricane Sandy by not returning to coastal areas. To be sure, such responses are more likely for people who have good information about alternative places to live and who are better able to afford the move, again suggesting that sacrificing income today may hinder adaptation in the future.

Even if the atmosphere as a greenhouse gas sink and greenhouse gas emissions themselves are not priced, prices correlated with the effects of climate change will induce adaptation. For example, if climate change reduces the productivity of land for certain wheat production, the price of land will be high relative to its productivity. This generates an incentive for wheat farmers to seek new places for wheat production where land prices are lower. Hence the 2012 Bloomberg news headline, "Corn Belt Shifts North with Climate as Kansas Crop Dies."

This is McKenzie Funk's thesis in his book titled *Windfall: The Booming Business of Global Warming* (Funk 2014). Changes in the arctic sea ice ("the Melt"), changes in water supplies ("the Drought"), and changes in coastal flooding ("the Deluge") are the three central categories into which Funk pigeonholes entrepreneurial responses to climate opportunities. He asserts that his book is an answer to the increasingly urgent question: "What *are* we doing about climate change?" (Funk 2014, 11). Here are a few examples of climate entrepreneurs who aren't just talking about the weather; they are doing something about it.

- Vintner Matthieu Elzinga moved from his vineyard in the Loire Valley of France to an emerging wine region in southern England. Such a move is consistent with the findings of a Conservation International and National Academy of Sciences study predicting that areas suitable for viticulture will decrease "25% to 73% in major wine producing regions by 2050" (Hannah et al. 2013).
- John Dickerson, founder and CEO of Summit Global Management and its subsidiary, Summit Water Development Group, is positioning his company for more frequent water shortages, extreme weather events, flooding, and shifts in growing seasons; water markets are beginning to flourish. In a conversation with Funk, Dickerson noted, "We still have the exact same amount [of water] in our ecosphere," so "the ultimate effect of global warming is that the percentage that is freshwater is getting smaller, the percentage that is salt water is getting larger, and the maldistribution of freshwater is getting much more severe" (as cited in Funk 2014, 119). Because these conditions are expected to lead to higher prices for water in areas receiving less rainfall, Dickerson has positioned himself well in the water market by purchasing water rights in Australia and the American West.
- Hedge fund managers are using derivatives to deal with climate variation. Ski resorts, for example, can purchase snow derivatives to hedge against low snowfalls. The resort essentially bets against other investors, with the ski resort being paid if snow falls below a level specified in the contract or paying if it is above that level. This helps spread the cost of the risk associated with climate uncertainty.

- Astute environmental entrepreneurs find innovative ways to achieve their conservation goals in the face of climate variation. For example, the Fresh Water Trust in Oregon uses option contracts to lower the cost of restoring and preserving stream flows and fish habitat. When there is an abundance of runoff, it has nothing to worry about, but when there is little rain or snow in the mountains, it must compete with irrigators to keep the streams flowing. In some cases, it simply purchases water rights and halts irrigation, but in others, it purchases options from farmers. When stream flows are low, the trust exercises its option and pays the farmer to stop irrigating, leaving the water for fish.

There is evidence that property owners who experience increased coastal flooding due to slowly rising sea levels are moving to higher ground. A paper by three Harvard University professors (Keenan, Hill, and Gumber 2018) tested the hypothesis "that the rate of price appreciation of single-family properties in MDC (Miami-Dade County) is positively related to and correlated with incremental measures of higher elevation." Using the value of 107,984 properties between 1971 and 2017, they found a positive relationship between price appreciation and elevation in 76 percent of the properties (82,068) in the sample.

A similar study by economists at the University of Colorado and Penn State (Bernstein, Gustafson, and Lewis 2019) found that beachfront homes in Miami exposed to rising sea levels sell at a 7 percent discount compared to properties with less exposure to coastal flooding. Moreover, the discount has risen significantly over the past decade. Comparing rental rates to selling prices of coastal homes, they found that the discount in selling prices "does not exist in rental rates, indicating that this discount is due to expectations of future damage, not current property quality."

Though not armed with large datasets and sophisticated regressions, Massachusetts realtors are coming to the same conclusions (Conti 2018). According to Jim McGue, a Quincy real estate agent, the nor'easter that "happened here in March certainly underscores what a 100-year flood map is all about" (as quoted in Conti 2018). Another broker, Maureen Celata from Revere, said a home that included a private beach sold for 9 percent less than its list price of nearly $799,000 and took 55 days to sell, which she called an "eternity."

Wine producers in California, Bordeaux, and Tuscany beware. A study by Conservation International published in the *Proceedings of the National Academy of Sciences* forecasts that wine production in California may drop by 70 percent and in regions along the Mediterranean by as much as 85 percent over the next 50 years (Hannah et al. 2013). The silver lining is that vintners will adapt by moving their grape production north, some predicting it will even move to places such as Montana, Wyoming, and Michigan, noted for their severe winters (Hannah et al. 2013).

In the future you may also see more signs on fruit saying, "Country of Origin—Canada." Canadian biologist John Pedlar sees more people in southern Ontario "trying their hand at things like peaches a little farther north from where they have been trying" (Charles 2012). This is consistent with the US Department of Agriculture's Plant Hardiness Zone Map, which shows tolerant zones moving north (Charles 2012).

CONCLUSION

Even without complete property rights to the atmosphere and with high transaction costs for market exchanges that would reflect incidental services or disservices, climate change connects in many different ways to asset rents, which in turn encourage adaptation. Changes in land rents are an example of how temperature, precipitation, sea level, and storms enter into landowners' decision-making as to how to use their property. Temperature and precipitation might increase or decrease agricultural productivity, sea levels affect suitability for beachfront housing, storms increase the risk of building in their path, and the probability of wildfires destroying property discourages building in the wildland–urban interface.

Of course, all of these examples are conditioned by policies that change the risk through insurance programs and subsidies that become part of the rent package. Is there subsidized crop insurance, flood insurance, or fire insurance? Hence, the structure of insurance markets becomes an important factor in whether and how people adapt to climate change. Similarly, unfettered finance markets would incorporate the variance due to climate change into investment decisions, unless the prices—interest rates—are distorted by political intervention.

Because water is a resource directly affected by climate, water markets could be crucial in determining whether and how agricultural, industrial, municipal, and environmental water users will adapt. Again, the relevant policy question is whether water rights are well defined and enforced and whether regulations on water trading unnecessarily raise the transaction costs of water marketing.

There are many ways in which climate change can and will be incorporated into market prices and individual decisions, and there is some evidence that people are already adapting. How adaptation will progress depends importantly on implementing policies that produce clear price signals regarding resource rents.

NOTE

1. For a discussion of the contrast between Pigou and Coase, see chapter 2 in this volume by Boudreaux and Meiners.

REFERENCES

Anderson, T. L., and D. R. Leal. 2015. *Free Market Environmentalism: For the Next Generation*. New York: Palgrave Macmillan.

Anderson, T. L., and G. D. Libecap. 2014. *Environmental Markets: A Property Rights Approach*. New York: Cambridge University Press.

Associated Press. 1989. "Industrial Nations Unwilling to Pay for Cleaner Ozone." *Billings Gazette*, March 8.

Bernstein, A., M. T. Gustafson, and R. Lewis. 2019. "Disaster on the Horizon: The Price Effect of Sea Level Rise." *Journal of Financial Economics* 134, no. 2: 253–72.

Botkin, D. B. 1990. *Discordant Harmonies: A New Ecology for the Twenty-First Century*. New York: Oxford University Press.

——. 2012. *The Moon in the Nautilus Shell: Discordant Harmonies Reconsidered*. New York: Oxford University Press.

Charles, D. 2012. "Gardening Map of Warming U.S. Has Plant Zones Moving North." National Public Radio, January 26. https://www.npr.org/sections/thesalt/2012/01/25/145855948/gardening-map-of-warming-u-s-has-plant-zones-moving-north.

Coase, R. H. 1960. "The Problem of Social Cost." *Journal of Law & Economics* 3: 1–44.

Conti, K. 2018. "Homes near Ocean Risk Losing Value, Even in Hot Market." *Boston Globe*, April 23. https://www.bostonglobe.com/business/2018/04/23/sunk-water-view-homes-near-ocean-risk-losing-value-even-hot-market/HskjAqt0acqHiBcbh4L0XL/story.html.

Demsetz, H. 2003. "Ownership and the Externality Model." In *Property Rights: Cooperation, Conflict, and Law*, edited by T. L. Anderson and F. S. McChesney. Princeton, NJ: Princeton University Press.

Ellis, E. C. 2011. "Anthropogenic Transformation of the Terrestrial Biosphere." *Philosophical Transactions of the Royal Society* 369, no. 1938: 1010–35.

Environmental Protection Agency, Office of Water. 2010. "State and Individual Trading Programs." http://water.epa.gov/type/watersheds/trading/tradingmap.cfm, accessed March 15, 2010.

Funk, M. 2014. *Windfall: The Booming Business of Global Warming*. New York: Penguin.

Hannah, L., P. R. Roehrdanz, M. Ikegami, A. V. Shepard, M. R. Shaw, G. Tabor, L. Zhi, P. A. Marquet, and R. J. Hijmans. 2013. "Climate Change, Wine, and Conservation." *Proceedings of the National Academy of Sciences* 110, no. 17: 6907–12.

Hayek, F. A. 1945. "The Use of Knowledge in Society." *American Economic Review* 35, no. 4: 519–30.

Kareiva, P., M. Marvier, and R. Lalasz. 2012. "Conservation in the Anthropocene: Beyond Solitude and Fragility." Breakthrough Institute, Winter 2012. http://thebreakthrough.org/index.php/journal/past-issues/issue-2/conservation-in-the-anthropocene, accessed April 2, 2014.

Keenan, J. M., T. Hill, and A. Gumber. 2018. "Climate Gentrification: From Theory to Empiricism in Miami-Dade County, Florida." *Environmental Research Letters* 13, no. 5.

Marris, E. 2011. *Rambunctious Garden: Saving Nature in a Post-Wild World*. New York: Bloomsbury.

Marsh, G. P. 1865. *Man and Nature: Or, Physical Geography as Modified by Human Action*. New York: Charles Scribner.

Molina, M., and D. Zaelke. 2012. "A Climate Success Story to Build On." *New York Times*, September 25. http://www.nytimes.com/2012/09/26/opinion/montreal-protocol-a-climate-success-story-to-build-on.html?_r=0, accessed June 2, 2014.

National Climate Assessment and Development Advisory Committee. 2013. *National Climate Assessment*, chap. 1: *Executive Summary: Draft for Public Comment*. Washington, DC: US Global Change Research Program. http://www.globalchange.gov/sites/globalchange/files/NCAJan11-2013-publicreviewdraft-chap1-execsum.pdf.

Pigou, A. C. 1920. *The Economics of Welfare*. London: Macmillan.

Pyne, S. 1982. *Fire in America: A Cultural History of Wildland and Rural Fire*. Princeton, NJ: Princeton University Press.

Ridley, M. 2009. "The Natural Order of Things." *The Spectator*, January 7. http://www.spectator.co.uk/features/3213246/the-natural-order-of-things/, accessed February 26, 2014.

Stern, N. 2006. *Stern Review: The Economics of Climate Change*. Cambridge: Cambridge University Press.

Wilson, S. G., and T. R. Fischetti. 2010. *Coastline Population Trends in the United States: 1960 to 2008*. Washington, DC: US Census Bureau.

Yandle, B. 1997. *Common Sense and the Common Law for the Environment*. Lanham, MD: Rowman & Littlefield.

CHAPTER 4
Bruce Yandle and the Art of Economic Communication

TODD J. ZYWICKI

Some years ago I watched the wolves of Yellowstone's Lamar Valley through a telescope, entranced by their beauty and fascinating social structure. I struck up a conversation with another observer on the hilltop. He asked what brought me to Yellowstone. I told him that I was spending a few days before heading to an "environmental economics" conference in Bozeman, Montana. At this point my new friend (or so I thought) shook his head disapprovingly and announced, "Aren't there some things that are too important to be left to economics?"

My jaw dropped. Having spent some time around the then–Political Economy Research Center and the Foundation for Research on Economics and the Environment, I was familiar with the ingenious role played by economics in making possible the reintroduction of the wolves after they had been hunted and driven from Yellowstone at the behest of neighboring cattle ranchers (Downey 2016). Working with Defenders of Wildlife, economists and environmentalists established a fund that provides compensation to any cattle rancher who loses any of their herd to roaming wolves. Through a common sense application of the Coase Theorem, what had been a seemingly unresolvable conflict that could have created years of strife and possibly stopped the reintroduction of wolves, instead turned into a harmonious market exchange. Today, the wolves not only provide a valuable contribution to Yellowstone's ecology, they generate millions of tourist dollars for the park and surrounding areas. Yet here was a well-educated man who dismissed the consideration of economics as degrading to environmental values.

The experience brought me back to memories of Bruce Yandle lecturing on environmental economics and public choice theory. Indeed, to this day I vividly recall Bruce using the Socratic method to teach the basic institutions of public choice theory through the example of Gary Libecap's case study of efforts by local businesses to use regulation to block competition from more efficient refrigerated boxcars (Libecap 1992). By turning Libecap's historical illustration into a story, Yandle succeeded in introducing public choice theory to a group of students who otherwise might have glazed over at a blackboard full of graphs or dismissed the concepts out of hand as ideologically uncongenial to their world view.

The juxtaposition brought me back to my experiences as a graduate student in Bruce's classroom in the 1990s. In particular, what I recognized was Bruce's omnipresent message that teaching students—and the citizenry—about economics is not just a matter of teaching economic concepts; it is recognizing the *moral* dimension that people bring to these debates. My wolf-loving interlocutor was not taking issue with the shape of the supply and demand curves of reintroducing wolves in the Yellowstone ecosystem. Instead, he was objecting to the moral premise that economics could and should play any role in environmental questions. Or as Bill Dougan has observed, "Arguing that recycling is economically inefficient is like arguing that communion wafers are not nutritious. It simply misses the point."

Over his long and extraordinary career, Bruce Yandle is a man who has rarely missed the point of anything. A brilliant economist and even more brilliant communicator of economic ideas, Bruce's influence is far-reaching. More importantly, Bruce's gifts as a teacher and economist are reflected in the influence he has had on many of those, like me, who work in areas outside of environmental economics. Bruce taught me the importance of sound communication of economics, and more important, to be alert to the differing moral structures that people bring to public policy debates and the different ways in which they process and weigh information.[1]

Bruce's lesson about the need to communicate in a fashion that speaks to people's moral and conceptual framework is one that I keep in mind every day as I teach my law students. Even more, it is a lesson that I keep in mind when I communicate with policymakers and the public about matters of public policy, especially in my chosen area of study, consumer finance and its regulation.

Other papers in this volume will speak to Bruce's brilliance as a technical economist and his influence on public policy and generations of students. I choose instead to focus on a less-appreciated element of Bruce's work—his attention to the importance of communicating economic concepts, which is a theme that runs through his work. I will then briefly discuss how I have applied the lessons I learned from Bruce to my own work, in an area that seems to be far removed from Bruce's work on environmental economics, but on closer inspection is more conceptually similar than first appreciated.

COMPETING VISIONS OF SOCIAL ORDER: WOLVES AND COMMUNION WAFERS REVISITED

In 1989 Yandle published *The Political Limits of Environmental Regulation: Tracking the Unicorn*. The book represented one of Yandle's earliest efforts to pull together in book form his overarching critique of environmental law and policy from an economic perspective. Yandle comments that when he first went to Washington in the 1970s to help craft environmental policy, he "was primarily an efficiency seeker, believing that good lessons in basic economics properly presented would sharply limit the number of federal regulations that seemed to cost so much but yield so little in the way of net social benefits" (Yandle 1989, xi). He admits, "After some experience working in Washington, I learned that economic ignorance was not the source of the problem. Indeed, the level of economic understanding among career bureaucrats, politicians, and their appointees was quite high" (Yandle 1989, xi). What had been neglected, however, was a careful analysis of the institutions that generate American environmental policy and the translation of these ideas into policy outcomes. Yandle's particular task in *The Political Limits of Environmental Regulation* was to try to explain the puzzling persistence of command-and-control environmental regulation as the dominant approach to regulation in the United States, despite its relative inefficiency as a matter of economic logic. Yandle contrasts command-and-control approaches to regulation with what he calls the "property rights" approach to addressing environmental issues. This is an approach that relies more heavily on property rights, markets, and private ordering solutions, rather than government mandates, enforcement, and other forms of direct governmental control. Yandle notes that solutions grounded in the property rights approach promise the potential to attain the same environmental goals at lower economic cost. In that sense, the property rights approach appears to offer a veritable "free lunch" to policymakers. Why, then, was environmental regulation so stubbornly resistant to reform?

Yandle argues that the problem is not one of *measurement*, but a problem of intellectual (and moral) *visions*, which cause many people to be inherently distrustful of the property rights approach to environmental regulation. Thus, instead of starting the book with a discussion of supply and demand or the Coase Theorem, Yandle begins chapter 1 by laying out "competing visions" of the world, focusing on the ideas of Thomas Sowell in his book *A Conflict of Visions* (Sowell 1987) and, more surprising, Robert Pirsig, author of *Zen and the Art of Motorcycle Maintenance* (Pirsig 1979). The lack of success of the property rights school in making headway in the policy realm, Yandle suggests, reflects an inability of proponents of greater use of economics in environmental policy to address the worldview, or "vision," of those who are distrustful of economics. Yandle writes, "Those who favor scientifically determined command and control regulation generally do not support the use of incentives that rely on unbridled individual choice in environmental matters. The property rights school and the regulation school are populated by people who think differently. They are naturally at odds with each other" (Yandle 1989, 11). In other words, too often the property rights school is arguing that communion wafers are not nutritious.

THOMAS SOWELL, *A CONFLICT OF VISIONS*

Consider first Sowell's "conflict of visions." As Yandle notes, Sowell "places people in two polarized camps," the "unconstrained view" of the world and the "constrained view." Yandle summarizes the fundamental characteristics of the two camps:

> Those in the first camp have an unconstrained view of man and believe accordingly that properly chosen knowledgeable people can find and impose regulatory solutions to social problems. The second camp is populated by people who have a constrained vision of man, believing that social systems evolve in complex ways that provide incentives for fallible people to achieve socially useful results, even when the social end is no part of the people's intentions. (Yandle 1989, 12)

According to Sowell, the constrained and unconstrained visions of the world provide coherent intellectual frameworks for addressing social and political problems. The constrained vision rests on several basic ideas. First, human beings are cursed with limited wisdom, limited altruism, and are more motivated by self-interest than general appeals to sentiment or public morality (Sowell 1987, 19–23). Self-interest, however, is not the same as "selfish"—as Yandle himself has said (in a line that I have invoked on multiple occasions), "self-interest" means that "you love yourself, your family, and your friends, more than you love perfect strangers." The "constrained vision" takes the limitations of human nature as given and tries to harness the power of self-interest to the benefit of society, rather than trying to pretend that human nature is infinitely malleable or, even worse, that individuals can be reeducated into ignoring their natural impulses.

Second, following from the initial observation about taking human nature as given, the constrained vision focuses on incentives and trade-offs instead of solutions, and particularly on the unintended consequences of efforts to "solve" social problems. Concepts such as cost-benefit analysis—which attempt to account for issues of unintended consequences—are thus inherently "constrained" vision approaches to social problems in seeking to consider all of the effects of a proposed regulation or legal rule. Sowell argues that those who hold the constrained vision hold a somewhat tragic view of the world—utopia is unattainable, and its pursuit frequently goes awry, thereby making mankind more miserable. The constrained vision, as articulated by thinkers such as Adam Smith and F. A. Hayek, also tends to have a great appreciation for decentralized processes, such as markets, which are social institutions that overcome the limited and dispersed knowledge and altruism of mankind, thereby enabling individuals to promote the public good even if that is not their design (Smith [1776] 1982, 456).

Good intentions are "the essence of virtue" for those who hold an unconstrained vision (Sowell 1987, 23). *Unintentional* social benefits, by contrast, are seen as suspect and ineffective by adherents of the unconstrained vision. Indeed, basing social policy on incentives and self-interest is worse than ineffective; it is seen as corrosive to individual character and morality, thereby promoting a deterioration of moral virtue, coarsening life, and reducing individual and social potential. Whereas adherents of the constrained vision "regard[] human selfishness as a given" and look to incentives to direct behavior to promote the public good indirectly, believers in the unconstrained vision see selfishness as being promoted by the very system of rewards used to cope with it. "The real solution," summing up the unconstrained vision, "toward which efforts should be bent was to have people do what is right because it is right, not because of psychic or economic payments—that is, not because someone 'has annexed it to a great weight of self-interest'" (Sowell 1987, 24).

Adherents of the unconstrained vision see human nature as largely a blank slate, to be shaped by education, socialization, and inspiration that can bring out man's inherent sociability. Thus, they are "not preoccupied . . . with what is the most immediately effective incentive under the current state of things. The real goal was the long-run development of a higher sense of social duty. To the extent that immediately effective incentives retarded that long-run development, their benefits were illusory" (Sowell 1987, 24).

The malleability of human nature implies the necessity of some organization to perform the molding function. Although earlier thinkers bestowed this responsibility on a variety of institutions, in the 20th century the "state" came to be charged with that responsibility. For Rousseau, the state would be the reflection of an enlightened democratic populace that would voluntarily transcend self-interest. For Woodrow Wilson and subsequent Progressive thinkers, the state would be administered by disinterested civil service professionals, whose moral virtue and intellectual development would be refined through a system of comprehensive education and training. Moreover, by protecting professional civil service employees from the distortions created by political (eliminating the spoils system) and economic incentives (through seniority-based compensation systems), they will be empowered to pursue the "public good."[2]

The constrained vision, by contrast, sees government officials as subject to the same biases, weaknesses of will and intellect, moral failings, and tendency toward self-interest as those they govern. Whereas the unconstrained vision leads directly to the normative proposals of the modern politically unaccountable administrative state, the constrained vision implies the public choice approach. In this approach, government officials are within the system, rather than standing outside the system looking in (as with the unconstrained vision). This vision implies the system of checks and balances and separation of powers of the Framers' Constitution, where in Madison's words, "ambition was to counteract ambition" (Zywicki 2016). Indeed, the project of constitutionalism itself is captured in Madison's recognition that government reflects a tension between two rival, but equally fearsome, forces—on the one hand the government must be powerful enough to control the governed (through a sufficient degree of independence of government officials such that they can withstand the gales of populist fury and majoritarian pressures to commandeer the power of the state to pursue their special interests instead of the public interest), but at the same time to "oblige the government to control itself" by placing sufficient constraints on government officials such that they do not become their own faction, perverting the power of the state for their own purposes (*The Federalist* 2001).

As this example of the tension between independence and accountability suggests, the constrained vision focuses on *trade-offs* (Sowell 1987, 25). The unconstrained approach, by contrast, focuses on "solutions" and sees the design of good policy as something like an engineering problem—hence its emphasis on the "technical expertise" of those who run the modern administrative state. For the constrained vision, every social benefit has some cost to some people, and even more important, every action has a ripple of unintended consequences—both good and bad. Thus, "solutions" are fundamentally impossible—social policy is not an engineering problem conducive to technical solutions. As suggested by Coase, the problem of pollution is not subject to a "solution," but is actually a question of allocating property rights to scarce resources among competing incompatible uses (and users). One cannot "solve" the question of whether dung-burning hut-dwellers in sub-Saharan Africa should be permitted access to fossil fuel–generated power in light of the marginal contribution of CO_2 that would be emitted into the environment from doing so.[3] One can only specify the trade-offs involved and propose some normative frame to adjudicate among competing uses. The constrained vision, therefore, is a science of trade-offs and unintended consequences, not a series of "solutions."

For Yandle, the implications of these two visions for environmental policy and regulation are straightforward (Yandle 1989, 12):

> Applying those incompatible visions to environmental control suggests that command-and-control regulation satisfies the unconstrained view of man. The evolution of property rights and markets where efficient environmental use is not directed, but occurs spontaneously through uncoordinated group actions satisfies the constrained view. As Sowell points out in his extensive discussion of the conflict, we should not expect one approach to emerge from the other.

Yandle argues that these visions animate the stories that are told about environmental regulation over time. Perhaps more important, these visions structure thinking about the *type* of solutions that can be contemplated over time. My Yellowstone acquaintance quite clearly adhered to the unconstrained vision—he was sincerely aghast at the idea that economics could and should be relevant to the design of environmental policy.[4] In this approach, regulation is fundamentally motivated by the public interest, and regulatory failures are caused by bad, selfish people putting their selfish desires ahead of larger social objectives. The implied solution is clear—more power should be given to public-spirited public officials buttressed and informed by "public interest" environmental groups. In turn, those same actors should be insulated from the pressures of greedy "industry" interest groups who seek to undermine the quest for greater environmental enlightenment and outcomes.

Those adhering to the constrained vision—notably many economists—tell a less optimistic story. Instead, environmental regulation is a story of tradeoffs. In the first instance, greater environmental protection is typically accompanied by economic growth. In turn, the allocation of those economic costs will have distributional consequences. For example, energy consumption is highly inelastic across the short and medium run, and thus lower-income households will be relatively more affected by increases in energy costs than wealthier households. Indeed, even something as simple as questions as to whether to pave roads in national parks or to allow snowmobiles in the winter will have adverse impacts on those who are handicapped or unhealthy and thus unable to hike to more remote regions that they could otherwise reach by car or snowmobile.

More important, the constrained vision holds that self-interest and strategic behavior simply cannot be wished away. It is inherent in human nature. Thus, while the creation of an independent regulatory agency can reduce the influence of the president over policy, it might heighten the influence of Congress over agency actors (Moran and Weingast 1983). And if steps are taken to reduce the influence of both Congress and the president, that in turn can increase the ideological influence of career agency staff (Muris 1986; Zywicki 2013). Contra Wilson and his later Progressive followers, there is no reason to believe that those who work within agencies are going to be animated to pursue the "public interest" (if they can even discern it) as opposed to their own personal agendas, whether ideological or otherwise (Niskanen 1971). Moreover, interest groups will be ubiquitous in the process, as the basic logic of economics suggests that if a firm or industry can gain a competitive edge and earn or save money by investing in influencing the political process, then they will rationally do so, or they will be selected out in a competitive market (Alchian 1950). Indeed, this same logic applies to so-called public interest environmental groups as well, as they will intrinsically prefer public policy solutions that increase their political influence and hence their claims for financial support from donors (Zywicki 2002).

ROBERT PIRSIG, *ZEN AND THE ART OF MOTORCYCLE MAINTENANCE*

More surprising than his invocation of Sowell, in *The Political Limits of Environmental Regulation* Yandle (1989) also invokes the complementary analysis of Robert Pirsig (1979) in his widely read book, *Zen and the Art of Motorcycle Maintenance: An Inquiry into Values*. "Like Sowell," Yandle writes, "Pirsig divides mankind into two camps, those who hold to a romantic view of the world and others who have a classical understanding." The romantic view, like the unconstrained vision, sees the world in an immediate and holistic sense, consciously aware of the aesthetic and immediate experience of nature and motorcycle riding. The classical view, by contrast, mirrors the constrained vision, and provides the rider with the "appreciation of the machine and the interconnected parts that deliver the experience." Those who hold the classical vision are "keenly aware of linkages and systems and see the world as 'underlying form itself'" (Yandle 1989, 12).

Although Pirsig is not an economist or a social scientist, the application of his duality to environmental matters mirrors Sowell's. Yandle writes:

> The romantics, chiefly interested in immediate appearances, seek environmental quality for its own sake, perhaps believing that rules can be designed and imposed to generate desired outcomes immediately. Their vision of human agents who might engage in strategic behavior when confronting the rules contains such unfortunate behavior as stemming from ignorance and immorality, things that have to be dealt with by more enlightened social servants.
>
> Those who see the world as built from complex intertwined relationships that reflect competing human values scoff at the idea of command and control, arguing that one cannot simply alter one part of the system without disturbing its entire mechanism. Unlike ecologists who have a supreme appreciation of the complex linkages that generate any natural life system, but who generally fail to include man's response to economic incentives in that system,

> those holding the classical view of the environment include man in all his manifestations in the ecological system. (Yandle 1989, 12)

As Yandle observes, those who hold the constrained/classical view thus gravitate toward market and property rights–based systems of dealing with environmental issues. Aligning incentives with desired outcomes is the most robust way to harness the power of self-interest and to attain desired social goals in the least expensive and least disruptive fashion. Attainment of the intended social goal, however, need not be the intent of the individuals within the system. Social benefits are merely a by-product of private individuals pursuing their self-interest.

Those who hold to the unconstrained/romantic view, by contrast, are "impatient with all this and can hardly be expected to accept an uncontrolled outcome for things as important to him as air and water quality" (Yandle 1989, 13). In their mind, the safest and most secure way to ensure that certain social outcomes are recognized is to design laws and regulations that are aimed at accomplishing those policies and then empower certain individuals with the authority to take the steps necessary to accomplish those ends. The idea that the accomplishment of important social ends can be trusted to emerge as the by-product of the interactions of decentralized, uncoordinated individuals pursuing their self-interest subject to constraint strikes those who hold the unconstrained/romantic vision as little more than playing Russian roulette with the planet's future.

SUMMARY AND IMPLICATIONS

Why does Yandle (1989) open *The Political Limits of Environmental Regulation* with an exploration of competing visions and how those visions map onto stories about environmental protection? Yandle's task in the book is to try to explain the puzzling persistence of the dominant command-and-control approach when economists have provided ample evidence of the relative inefficiency of such a system and the potential for rent-seeking and special interest activity that followed from it.[5] Of course, Yandle's analysis of the inability of economists to persuade the general public of the superiority of property rights approaches should not be read to exclude the importance of interest groups in the shaping of environmental law and regulation, but instead should be read as an explanation as to why "Baptists"—the average citizen who cares about clean air and water—cling to command-and-control regulatory approaches.

Yandle suggests that economists' lack of influence stems from a failure to account for these competing visions of the world when making the public case for a property rights approach. Facts and data do not speak for themselves; instead, they must be sifted and processed through preexisting analytical frameworks. Moreover, as Sowell and Pirsig suggest, these analytical frameworks are often unrecognized and unconscious; thus, most people are never even aware that they are applying those mental constructs to the facts that they encounter. They believe that they are simply analyzing "the facts" in an unbiased and open-minded fashion. Yet if the mindset one brings to a question is the direct, immediate problem–solution metric of the unconstrained vision, which seeks certainty and solutions, then one is unlikely to appreciate stories and evidence that point to the superiority of indirect, incentive-based systems that focus on trade-offs between competing social goals. The task of the environmental economist who seeks to improve the world, therefore, is one of communication as much as scientific proof—analysis must be packaged in terms that will resonate with the public and others or it will be dismissed as irrelevant to the concerns offered.

ADDITIONAL PERSPECTIVES ON ECONOMIC COMMUNICATION

Yandle's discussion of Sowell and Pirsig is used in *The Political Limits of Environmental Regulation* to establish that the initial challenge of those seeking to provide more efficient and effective environmental policies must account for the different cognitive visions that human beings bring to social questions. But my fellow Yellowstone wolf-watcher's objection was not just that economics was not an effective tool for designing environmental policy. Instead, the tone and import of his comment was that economic approaches to environmental policy were not just analytically incorrect but *morally* incorrect—that is, that only an immoral person would think that environmental purity and natural beauty should be subject to crass economic calculation and self-interested incentives.

Although this normative, moral tinge is suggested by both Sowell and Pirsig, it is largely hinted at, rather than explored in detail. Subsequent thinkers, however, have explored the moral and psychological implications of holding different visions of the world. In this section I will discuss two perspectives that are complementary to Yandle's analysis and extend the idea of competing visions into the moral and psychological realms. Of particular relevance, both of these models of human thinking make explicit what is implicit in Sowell's and Pirsig's analyses, namely that these visions are subconscious and, perhaps more important, that they condition how individuals interpret and weigh the facts and information that confront them on a daily basis. I focus on two approaches that supplement Yandle's initial intuitions—personality types, notably the Myers-Briggs Type Indicators and the "Big 5" personality types, and moral intuitions as described by Jonathan Haidt. Both of these models help to explain why individuals are often so resistant to new modes of thinking and why they often imbue with normative moral significance what could be understood as simply different modes of thinking and cognition.

Personality Types and Social Cognition

The science of personality types has been around for decades, at least since Jung, but has taken on increasing scientific rigor and influence in recent decades. Personality attributes are heterogeneous among individuals and are also often predictable and stable over time. Two of the most frequently used personality type categorization systems are the Myers-Briggs Type Indicator and the Big 5 personality traits (Caplan 2003). The origins of personality are unclear, most notably the relative contribution of genetics, environment, and character (i.e., "nature versus nurture") to the development of different models of personality. Regardless of their source, however, understanding the reality of personality differences can provide an important insight into how individuals think. It illuminates Yandle's observation that different narratives about the nature of environmental regulation are actually not debates about the actual data or application of underlying economic concepts but are debates about how to interpret that data and the normative implications to draw for regulatory structures, that is, command-and-control government regulation versus decentralized market-based and property rights approaches to the problem. On the other hand, although personality types provide their own dichotomy in terms of categorizing people, these views do not line up along the same dividing lines as Sowell and/or Pirsig.

Personality typing remains controversial in some quarters. As Caplan notes, however, much of this skepticism is overstated. Over time, psychological personality typing has become more rigorous, precise, reliable, and empirically validated (Caplan 2003). Personality tests have a high degree of reliability (producing consistent answers when the tests are taken some time apart) and stability (producing consistent overall results at different stages of life). In his article, Caplan focuses primarily on the Big 5 (the "Five Factor Model" or FFM) personality types in his article, which categorizes individuals according to their levels of "openness to experience," "conscientiousness," "extraversion," "agreeableness," and "neuroticism," and draws implications for how those personality characteristics can provide alternatives to traditional economic explanations for behaviors such as investments in education, occupational choice, and workplace productivity.

With respect to analyzing individual narratives about environmental regulation, however, the Myers-Briggs Type Indicator (MBTI) appears to be more relevant. The MBTI classifies personality types according to four fundamental personality attributes, creating a bilateral classification system within each quadrant (McCaulley 2000). These four attributes are as follows: (1) Extraversion-Introversion (EI), (2) Sensing-iNtuition (SN), (3) Thinking-Feeling (TF), and (4) Judging-Perceiving (JP). EI identifies whether one is an "extravert" or "introvert," terms that the MBTI describes as whether one draws energy from interacting with other people (extravert) or loses energy when interacting with others (introvert). SN examines whether one's analytical processes are "sensing," which in MBTI means preferring to trust information that is tangible and concrete, such as information that can be *sensed* and understood by the five senses, and to rely on particular facts and details, such as anecdotes and other concrete examples. Those who score high on N or "intuitive" are more abstract thinking, looking for larger patterns and associations. They tend to be more imaginative in terms of contemplating future possibilities and more hypothetical scenarios. TF refers to whether one's primary cognitive approach is "thinking" and reasoning or "feeling." Thinkers are more detached, considering decisions according to what is logical, consistent, and causal. Feelers, by contrast, reach decisions through the application of empathy or forming connections and crafting consensus and harmonious resolutions. Finally, "judging" refers to someone who is regular and rule-bound, while those who are classified as "perceiving" tend to be more fluid and adaptable.

Although the Myers-Briggs preference classification scheme is frequently criticized for being unreliable, many of these criticisms are unsupported, overbroad, or overstated.[6] According to the Myers-Briggs Company, the publisher of the Meyers-Briggs official *MBTI Manual*, the reliability of the official MBTI test is similar to that of other personality tests and that retesting generates consistent type preferences 75–90 percent of the time (Myers-Briggs n.d.).[7] Other studies have found reliability results in a similar range, finding reliability coefficients of about 0.85 to 0.90 for most attributes for tests taken some time apart (Hammer et al. 1998, 162–65; Johnson 1992). According to one study, "Overall, the MBTI tended to yield acceptable score reliabilities" (Capraro and Capraro 2002, 596).[8] Recent and more sophisticated analyses of the reliability of the MBTI find that not only does it show high reliability and stability across time, more sophisticated measures of reliability reveal the test to be more reliable than previously thought (Evans, Forney, and Salter 2005).

As mentioned above, the category classifications of the MBTI are more intuitively relevant to the current discussion than the FFM. For those who prefer or are more familiar with the FFM, however, the discussion here can be readily recharacterized within that scheme to approximate the same analysis. Research has found high correlations between MBTI and four of the five dimension scales in the FFM.[9] Of particular relevance to the discussion that follows, measurements of openness are highly correlated with the SN dimension, with higher levels of openness being positively correlated with higher measures of intuition and lower measures of sensing (Crump, Furnham, and Moutafi 2003).[10] Although the MBTI and FFM show correlations and overlaps, Crump, Furnham, and Moutafi (2003, 583) caution, "This does not necessarily mean that the MBTI should be reinterpreted in terms of the FFM." Instead, they should be viewed as complementary to "provide a more comprehensive picture of the construct of personality" (Crump, Furnham, and Moutafi 2003, 584). For many of the particular purposes for which psychologists use personality testing, there is a clear preference for use of the FFM instead of MBTI for a variety of reasons (see McCrae and Costa 1989). Critics also object to the theoretical structure of the MBTI and its bimodal four-factor classification scheme.[11] This preference among psychologists to use the FFM for certain purposes should not be interpreted, however, as implying that the MBTI is not useful for other purposes.[12]

Beyond their reliability, personality tests have been found to be valid predictors of certain manifestations of personality.[13] Caplan (2003) summarizes many of the correlates between scores on the Big 5 personality test and outcomes such as levels of educational achievement, occupational choice, and vulnerability to addictive behavior.[14] Researchers have similarly found the MBTI to be valid in predicting behaviors such as personal interests (Hammer et al. 1998, 258–59), occupational choice,[15] and preferences in learning style.[16] These insights about personality type drawn from MBTI and potentially the FFM might provide additional support for Yandle's observation that the difficulty of market-based approaches in getting traction in public policy reflects the manner in which individuals take in and process information, as captured by MBTI, not the underlying facts themselves.

The SN distinction seems particularly relevant to the question of whether voters and politicians will prefer command-and-control–style regulatory strategies or more decentralized market-based strategies.[17] Command-and-control–style regulatory policies will tend to be naturally appealing to S types, as they present a direct relationship between the identified problem and the proffered solution. Passing a law and regulation and empowering a government agency to carry out those mandates is a simple, straightforward way of addressing the problem. This is especially so for those who are S types but also fall in the J category of judging.

Indirect responses to identifiable problems, such as property rights and incentive-based mechanisms, strain the imagination of S types. The lack of a concrete, tangible direction to address the problem makes it difficult for them to envision how these mechanisms will work in practice to accomplish the desired goal. Markets and incentives are the realm of the N-type thinker (indeed, most economists are N-type thinkers, while many business school graduates are S-type thinkers).

This preference for S- or N-type thinking about social problems supports Yandle's argument that something is going on at a cognitive and psychological level for many people and not merely a disagreement about the interpretation of data. Moreover, the distribution of responses within MBTI categories is approximately equal in the aggregate for EI, TF, and JP.[18] The only exception to this equal distribution is the SN distinction—roughly three-quarters of the population is S type and a mere one-quarter are N types.[19] The difficulty of the public in accepting market-based approaches to environmental regulation may simply reflect the difficulty of explaining and understanding how markets and other decentralized processes might work to address social problems, but especially in new and novel areas where they have not been previously tried and thus there are no concrete examples or anecdotes to draw on. Moreover, S types may be more likely to dismiss arguments about unintended consequences caused by regulatory interventions if they are postulated to result from a chain of causation and are not closely related to the proposed intervention.

Indeed, the implications of this lopsided distribution of cognitive approaches in the population may have even more profound results for regulatory policy, as it may undergird the natural tendency of the media (which tends to be S type in its focus on particular, verifiable facts) and the public to think of regulatory policy in zero-sum terms, that is, "more" or "less" regulation. Yandle's suggested approach to environmental policy, however, is not easily placed on a regulation versus deregulation spectrum—instead, it is grounded in different approaches to the system of regulation. An important example is Yandle's works that he penned years after *The Political Limits of Environmental Regulation*, in which he explored the possibility of greater use of common law and private liability models for dealing with incompatible uses of environmental resources (Yandle 1997). The liability system is quite obviously a system of regulation, yet in common parlance few think of it as such. Indeed, some historical evidence suggests that the liability system historically was more restrictive than regulation in terms of limiting pollution and other environmental harms. Yet one suspects that the response of many to Yandle's proposal to *substitute* the common-law liability system in place of command-and-control regulation would be to characterize it as "deregulation." Yet this characterization betrays a lack of imagination. For just as Yandle's early work focused on property rights, markets, and incentive-based approaches to the environment, his later advocacy of enhanced use of the common law is grounded in describing an alternative regulatory system that could harness the power of decentralized information and private incentives, while avoiding the public choice problems inherent in traditional command-and-control regulatory approaches.[20]

These different cognitive strategies matter because personality analysis concludes that one's personality type conditions the way in which people take in and analyze information and facts (Keirsey 1978). Thus, as with the conflict of visions, those who are grounded in concrete, tangible approaches to understanding the world are going to discount facts and information that speak to abstract systems and hypothetical alternative regulatory regimes. Researchers have found correlations between personality traits and ideological and political views.[21] Moreover, research indicates that some personality types tend to express stronger moral preferences than other types. Those classified as Feelers on the TF dimension will also tend to approach issues from a less detached perspective than those who are Thinkers, leading to a greater tendency to process policy questions in more moralistic terms.

In this context, it is interesting to note that researchers have found that the personality types of climate scientists are also not representative of the population as a whole, and it is posited that this difference may contribute to the inability of climate scientists to communicate effectively with the public. A survey of 209 interdisciplinary early-career PhD researchers in climate science by Keller, Olex, and Weiler (2012) found that 82 percent of climate researchers indicated a preference for Intuition over Sensing, in contrast to the US population at large, of which only 27 percent prefer Intuition (compared to 73 percent who prefer Sensing). In addition, 76 percent of climate scientists show a preference for Judging rather than Perceiving, in contrast to a national sample in which only a slight majority (54 percent) prefer Judging.

Keller, Olex, and Weiler (2012) argue that this divergence between the abstract "intuitive" cognitive styles of climate researchers and the concrete "sensing" preference of the majority of the public interferes with effective communication between climate researchers and the public. For example, "climate impacts beyond the present or readily foreseeable future may lack relevance among the general public." This suggests that scientists can bridge the communication divide by starting with concrete and short-term effects and "building towards the big picture without any leaps in cause and effect," making the bigger picture and more far-off effects easier for Sensing individuals to understand and appreciate (Keller, Olex, and Weiler 2012, 240). The effects of climate on a person's local weather patterns may also be more resonant with Sensing types than "the plight of polar bears" (241).

Perhaps more surprising is Keller, Olex, and Weiler's (2012) finding that climate scientists show a dramatically higher propensity for Judging rather than Perceiving, which the authors claim may also contribute to the difficulty of climate scientists in communicating with the public. As they frame it, "This suggests that on average, climate change researchers will prefer to reach a decision or come to closure and 'move on' to the next step more quickly than the general population" (241). By contrast, "The general population, with a higher proportion of Perceivers, is more likely to see room for doubt, or want to take more time to explore possible alternatives, especially when outcomes are not likely to be positive. When presenting climate change to the general public, it is important for researchers to confirm what information is still unknown and what areas are still being studied" (240). The interaction of these pronounced tendencies toward Intuition and Judging may explain the often-noted tendency of climate scientists to communicate in excessively doctrinaire terms that demand that the "science is settled" and that debate should be ended, and to move on to "solutions" (which are often also equally doctrinaire and theoretical).[22] Environmental economists can learn from the failures of climate scientists and should be careful not to fall into the same traps of excessive abstraction and premature finality that fail to acknowledge unanswered questions.

Yandle does not explore the possible implications of Myers-Briggs or other personality types for communicating about environmental policy. His observation, however, that much of the debate over regulatory approaches to social problems is actually driven by unconscious "visions" of the world should be a catalyst for economists to consider their failure to communicate other complicated and counterintuitive ideas about the world, such as comparative advantage and the value of international trade. The importance of personality type for structuring approaches to regulatory policy is something that calls out for further exploration, just as Caplan (2003) had previously called for drawing on personality typing to help economists develop a more robust model of individual preferences, a call that seems to have been largely ignored in the 15 years since he first expressed the idea.

JONATHAN HAIDT AND THE MORALIZATION OF POLITICS

The work of psychologist Jonathan Haidt provides another complementary approach to Yandle's analysis of the role of "visions" in crafting and communicating about environmental policy. Haidt's work is particularly important and relevant to economists, as Haidt suggests that economists' distinction between "positive" and "normative" analysis does not come naturally to noneconomists. Instead, most people interpret and analyze facts through the lens of a preexisting normative framework. Haidt observes that this leads most people to overvalue facts and ideas that are compatible with their already existing moral framework and to downplay or overlook facts that are inconsistent with their existing framework. This heightens the difficulty of communicating about new ideas like using markets and property rights to help to resolve questions of incompatible uses of environmental and natural resources. Beyond that, however, this tendency to "moralize" policy, and even the facts and analysis that go into it, might explain the shocked reaction of my Yellowstone acquaintance—he was not merely confused and intellectually opposed to the idea that economics should be brought to bear on the issue of environment policy, he was *morally* opposed to the idea that environmental resources should be subject to the market and property rights.

In his book *The Righteous Mind: Why Good People Are Divided by Politics and Religion*, Haidt (2012b) develops a theory of moral "intuitions" that drive people's thinking and emotions. Moreover, as with the other models that have been discussed, Haidt suggests that these models operate at a subconscious, psychological level, not a conscious level. As Haidt titles part I of the book, "Intuitions Come First, Strategic Reasoning Second." According to Haidt, our "conscious reasoning—the stream of words and images of which we are fully aware" explains only a very small part of our behavior and beliefs; "99 percent of mental processes . . . occur outside our awareness but . . . actually govern most of our behavior" (Haidt 2012b, xiv). Haidt argues that the dominance of this subconscious reasoning function explains why many people believe so many incorrect, indeed demonstrably goofy, ideas about the world and why it is so difficult for people to persuade one another.

Haidt puts particular emphasis on the role of "disgust" in forming people's moral intuitions. Disgust is a visceral reaction to something, not a conscious, considered reaction. In this sense, my mention at Yellowstone Park of the concept of environmental economics triggered a disgust response—a visceral, subconscious response that indicated his view that only a bad person could seriously think that economics was relevant to something as sacred as the environment and natural resources. And indeed, Haidt also develops a theory of the "sacred" which is connected to the idea of disgust. The sacred items or ideas of a culture or subculture are those that come to take on a particularly powerful symbolic role or embody a narrative about the meaning of a group that serves to bind the group together.

Much as Yandle describes the history of environmental regulation as a tale of two competing narratives, Haidt describes the narratives of American history and society writ large through a similar lens. Writing in the *New York Times* during the 2012 presidential election, Haidt summarizes the competing narratives of the American left and right and the sacred symbols and ideas that they embody (Haidt 2012a). The left's rendition of American history is the "heroic liberation narrative": the history of the United States is one founded in repression and injustice toward women, minorities, gays, and the environment. Capitalism exploited workers and destroyed the environment. The history of the United States in this vision has been to overcome inequality, repression, and exploitation. In this telling, "African-Americans, women and other victimized groups are the sacred objects at the center of the story. As liberals circle around these groups, they bond together and gain a sense of righteous common purpose." An active federal government that rights the historic wrong is the hero of this version of the story.

The conservative narrative, by contrast, is one of the United States founded as a shining city on a hill (to invoke Ronald Reagan's famous metaphor). Founded in liberty, strength, and independence, over time the country's innocence and vitality have been eroded through bureaucratic overreach, arrogant politicians, and cultural decline. The sacred vision—to invoke an even more recent slogan—is to "Make America Great Again." Haidt notes that in this narrative "it's God and country that are sacred," but that the underlying narrative is about moral order, which also elevates religion and traditional family. For more libertarian-leaning conservatives, "liberty" is the sacred idea at the heart of the American narrative. But as Haidt notes, Reagan's political genius was to craft a narrative of American history that united these two seemingly incompatible sacred visions into one narrative and to define liberalism and big government as the "single devil that is eternally bent on destroying two different sets of sacred values—economic liberty and moral order" (Haidt 2012a).

Haidt's analysis is relevant to the current discussion because it highlights the competing roles of narratives in Yandle's story about the history of environmental regulation. Indeed, Haidt has cited Sowell's *Conflict of Visions* as a profound influence on his own thinking on these matters (Jenkins and Holman 2012). Haidt's research reinforces Sowell's view that certain visions or psychological constructs about the world condition not only the manner in which people process information, but even their willingness to seek out new information about the issue. As Haidt summarizes, "We make our first judgments rapidly, and we are dreadful at seeking out evidence that might disconfirm those initial judgments" (Haidt 2012b, 47). According to Haidt, people respond to certain issues with "gut feelings" and then "automatically fabricate justifications" for those gut feelings without even recognizing that they are doing so (Haidt 2012b, 54). Moreover, Haidt emphasizes that social and political judgments are "particularly intuitive" and particularly prone to motivated reasoning. Once a person adopts a position—one that is also believed to be the morally correct position—there is little motivation to revise that position in light of subsequent adverse evidence. After all, unlike holding an irrational position on something like the germ theory of disease, there is little personal benefit to correcting one's understanding of policy issues and a potentially good deal of psychological pain for many people in admitting that a position they hold is not just intellectually, but morally, correct. Instead, Haidt claims, people will tend to seek out and accept facts that confirm what they already believe, and to avoid and discount adverse facts.

Haidt identifies five moral vectors that he claims underlie the moral frameworks of most people and, as a result, underlie the political framework of most people as well. The five factors that he identifies are (1) Care, (2) Fairness, (3) Loyalty, (4) Authority, and (5) Sanctity. The Care/harm foundation focuses on one's sensitivity to signs of suffering and triggers an impulse to help those in need. The Fairness/cheating foundation measures one's outrage at social free riders and those who treat others unfairly by taking more than they give. Loyalty/betrayal focuses on one's loyalty to the group or team, and measures our desire to punish those who betray our group. The Authority/subversion foundation measures an individual's sensitivity to status and the proper "chain of command" and whether people are acting properly in their given role. Finally, the Sanctity/degradation foundation relates to issues of purity and cleanliness, not only in the physical sphere (making sure that food is pure, for example) but also in the moral and social sphere (keeping one's morality pure).

Haidt finds that scores on the amount of emphasis individuals place on these various attributes predict their political views. Liberals, for example, place higher weight on the Care and Fairness dimensions of the scale than they do on the other three. While conservatives place a high value on the Care and Fairness dimensions too, they also place a high value on the foundations of Loyalty, Authority, and Sanctity as well. Thus, while liberals tend to process political, social, and moral arguments in just two moral dimensions (Care and Fairness), conservatives generally process moral arguments across all five dimensions. This suggests that in a purely descriptive sense, conservatives tend to have a richer moral vocabulary and concepts than liberals. This also suggests that conservatives might be better equipped to navigate intellectual trade-offs among potentially competing social goals than liberals.

Haidt's model readily explains the difficulty of economists like Yandle in persuading environmentalists to take market-based ideas seriously. In the pantheon of the modern American left, environmentalism holds a major sacred status. When sacred items are threatened, Haidt suggests, the response is to fight to protect the sacred entity and to repel anything that could be construed as an attack on the sacred item. Many commentators have observed that modern environmentalism has come to resemble a religion, with its own priesthood and millenarian and apocalyptic myths. If Haidt is correct, this explains why environmental economics is often seen not merely as a bad idea intellectually, but a bad idea *morally*.

Environmental economics, by contrast, more easily fits into a conservative moral framework. While conservatives care about polar bears, whales, and clean air as much as liberals, conservatives also care about other values, such as liberty, fairness, and the role of private property rights in upholding the social and political order. For example, conservatives can more easily maintain a moral framework in which they simultaneously value wildlife but also the symbolic, historical, and practical value of firearms and hunting wildlife.

Haidt's analysis suggests that it should be easier to communicate about environmental economics with conservatives than liberals. Even if conservatives are predisposed to think in terms of standard command-and-control regulation—simply less of it—it may be possible to persuade conservatives to try market and common-law approaches if they are shown to further other moral goals, such as liberty and protection from arbitrary government overreach. The task of reaching liberals, by contrast, is likely to be more difficult. Whereas for conservatives, environmental economics touches on several values that conservatives consider sacred and that can temper one another, liberals elevate environmentalism to a place of sacredness that is largely unrivaled, except by other sacred values, such as civil rights.

One possible line of argument for reaching economics skeptics might be to identify how environmentalism conflicts with the interests of other sacred groups, such as low-income families, union workers, or the disabled. For example, energy consumption is largely inelastic, which means that increases in energy prices will be felt much more heavily by low-income than upper-income families. Inefficient environmental policies can also harm workers, especially union workers, if those policies lead to a reduction or exportation of manufacturing jobs. In fact, in 2018 a coalition of California civil rights organizations sued the California Air Resources Board, claiming that the cost of implementing the state's climate policies fell disproportionately heavily on lower-income and minority residents by driving up the cost of electricity, housing, and transportation, while also driving "gateway" jobs to the middle class without college degrees, such as manufacturing and logistics, to other states (Shellenberger 2018). Consideration of how Haidt's analysis might reinforce Yandle's approach to these issues should be considered more concretely in future research.

WHAT I LEARNED FROM BRUCE YANDLE ABOUT THE ART OF ECONOMIC COMMUNICATION

In this final section, I would like to say a few more personal and autobiographical notes about why I picked this particular topic as the focus of my essay. After all, even though I had the great fortune to have Bruce as a professor when I was in graduate school and have had the great privilege of calling him a friend ever since, most of my work is not in the field of environmental economics. Nevertheless, I took my environmental economics class with Bruce in the fall of 1989—almost thirty years ago. Why is it that after all of these years and Bruce's thousands of pages of scholarly output, one of the first things that came to mind to write on for this conference was the dozen or so pages that he wrote in the introductory material to *The Political Limits of Environmental Regulation*—especially the seeming digression into the thought of Thomas Sowell and Robert Pirsig on "visions"?

Yandle is one of the great economic communicators that I have ever witnessed in action. He has an ability to break outside of the economist's "bubble" and express ideas in a fashion that is intuitive and compelling to all students. And so, while I have not followed in his footsteps in focusing heavily on environmental law and economics, I have tried to follow in his footsteps to try to take to heart his lessons about communicating economic ideas. As such, I continue to think about the implications of his focus on different visions, and particularly what that insight means for those who seek to influence public policy and to communicate with the public.[23] I have tried to adopt these concepts and apply them in my own efforts to communicate with students, policymakers, and the public. The difference is that I do much of my work in the field of consumer finance and its regulation instead of environmental economics. As with the environment, people hold strong views about the morality of consumer credit and its regulation. Indeed, "usurious" interest rates have been prohibited for most of history, and charging usurious rates was condemned for most of Judeo-Christian history (Durkin et al. 2014, 483–86). Virtually every adult has some interaction with the world of personal finance, such as mortgages, credit cards, and the like. People bring strong moral intuitions about the role of personal responsibility in managing one's finances as well as the government's role in paternalistically reducing choices for grownups who are thought to lack the willpower or wherewithal to avoid the misuse of certain products, including middle-class products such as credit cards, but especially products used particularly heavily by lower-income consumers, such as payday loans and auto title loans (Ekins 2017).

In 1972, Anthony "Fat Tony" Salerno, the head of the Genovese crime family, was convicted on 14 counts of loan-sharking, one count of conspiracy, and, according to the front page of New York's *Daily News* on May 31, 1972, "a charge of criminal solicitation involving Salerno's alleged order to have a unidentified victim's leg broken" (Fleysher 1972). According to investigators, Fat Tony's overall operations had approximately $80 million outstanding in just his territory on a daily basis (amounting to about $463 million in inflation-adjusted dollars). Although striking, Fat Tony's operations were far from unique. According to a 1968 Senate committee report, illegal loan-sharking operations were the second-largest revenue source of organized crime, trailing only illegal gambling (US Senate 1968). And in the same vein, Richard Nixon's speech accepting the 1968 Republican nomination for president contained a pledge to appoint an attorney general who would be "an active belligerent against the loan sharks and the numbers racketeers that rob the urban poor in our cities" (Nixon 1968).

Today, of course, we hear few reports of illegal loan-sharking, much less organized crime bosses breaking people's legs in order to collect debts. What happened?

To a large extent, what happened was that economists were able to persuade the public that the presence of loan sharks was an unintended consequence of well-intentioned usury regulations that were designed to "protect" consumers from paying high interest rates for access to credit. Instead, by shutting off access to high-cost—but legal—forms of credit, desperate consumers turned to Fat Tony and his business rivals for needed funds. Regulation was able to reduce the supply of credit for many consumers, but the demand for credit persisted. Economists ranging from Milton Friedman (1970) to Paul Samuelson (1969) pointed to the academic consensus that usury restrictions harmed those that they were intended to help and in so doing facilitated organized crime. For example, testifying before the Massachusetts state legislature's judiciary committee in 1969, Samuelson stated, "The concern for the consumer and for the less affluent is well taken. But often it has been expressed in a form that has done the consumer more harm than good. For fifty years the Russell Sage Foundation and others have demonstrated that setting too low ceilings on small loan interest rates will result in drying up legitimate funds to the poor who need it most and will send them into the hands of the illegal loan sharks. History is replete with cases where loan sharks have lobbied in legislatures for unrealistic minimum rates, knowing that such meaningless ceilings would permit them to charge much higher rates" (Samuelson 1969). As Samuelson noted as well, the understanding that usury regulations promote the interests of organized crime dated back decades, to the earlier efforts of the Russell Sage Foundation to attack the organized crime problem by permitting small-loan companies to charge reasonable rates for their products. Indeed, in 1964 even Senator-Elect Robert Kennedy said that in order "to drive the racketeers from loan-sharking" the New York legislature should "alter[] the state laws on usury so that an insolvent person who needs money for legitimate purposes might borrow it at rates that were not exorbitant" (*New York Times* 1964).

Yet some bad ideas die hard. Despite the centuries-long understanding among economists on the harmful effects of price controls on the price of credit, the idea continues to revive itself. Writing in 2014, for example, the *New York Times* editors wrote (Editorial Board 2014):

> The Obama administration has proposed much-needed improvements in federal rules that are supposed to protect service members from predatory loans that trap them in debt and, in certain circumstances, can end their military careers. The changes would repair glaring weaknesses in the rules used to carry out the Military Lending Act of 2007. But the administration and Congress should not stop there. Millions of civilians are also exposed to ruinously priced loans. What is needed is a national consumer lending standard—and interest rate cap—to ensure fair credit in the country as a whole.

> Poor and working-class people across the country are being driven into poverty and default by deceptively packaged, usuriously priced loans. The obvious solution is a national standard for consumer lending. Both the House and Senate have bills pending that would adopt the 36 percent standard for all consumer transactions, including those involving payday loans, mortgages, car loans, credit cards, overdraft loans and so on.

The simple-minded reasoning of the *Times* immediately brings to mind Thomas Sowell's characterization of the "unconstrained" vision of society—there is a problem in society, namely that interest rates are "too high," and that as a result, "poor and working-class people across the country are being driven into poverty and default." The solution is obvious—if prices are too high, then simply order the prices to be lower!

The obvious response comes from the constrained vision—"Yeah, but. . . ." What about trade-offs? What about unintended consequences? What about consumer demand for credit? Where will consumers turn if they are unable to obtain loans? Will they turn to products such as overdraft protection, which is more expensive to use in some instances?[24] More important, regulation can eliminate the supply of certain financial products, but it doesn't eliminate the demand, meaning that most consumers will either turn to less-preferred options that still exist or be forced to forego the advantages associated with credit (Durkin et al. 2014). Unintended consequences are widespread and profound, yet the *Times* editors show no awareness of those problems. Does the *Times* editorial board lack access to its newspaper's archives, where it can discover what happens when overly strict usury ceilings are adopted?

In addition to the conflict of visions between economists and the *Times* writers, we also see the moralization of the analysis and the tendentious connection of cause and effect predicted by Haidt's analysis. For the *Times* editors, usury ceilings are not merely a question of correcting a purported market failure, they are a moral necessity to counter "predatory loans" that are "ruinously priced." A price control of 36 percent, however, will ensure that credit is "fair" for all—or at least those who are still able to obtain credit on those terms. Left unmentioned, but implied, is that lower-income consumers really cannot be trusted to manage credit responsibly and that high-rate credit should not be available.

I submit that what we have here is "a failure to communicate" (*Cool Hand Luke* 1967). But the failure of economists to adequately communicate the folly of interest rate ceilings mirrors the tension that Yandle points to in the first chapter of *The Political Limits of Environmental Regulation*—the *Times* editorial board's editorial is the virtual exemplar of the unconstrained vision combined with Haidt's moralization of politics and economics. The *Times* editors do not merely think that allowing the market to set the price of credit is unwise public policy; they are morally outraged and even disgusted by the "predatory" lenders who provide money to low-income consumers who need it at prices that the upper-middle-class *Times* editors find offensive.

Enter Fat Tony. The challenge for those who ground their policies in the constrained vision is to make clear the concrete and tangible injustice caused by ostensibly well-intentioned policies. The real choice, history reveals, is a tragic one: between high-cost small-dollar lenders or illegal leg-breakers.[25] Economic analysis can then be provided to explain why these historical examples are not merely anecdotes but are inevitable in a system of price controls on credit provision. But supply and demand curves should be understood as the *last* step in the explanation of why usury laws are counterproductive and harmful to those they are intended to help. That's an easy sell for those who hold the constrained view or hold Intuitive preferences in the Myers-Briggs framework. More difficult to educate are those who hold Sensing preferences, an unconstrained vision of cosmic justice, and a particular understanding of "fairness" in Haidt's taxonomy. For the latter types of people, it is necessary to first explain the concrete harm and injustice that are caused by the policies, which are more harmful than the harm to be ameliorated in the first place. Notably, this approach of moving from the specific to the more general is often foreign to most academic economists.

Return to Yandle's masterful use of the Socratic method with college students. He started by engaging with the students to capture their intuition (in the non-MBTI sense) about how they would respond if they were in the shoes of a small, local meat distributor and how they might turn to the government for protection from more efficient, larger meat distributors. From there, he could explain the logic of public choice and regulation.

What I really learned from Bruce Yandle, therefore, was the value of economic communication, and particularly the value of economic communication with people who are not natural economists. On issues from international trade, to environmental regulation, to consumer credit regulation, economists face particular challenges in communicating with people who do not think like economists. We can learn much from Bruce Yandle on that score.

NOTES

1. Bruce's paper in this volume is a good example of his art as an economic communicator: who else would think of modeling the progress of economic ideas as a series of "idea tournaments"? (Yandle, this volume).

2. There are obvious parallels to the normative proposals of modern behavioral economists such as Richard Thaler and Cass Sunstein, who propose to empower the state to "nudge" citizens to undertake desired behaviors, in that their framework implicitly assumes that government officials empowered to impose the nudges are not subject to the same biases and prejudices as those subject to the nudges (Thaler and Sunstein 2009).

3. One can note, however, that by almost any moral standard it is depraved to reduce access to relatively cleaner sources of energy for those who are forced to cook with animal dung or other unclean sources of fuel. One source estimates that use of indoor fires for cooking, heating, or lighting is responsible for approximately 3.5–4 million premature deaths worldwide every year (Gordon et al. 2014).

4. As I recall, he actually was an employee of some Washington, DC, regulatory agency and was vacationing in Yellowstone.

5. Ackerman and Hassler's (1981) classic study *Clean Coal/Dirty Air* is a good example of the genre. Ackerman's criticism of command-and-control regulation is especially notable in that he is a notable leftist academic, which illustrates that the competing visions do not map neatly onto ideological categories, but are instead modes of thought. Zywicki (1999) explains why interest groups tend to prefer command-and-control regulatory approaches instead of property rights approaches.

6. Much of the animus of academic psychologists toward the MBTI appears to be motivated by the fact that the test has commercial value and is widely used by many major corporations and other institutions as well as the founders' lack of standard academic credentials.

7. Several other early studies found similar reliability. See Boyer et al. (1984), Carlyn (1977), and Carlson (1985).

8. The general reliability of the MBTI, however, is subject to some caveats. First, although the MBTI is largely reliable and stable, not all four elements of the MBTI are equally so. According to Myers and McCaulley (1989, 164), the Thinking-Feeling (TF) dimension is predicted to be slightly less stable and predictable over time than other dimensions. Hammer et al. (1998) report lower test-retest correlations over a 30-month period for the TF preference (0.62), compared to the other three preferences (which range from 0.79 to 0.83). Capraro and Capraro (2002) similarly found the TF dimension to have a lower mean reliability coefficient than the other characteristics and a higher standard deviation. Still, they found that a reliability coefficient of 0.764 for the TF dimension, only slightly lower than the mean values of the other three dimensions, which fell within a range of 0.822 to 0.843 (597, table 1). Where respondents do exhibit a change in type over time, it usually is only in one dimension, and typically where they were not strongly differentiated initially (Myers and McCaulley 1985). Personality types in general, including the MBTI, also tend to be less stable and reliable at younger ages, but become more stable over time (Caplan 2003). Some evidence suggests that the reliability of the test across time is higher for women than for men (Harvey 1996). Some of the popular belief in the unreliability of personality derives from the tendency of individuals to misremember their prior scores, thereby leading them to erroneously believe that their scores have changed more than they actually have. As Caplan notes, "researchers have found that people are more likely to mistakenly *believe* that they changed their response than they are to actually do so" (Caplan 2003, 397, citing Costa and McCrae 1997). Some of the popular belief in the lack of reliability of the MBTI also may be due to the frequency of use of easy (but unreliable) online personality tests.

9. The EI dimension of MBTI is correlated with extroversion in the FFM, SN with openness, TF with agreeableness, and JP with conscientiousness (Levitt 2011; Crump, Furnham, and Moutafi 2003; Furnham 1996; MacDonald et al. 1994; McCrae and Costa 1989). The FFM also measures levels of "neuroticism," which may be useful for other purposes but is not

relevant to the current discussion. Levitt (2011) and Crump, Furnham, and Moutafi (2003, 580), however, find that neuroticism in the FFM is highly correlated with the MBTI EI dimension, being negatively correlated with extraversion and positively correlated with introversion.

10. On the other hand, Crump, Furnham, and Moutafi (2003) report that the highest correlations between the SN dimension and openness measure were in the realm of "Ideas, Fantasy and Aesthetics," which do not precisely capture the same range of cognitive questions that is discussed here.

11. Pittenger (2005, 1993) summarizes many of these objections. None of them are particularly relevant for the limited purposes of the current discussion.

12. As MacDonald et al. (1994, 343) note, simply because the FFM and MBTI show high levels of correlation and the FFM is more useful for some purposes, this does not necessarily imply the construct validity of either measure. Thus, even if the MBTI is only an imperfect application of a Jungian approach, it nevertheless might provide distinct insights for other purposes from the FFM's analytical construct.

13. Hammer et al. (1998, chap. 9) review the findings of multiple studies of validity.

14. Caplan (2003, 402) also suggests that with respect to understanding the validity of personality tests in predicting certain outcomes, by eliminating outliers, median results may be more predictable than mean results.

15. Myers and Myers (1993) present extensive evidence of correlations between MBTI preferences and occupational choice. Capraro and Capraro (2002, 594) and Myers-Briggs Company (n.d.) summarize several studies of validity. See also McCaulley (2000), who presents data on the relationship between MBTI classifications and populations of counselors and leaders of organizations.

16. In a study of student learning styles, Harrington and Loffredo (2010) found that introverts prefer online classes, whereas extraverts prefer face-to-face instruction.

17. Myers and McCaulley (1989) and Capraro and Capraro (2002) found the SN scale to have high reliability in terms of consistency over time.

18. TF is approximately equal in the aggregate, although women are more likely to be F and men are more likely to be T, thus balancing out in the aggregate.

19. See, for example, Podolyak (2017), who reports that SJs are 43 percent of the population and SPs are 33 percent of the population, meaning 76 percent of the population are S types, whereas NTs are 10.6 percent and NFs 11 percent. Note that this unequal distribution of cognitive preferences also suggests that those politicians who are elected to office are statistically more likely to hold a Sensing preference, which will reinforce the tendency toward those sorts of regulatory approaches.

20. Elinor Ostrom's (1990) analysis of how voluntary and spontaneous social arrangements can address social problems also fits within this tradition.

21. Fenton-O'Creevy and Furnham (2018) find correlations between personality traits as measured by the FFM and political and ideological views. Other commenters have noted apparent relationships between Myers-Briggs typology and partisan and ideological affiliation. While such connections are plausible and have at least some support in data, my focus here is not on Republican-Democrat or liberal-conservative approaches but rather on what appears to be a more fundamental distinction along the SN dimension. For analysis of the relationship between MBTI type and political ideology, see Boozer (2017) and Darrell (2016).

22. Overall, Keller, Olex, and Weiler (2012) found that over 20 percent of climate scientists in their survey were of the ENFJ personality type, in contrast to 3 percent of the general population of the United States. In addition, the INTJ (15 percent), ENTJ (12 percent), and INFJ (12 percent) personality types were much more common among climate researchers than in the general population. Overall, almost 60 percent of climate researchers exhibited preferences for Intuition-Judging combinations, in contrast to the population as a whole, in which

those represent the four rarest personality types, totaling approximately 10 percent of the population (Hammer et al. 1998, 298, table 12.13).

23. As noted in Keller, Olex, and Weiler (2012), communication problems arise only when communicating with people with different modalities of thinking and reasoning. Thus, the heavily disproportionate number of climate science researchers who feature Intuition-Judging preferences means that in communicating with other climate science researchers, those who hold those preferences can communicate easily and persuasively. Members of the public, however, have vastly different preferences on such issues; as a result, the modes of communication that are suitable for discussions with other climate researchers are unlikely to be as appreciated by members of the general public.

24. The answer is yes, of course, as usage of overdraft protection increases when payday loans are effectively outlawed by usury regulations (Clarke and Zywicki, 2013). Notably, it appears that in choosing between payday loans and overdraft protection, consumers typically act in a cost-minimizing fashion.

25. Indeed, violence and threats of violence were commonplace in the heyday of illegal loan sharks before the deregulation of lending markets. For myriad examples, see Goldstock and Coenen (1978).

REFERENCES

Ackerman, B. A., and W. T. Hassler. 1981. *Clean Coal/Dirty Air*. New Haven, CT: Yale University Press.

Alchian, A. A. 1950. "Uncertainty, Evolution, and Economic Theory." *Journal of Political Economy* 58, no. 3: 211–21.

Boozer, B. 2017. "Types and U.S. Political Party Affiliations." *PoliticalTypes*. http://politicaltypes.com/index.php/public-politics/public-politics-articles?layout=edit&id=79, accessed October 4, 2018.

Boyer, S. L., D. Landis, D. Outcalt, O. C. S. Tzeng, and R. Ware. 1984. "Item Validity of the Myers-Briggs Type Indicator." *Journal of Personality Assessment* 48, no. 3: 255–56.

Caplan, B. 2003. "Stigler-Becker versus Myers-Briggs: Why Preference-Based Explanations Are Scientifically Meaningful and Empirically Important." *Journal of Economic Behavior & Organization* 50: 391–405.

Capraro, M. M., and R. M. Capraro. 2002. "Myers-Briggs Type Indicator Score Reliability across Studies: A Meta-Analytic Reliability Generalization Study." *Educational and Psychological Measurement* 62, no. 4: 590–602.

Carlson, J. G. 1985. "Recent Assessments of the Myers-Briggs Type Indicator." *Journal of Personality Assessment* 49, no. 4: 356–65.

Carlyn, M. 1977. "An Assessment of the Myers-Briggs Type Indicator." *Journal of Personality Assessment* 41, no. 5: 461–73.

Clarke, R., and T. J. Zywicki. 2013. "Payday Lending, Bank Overdraft Protection, and Fair Competition at the Consumer Financial Protection Bureau." *Review of Banking and Financial Law* 33, no. 1: 235–81.

Cool Hand Luke. 1967. Jalem Productions.

Costa, P. and P. McCrae. 1997. "Longitudinal Stability of Adult Personality." In *Handbook of Personality Psychology*, edited by Robert Horgan, John Johnson, and Stephen Briggs, 269–90. New York: Academic Press.

Crump, J., A. Furnham, and J. Moutafi. 2003. "The Relationship between the Revised Neo-Personality Inventory and the Myers-Briggs Type Indicator." *Social Behavior and Personality* 31, no. 6: 577–84.

Darrell. 2016. "The U.S. Political Personalities (I): Parties." *16Personalities*. https://www.16personalities.com/articles/the-us-political-personality-i-parties, accessed October 4, 2018.

Downey, H. 2016. "The Wolf at the Rancher's Door." Property and Environment Research Center. https://www.perc.org/2016/09/01/tbt-the-wolf-at-the-ranchers-door/, accessed October 4, 2018.

Durkin, T. A., G. Elliehausen, M. E. Staten, and T. J. Zywicki. 2014. *Consumer Credit and the American Economy*. New York: Oxford University Press.

Editorial Board. 2014. "Opinion: A Rate Cap for All Consumer Loans." *New York Times*, October 18. https://www.nytimes.com/2014/10/19/opinion/sunday/a-rate-cap-for-all consumer-loans.html.

Ekins, E. 2017. "Wall Street vs. The Regulators: Public Attitudes on Banks, Financial Regulation, Consumer Finance, and the Federal Reserve." Cato Institute, September 19. https://www.cato.org/survey-reports/wall-street-vs-regulators-public-attitudes-banks-financial-regulation-consumer.

Evans, N. J., D. S. Forney, and D. W. Salter. 2005. "Two Approaches to Examining the Stability of the Myers-Briggs Type Indicator Scores." *Measurement and Evaluation in Counseling and Development* 37, no. 4: 208–19.

The Federalist. 2001. Edited by G. W. Carey and J. McClellan. Indianapolis, IN: Liberty Fund.

Fenton-O'Creevy, M., and A. Furnham. 2018. "Personality and Political Orientation." *Personality and Individual Difference* 129: 88–91.

Fleysher, E. 1972. "Fat Tony Indicted in Loan Sharking." *Daily News*, May 31.

Friedman, M. 1970. "Defense of Usury." *Newsweek*, April 6, 79. https://miltonfriedman.hoover.org/friedman_images/Collections/2016c21/NW_04_06_1970.pdf.

Furnham, A. 1996. "The Big Five versus the Big Four: The Relationship between the Myers-Briggs Type Indicator (MBTI) and NEO-PI Five Factor Model of Personality." *Personality and Individual Differences* 21, no. 2: 303–7.

Goldstock, R., and D. T. Coenen. 1978. "Perspectives on Investigation and Prosecution of Organized Crime, Extortionate and Usurious Credit Transactions: Background Materials." Cornell Institute on Organized Crime, Summer Seminar Program, August. https://www.ncjrs.gov/pdffiles1/Digitization/51183NCJRS.pdf.

Gordon, S. B., et al. 2014. "Respiratory Risks from Household Air Pollution in Low and Middle Income Countries." *The Lancet Respiratory Medicine* 2, no. 10: 823–60.

Haidt, J. 2012a. "Forget the Money, Follow the Sacredness." *New York Times*, March 17. https://campaignstops.blogs.nytimes.com/2012/03/17/forget-the-money-follow-the-sacredness/.

——. 2012b. *The Righteous Mind: Why Good People Are Divided by Politics and Religion*. New York: Pantheon.

Hammer, A. L., M. H. McCaulley, I. Briggs Myers, and N. L. Quenk. 1998. *MBTI Manual: A Guide to the Development and Use of the Myers-Briggs Type Indicator*, 3rd ed. Palo Alto, CA: Consulting Psychologists Press.

Harrington, R., and D. A. Loffredo. 2010. "MBTI Personality Type and Other Factors that Relate to Preference for Online versus Face-to-Face Instruction." *Internet and Higher Education* 13: 89–95.

Harvey, R. J. 1996. "Reliability and Validity." In *MBTI Applications*, edited by A. L. Hammer, 5–29. Palo Alto, CA: Consulting Psychological Press.

Jenkins, J., and W. Holman. 2012. "Jonathan Haidt: He Knows Why We Fight." *Wall Street Journal*, June 28. https://www.wsj.com/articles/SB10001424052702303830204577446512 5225826488.

Johnson, D. A. 1992. "Test-Retest Reliabilities of the Myers-Briggs Type Indicator and the Type Differentiation Indicator over a 30-Month Period." *Journal of Psychological Type* 24: 54–58.

Keirsey, D. 1978. *Please Understand Me*. Carlsbad: Prometheus Nemesis.

Keller, J. K., C. Olex, and S. C. Weiler. 2012. "Personality Type Differences between Ph.D. Climate Researchers and the General Public: Implications for Effective Communication." *Climate Change* 112: 233–42.

Levitt, T. 2011. "Myers–Briggs Inventories." In *Encyclopedia of Clinical Neuropsychology*, edited by J. S. Kreutzer, J. DeLuca, and B. Caplan. New York: Springer.

Libecap, G. D. 1992. "The Rise of the Chicago Packers and the Origins of Meat Inspection and Antitrust." *Economic Inquiry* 30, no. 2: 242–62.

MacDonald, D. A., P. E. Anderson, C. I. Tsagarakis, and C. J. Holland. 1994. "Examination of the Relationship between the Myers-Briggs Type Indicator and the NEO Personality Inventory." *Psychological Reports* 74, no. 1: 339–44.

McCaulley, M. H. 2000. "Myers-Briggs Type Indicator: A Bridge between Counseling and Consulting." *Consulting Psychology Journal: Practice and Research* 52, no. 2: 117–32.

McCrae, R. R., and P. T. Costa. 1989. "Reinterpreting the Myers-Briggs Type Indicator from the Perspective of the Five-Factor Model of Personality." *Journal of Personality* 57: 17–40.

Moran, M. J., and B. R. Weingast. 1983. "Bureaucratic Discretion or Congressional Control? Regulatory Policymaking by the Federal Trade Commission." *Journal of Political Economy* 91, no. 5: 765–800.

Muris, T. J. 1986. "Regulatory Policymaking at the Federal Trade Commission: The Extent of Congressional Control." *Journal of Political Economy* 94, no. 4: 884–89.

Myers, I. B., and M. H. McCaulley. 1985. *Manual: A Guide to the Development and Use of the Myers-Briggs Type Indicator*. Palo Alto, CA: Consulting Psychologists Press.

——. 1989. *Manual: A Guide to the Development and Use of the Myers-Briggs Type Indicator*. Palo Alto, CA: Consulting Psychologists Press.

Myers, I. B., and P. B. Myers. 1993. *Gifts Differing: Understanding Personality Types*. Palo Alto, CA: Consulting Psychologists Press.

Myers-Briggs Company. n.d. "History, Reliability and Validity of the Myers-Briggs Type Indicator (MBTI) Assessment." https://www.cpp.com/en-US/Support/Validity-of-the-Myers-Briggs-assessment, accessed August 16, 2018.

New York Times. 1964. "Inquiry Is Begun on Loan Sharks; Underworld's Investment in Racket Is Put at Billion." *New York Times*, December 2. https://www.nytimes.com/1964/12/02/archives/inquiry-is-begun-on-loan-sharks-underworlds-investment-in-racket-is.html.

Niskanen, W. A. 1971. *Bureaucracy and Representative Government*. New Brunswick, NJ: Transaction.

Nixon, R. 1968. Speech of Richard Nixon Accepting the Nomination of the Republican Party for President of the United States. *New York Times*, August 9.

Ostrom, E. 1990. *Governing the Commons: The Evolution of Institutions for Collective Action*. New York: Cambridge University Press.

Pirsig, R. 1979. *Zen and the Art of Motorcycle Maintenance*. New York: William Morrow.

Pittenger, D. J. 1993. "The Utility of the Myers-Briggs Type Indicator." *Review of Educational Research* 63: 467–88.

——. 2005. "Cautionary Comments Regarding the Myers-Briggs Type Indicator." *Consulting Psychology Journal: Practice and Research* 57, no. 3: 210–21.

Podolyak, P. 2017. "Myers Briggs Personality Type and Political Affiliation." *USA Daily Times*, December 26. https://www.usadailytimes.com/2017/12/26/myers-briggs-personality-type-and-political-affiliation/.

Samuelson, P. 1969. "Statement before the Committee of the Judiciary of the General Court of Massachusetts in Support of the Uniform Consumer Credit Code." January 29.

Shellenberger, M. 2018. “Sweeping Civil Rights Lawsuit Alleges Racial Bias in Implementation of California Climate Policies.” *Forbes.com*, September 13. https://www.forbes.com/sites/michaelshellenberger/2018/09/13/sweeping-civil-rights-lawsuit-alleges-racial-bias-in-implementation-of-california-climate-policies/#3777a7913c07.

Smith, A. [1776] 1982. *An Inquiry into the Nature and Causes of the Wealth of Nations*, vol. 1. Edited by R. H. Campbell and A. S. Skinner. Indianapolis, IN: Liberty Fund.

Sowell, T. 1987. *A Conflict of Visions: Ideological Origins of Political Struggles*. New York: William Morrow.

Thaler, R. H., and C. R. Sunstein. 2009. *Nudge: Improving Decisions about Health, Wealth, and Happiness*. New York: Penguin Books.

US Senate. 1968. “Report of Agency Operations.” Committee on Government Operations, Subcommittee on Legal and Monetary Affairs, Federal Effort against Organized Crime, June.

Yandle, B. 1989. *The Political Limits of Environmental Regulation: Tracking the Unicorn*. New York: Quorum.

——. 1997. *Common Sense and Common Law for the Environment*. Lanham, MD: Rowman & Littlefield.

Zywicki, T. J. 1999. “Environmental Externalities and Political Externalities: The Political Economy of Environmental Regulation and Reform.” *Tulane Law Review* 73: 845–921.

——. 2002. “Baptists: The Political Economy of Environmental Interest Groups.” *Case Western Reserve Law Review* 53, no. 2: 315–51. https://scholarlycommons.law.case.edu/caselrev/vol53/iss2/7.

——. 2013. “The Consumer Financial Protection Bureau: Savior or Menace?” *George Washington Law Review* 81, no. 3: 856–928.

——. 2016. “Rent-Seeking, Crony Capitalism, and the Crony Constitution.” *Supreme Court Economic Review* 23: 77–103.

CHAPTER 5
Yandle, Coase, Pigou, and Irrigation in the American West

RANDY T. SIMMONS

Irrigation is an art. Ask anyone who has plowed a ditch, set irrigation dams, used siphon tubes, changed sprinkler lines, laid drip line, or programmed center pivot systems. Farmers decide individually how best to practice that art depending on experience, terrain, soil type, elevation, available water, temperature, time of year, and type of crop. They skillfully manipulate the timing and amount of water to produce crops with a particular flavor and color and a high sugar or protein content. Farmers can make those decisions only after water is delivered to their fields by irrigation systems—dams, stream diversions, or wells. Water allocation systems and rules (institutions) determine who gets water when, how, and for how long.

This is a story of how water distribution systems and governing institutions affect the use and distribution of agricultural water in the western United States. In most western states, about 75 percent of the available water is used in agriculture, even though the marginal acre foot of water is often far more valuable in municipal or industrial uses. Transferring water rights from agriculture to urban uses is difficult and costly in time and money. The reason, I argue, is that the rules that successfully created property rights to water and reduced transaction costs for developing agricultural water delivery systems create very high transaction costs for moving water to different uses.

My guides in trying to understand how clear property rights and transaction cost–reducing institutions developed are Bruce Yandle and Ronald Coase. I examine externalities, transaction costs, and water markets through Yandle's parable of a river, a mill, and downstream water users. Yandle looked at competition for the river's water through the lens of what we might call Coase-colored glasses (Anderson 2004). He developed some nonobvious lessons from wearing those glasses, lessons that are useful for understanding western water today.

COASE, PIGOU, AND YANDLE

Bruce Yandle's analysis in his chapter titled "Coase, Pigou, and Environmental Rights" makes Ronald Coase's "The Problem of Social Cost" clearer than anything else I have read on the subject. The chapter is found in *Who Owns the Environment*, edited by Peter J. Hill and Roger E. Meiners (Hill and Meiners 1998). In that chapter, Yandle presents the standard, widely accepted economics textbook approach to externalities as developed by A. C. Pigou. Yandle also presents the less widely accepted property rights counterpoint to Pigou, developed by Ronald Coase.

Pigou was an English economist who launched the concept of externalities—costs and benefits imposed on others without their consent. The economic problem created by externalities is that the person creating the costs or benefits does not take them into account when choosing a course of action. Thus, a mill owner might not consider how dumping waste into a river imposes costs on downstream users, or an irrigator who diverts an entire stream might not consider the costs imposed on a downstream irrigator who is left with no water. Pigou said, "Smoke in large cities inflicts a heavy uncharged loss on the community, in injury to buildings, vegetation, expenses for washing clothes and cleaning rooms, expenses for the provision of artificial light, and in many other ways" (Pigou 1920, 84). He suggested that government tax actions it wants to discourage. The right amount of tax would, by aligning private costs with social costs, encourage those being taxed to produce the (socially) correct combination of products and pollution. Any further reduction would be costlier than paying the tax.

Modern Pigovians' enthusiasm for Pigovian taxes ought to be tempered by what Pigou had to say about Pigovian taxes. Although he established the theoretical groundwork for taxing externalities, when he moved from theory to practice, he no longer sounded like a Pigovian. He warned:

> It is not sufficient to contrast the imperfect adjustments of unfettered private enterprise with the best adjustment that economists in their studies can imagine. For we cannot expect that any public authority will attain, or will even whole-heartedly seek, that ideal. Such authorities are liable alike to ignorance, to sectional pressure and to personal corruption by private interest. A loud-voiced part of their constituents, if organised for votes, may easily outweigh the whole. (Pigou 1920, 331–32)

Pigou was reminding economists that the world outside their models acts quite differently than the theoretical world that fascinates them. Politicians and bureaucrats are as imperfect as those they seek to regulate. In the same paragraph as the citation above he cautions, "A hostile, lax, or ignorant city council, or even a state legislature, may vary the terms of the agreement in such a manner as totally to destroy or seriously impair its value" (Pigou 1920, 332). He could have added members of Congress and regulators to his list of the lax, hostile, or ignorant. He did add, "Every public official is a potential opportunity for some form of self-interest arrayed against the common interest" (Pigou 1920, 332). Yandle adds, "if Public Choice theory has taught us anything, it is that government is endogenous to the political economy" (Hill and Meiners 1998, 149).

Pigou simply did not believe that politicians could or would get the calculations of the proper level of taxation correct. He worried that politicians and regulators would end up crafting loopholes for their favorite interest groups at the same time they looked for ways to generate more revenue. Yandle, may have said it best: "It would seem that Pigou was not much of a Pigouvian" (Yandle 2010, 4).

Yandle explains that in Ronald Coase's 1960 paper, "The Problem of Social Cost," Coase "focused very tightly on the Pigouvian solution and arrived at a very different way of looking at the same pollution problem, as well as every other problem of social cost" (Hill and Meiners 1998, 132). Externalities, according to Coase, are reciprocal. That is, viewing externalities simply as the costs produced by polluters and consumed by victims misses the reciprocal nature of many externalities. Coase's point is that legal rules that assign blame to me and victim status to you can be inefficient. He explained, "We are dealing with a problem of a reciprocal nature, to avoid the harm to B would inflict harm to A. The real question to be decided is: should A be allowed to harm B or should B be allowed to harm A?" (Coase 1960, 2).

Yandle illustrates this with a story about a mill, a river, and a downstream community. The river is a common-access resource. A paper mill is located on the river and uses the river to power the paper-making machinery and as a place to discharge the waste produced in that process. If, as was usually the case, the mill were not charged for using the river, it will produce more paper than it would if it had to pay for disposing of the waste. In all likelihood, the mill would find that reducing its discharges into the river to zero would be very costly, while reducing the first units of waste might be relatively cheap.

He then introduces downstream users in "a charming location, set on the hills that slope down to the river" (Hill and Meiners 1998, 133). The community has a boat dock and other recreational facilities. These downstream users value an unpolluted river, and while they might not notice a small amount of discharge from the mill, they will notice if the river becomes a waste dump.

When an upstream polluter sends pollution downstream, it seems only logical that the upstream entity is at fault and must pay or curtail their use of the river in ways that harm the community downstream. But Yandle, putting on his Coase-colored glasses, says, wait a minute, if there were no downstream users, the mill would not impose costs on anyone. Their attempt to curtail the upstream mill's use of the river imposes a cost on the owners of the mill. Even though rivers flow in one direction, externalities flow up and downstream.

In this story, appealing to government to impose a Pigovian tax is unnecessary. The mill can invest in treatment or the downstream neighbors can pay the mill to make the investment. If, and this a crucial "if," property rights are clear, the parties can negotiate mutually agreeable and enforceable contracts. In doing so, they will arrive at an efficient solution to the conflict. It doesn't even matter who gets the property rights initially. Whether the mill invests in better water treatment facilities or the downstream neighbors pay the mill to build them, the outcome is the same—a river clean enough to reflect the values of those doing the bargaining.

The reciprocal nature of externalities was new in 1960 and continues to be new to many social scientists today. In Yandle's words, "Externalities flow both ways because costs and benefits flow both ways. There is no such thing as a one-sided externality" (Hill and Meiners 1998, 137). To Coase, externalities simply are evidence of incomplete property rights. If there were property rights to water quality in a river,[1] for example, bargaining among all who had an interest in the quality of the water would result in a better social outcome than if pollution controls were mandated by government.

If externalities really do flow both ways, a forward-looking approach is for users to ask themselves if more efficient ways of using their environment are available: are there new technologies, and what are the alternative ways of using the resource, in this case the river? In fact, Yandle concludes his discussion of Coase with a "final key point." A property rights system is "forward- not backward-looking. Instead of looking at current users and finding solutions that fit the needs of existing technologies and plans, the more dynamic approach encourages all users to focus on the future" (Hill and Meiners 1998, 137).

Coase wrote a sequel to "The Problem of Social Cost" because people drew incorrect conclusions about his central message. He called the second paper "Notes on the Problem of Social Cost" (Coase 1988). Coase explained:

> The world of zero transaction costs has often been described as a Coasian world. Nothing could be further from the truth. It is the world of modern economic theory, one which I was hoping to persuade economists to leave. What I did in *The Problem of Social Costs* was simply to bring to light some of its properties. . . . Economists, following Pigou whose work has dominated thought in this area, have consequently been engaged in an attempt to explain why there were divergences between private and social costs and what should be done about it, using a theory in which private and social costs were necessarily always equal. It is therefore hardly surprising that the conclusions reached were often incorrect. The reason why economists went wrong was that their theoretical system did not take into account a factor which is essential if one wishes to analyze the effect of a change in the law on the allocation of resources. The missing factor is the existence of transaction costs. (Coase 1988, 174–75)

Many readers of Coase miss the transaction costs[2] of the story and focus on property rights. Coase's fans, for example, concentrate on his claim that property rights are the key to moving assets to their highest and best uses and, regardless of who received the property rights initially, through time and sufficient trades, the resource will move from lower-valued to higher-valued uses. Coase's critics note that Coasean solutions to externalities might work well in small groups, but not in the larger world because it is impossible to get voluntary agreement to pay without the coercion of government.[3] But that was precisely his point, as he explained in the quotation above from "Notes on the Problem of Social Cost"—initial allocations can matter because of transaction costs. In fact, both essays are about property rights *and* transaction costs.

Yandle briefly addressed the large-number problem when he said, "we should recognize that large numbers can become smaller numbers when the large numbers form associations, clubs, or firms, such as river basin associations" (Hill and Meiners 1998, 148). This will become an important insight as we discuss how irrigation systems moved from solving problems involving small numbers to large numbers of users.

Coase did not claim that markets would handle everything. He identified two causes of inefficiency—insufficiently developed property rights and high transaction costs. Coase and Yandle suggest that, rather than turning automatically to Pigovian taxes, policy should focus on fixing those causes of inefficiency so that individuals may come up with solutions entirely outside of government approaches.

Solutions that focus on property and transaction-cost problems may be very different from solutions that focus on externalities. As Yandle wrote:

> Coase explains how an appropriate interpretation of market forces could eliminate the need for specialized statutes for handling "the problem of social cost." In doing so he calls attention to institutions for reducing the inevitable costs that are generated in communities. Government regulation is just one of the many approaches that might be taken. The cost of organizing and running the various institutions dictates which, if any, approach might be utilized. (Hill and Meiners 1998, 121)

WATER IN THE WEST

Institutions for managing water in the American West provide several examples of how "government regulation is just one of many approaches that might be taken." In what follows, I review some history and consider how water institutions emerged to handle the problem of social cost in the late 19th and early 20th centuries, along with how those same institutions may now be getting in the way of Coasean solutions to modern challenges.

Western Water, Externalities, Property Rights, and Transaction Costs

Early colonizers of the American West faced climate conditions entirely unlike those they had experienced in the eastern half of the country. The semiarid climate required diverting water to where it could be used, often over long distances. This was especially true for industries like mining and farming, where water was needed far from the only available sources. Farming, for example, could occur only "under the ditch," meaning downhill from an irrigation canal or ditch.

The system of water rights in the eastern United States was and continues to be the common-law doctrine of riparian rights, a system poorly suited to the arid West. Riparian water rights grant the owners of land adjoining bodies of water the right to withdraw water as long as they do not impair the rights of other landowners to use of the same water resource. Riparian land is land adjacent to a watercourse. Most of the fertile and mining lands in the West were not adjacent to water, however, so the riparian doctrine had to be scrapped in favor of a different system. The system that emerged in both mining camps and farming communities became what is known as the prior appropriation doctrine.

Long before European contact, Native Americans built extensive irrigation networks, but most were abandoned before the Europeans arrived. Some of the Spanish missions developed a few small irrigation joint ventures with Native Americans, usually using preexisting Native American canals. The first community-scale European systems were built in Utah by the Mormon settlers. On July 23, 1847, a company of pioneers entered the Salt Lake Valley and plowed some land, diverted water from City Creek to irrigate it, and planted potatoes. From that initial experiment, irrigation communities developed wherever water was flowing that could be diverted and spread on fields.

The early irrigators faced three institutional problems. The first was developing a system for allocating the available water. That question was addressed first in the mining camps and then in Mormon communities where the doctrine of "first in time, first in right" was developed. That doctrine remains the cornerstone of western water law. What first in time, first in right means is that those who first put the water to use had priority access to that water in the future. That priority was, in fact, a property right that became recognized by judicial decree or statute and provided certainty in water resource availability.

A second problem was similar to Yandle's story of the mill, the river, and downstream users. Downstream users got no water if the upstream user diverted it all for his own use. Prior appropriation solved that problem as well. The senior property right owner had rights to first use. If downstream users wanted water, they had to buy, trade, lease, or rent it from the senior right holder. Given clear property rights assignments and the freedom to trade those rights, no externalities arose, as externalities simply are caused by unclear or poorly developed property rights.

A third problem is the transaction costs of organizing people to cooperate in developing a resource, what to do about free riders, how to deal with opportunistic behavior, and how to match farm size to irrigation system size. In Yandle's story, the problem was solved contractually. In the West, irrigators solved, or at least reduced, that problem by inventing new organizational forms.

Developing Water Rights and Institutions

Pioneer Irrigation. The Mormon pioneers developed water codes that became the basis for the prior appropriation doctrine. One early writer explained:

> The Utah pioneers laid down the fundamental principle that since in an arid country the use of water for irrigation is the most important concern of the people, the doctrine of riparian rights must be abrogated, and the proper use of water in irrigation must constitute the fundamental claim of the individual upon the use of the freely flowing waters of the state. This doctrine which now seems axiomatic, represents a great contribution to the conquest of the arid West by irrigation. (Widtsoe 1928, 2–3)

A noted above, the Mormons get only partial credit for the prior appropriation doctrine as it also developed at roughly the same time in the gold mining camps. Under prior appropriation, whoever was the first to divert water from a source established the right to keep diverting that same *amount* of water regardless of whether the flow was high or low. Once the right to first use was established, other users had the right to divert water not already used. The first diverter had a "senior" right and users who came later had legally recognized "junior" rights. An even more extensive ranking of rights eventually was adopted, running from primary or senior rights to secondary junior and tertiary junior rights. Some rights are based on water that returns to a river after having been diverted by a prior user.

During the early years of irrigation, many thought that the water right was connected to a particular piece of land, and that the only way to purchase a water right was to purchase the land where it was used. It is true that the value of a farm often is determined more by the water right owned by the farmer than by the land itself. But it is also true that water rights now can be bought and sold independently of land ownership.[4] The caveat is that the water rights purchaser not interfere with the rights of other senior and junior users.

The early irrigation systems in Utah and other western settlements were built cooperatively. Dam and diversion sites were identified and dams and ditches were built by the people who were to use the water. John A. Widtsoe, who assisted in forming the College of Biology and Agriculture at Brigham Young University and then was president of Utah State University and then the University of Utah, wrote about those early efforts:

> Such cooperative efforts fit the nature of irrigation itself, for, after a ditch has been built, its maintenance becomes the joint concern of all who use water from it. Pioneer reclamation is always cooperative reclamation. The principles recognized, the rules and regulations set up and the cooperative spirit developed made it possible to create under the ditch, in full accord with the American spirit, a civilization conforming to the best knowledge and thought of the day. (Widtsoe 1928, 3)

Utah's pioneer irrigation efforts were so extensive that by 1865, 17 years after arriving in the Salt Lake Valley, they had dug 277 canals, 1,044 miles in length, at a cost, including the cost of dams, of $1,766,959,[5] by which 155,949 acres were irrigated at an average cost per acre of not quite $12;[6] the estimated cost of canals in progress was $877,730 (Widtsoe 1928, 4).

Speculative Reclamation. The pioneers developed the easiest projects first and were so successful that irrigation in the West soon attracted capital from eastern investors. The era of speculative reclamation (to use Widtsoe's phrase) was quite different in that the projects were more expensive, were not built as cooperative efforts, water users did not own the infrastructure, and interest on crops irrigated went to a capitalist-builder, not a farmer-builder who farmed under the ditch. Those ventures failed more often than not. The investors had little local knowledge about the harsh realities of the arid West and project owners were too distant from the water users. Because the water users did not own the infrastructure, they had little incentive to maintain it. Developing water projects in the more difficult places was more expensive than investors had expected, and the per acre cost rose more and more, which drove capital in other directions. In addition, some commercial companies tried covering the rising costs by charging higher and higher fees. Bretsen and Hill cite an observer who noted that commercial irrigation companies could sell land under the ditch, wait while farmers improved their farms, refuse to deliver water when crops needed it, take over the farms when farmers could not make payments, and then resell to other farmers (Bretsen and Hill 2006, 300). Farmers responded by refusing to buy water and went to their state legislatures for relief; several states passed laws regulating the sale of water rights by commercial irrigation companies.[7]

Mutual Irrigation Companies

The main transaction cost problem for irrigation is that farms need to be a certain size to capture economies of scale, but irrigation infrastructure must be on a larger scale to serve multiple farms. That is, irrigation presents a collective action problem. Getting the farmers or potential farmers together to create the infrastructure was accomplished in pioneer times by cooperative reclamation. Commercial irrigation companies built a lot of infrastructure, but many failed. They gradually were taken over by local mutual irrigation companies. In an effort to overcome the free-rider problems that came with funding and building irrigation infrastructure, farmers formed mutual irrigation companies to construct, maintain, and manage that infrastructure. Bretsen and Hill argue that mutual irrigation companies were successful at "reducing or eliminating transaction costs in areas where the commercial irrigation company had failed" (Bretsen and Hill 2006, 302). Mutual irrigation companies acquired appropriative water rights, either from other companies or from the members of the association, and redefined those rights as shares.

The concept of shares in a flow rather than a senior or junior right was another innovation in western water law. When farmers joined a mutual association, they no longer owned a property right; the right to divert water was owned by the association. What the farmers owned was a share of the flow from the association's water right. The concept of shares solved the conflict (some would say "externality") between senior and junior rights holders as no one was senior or junior. They each had a right to a share of the water right owned collectively by the association. The shares were allocated by time of water use. My shares of the Spring Creek Irrigation Company, for example, identify the time each week that my access to water starts and stops. The next person below me on the ditch has the next turn and so on all the way to the end of the ditch.

The mutual irrigation companies, as well as the pioneer organizations, faced a free-rider problem over the operation and maintenance of irrigation. Being one of the people at the head of the ditch meant there was little or no incentive to worry about users farther down the ditch. Why should water users, for example, be concerned about the status of the ditch beyond the boundary of their farm? Even if the ditch below them fails for lack of maintenance or any other reason, they will still get their water. Another problem is that those at the head of the ditch could not be relied on not to steal some water as it flowed past.

Bretsen and Hill cite Elwood Mead, Wyoming territorial and state engineer in the late 19th century and the head of the USDA Office of Irrigation Investigations from 1898 to 1907. He helped structure Wyoming's water code and federal irrigation legislation. He noted:

> Enthusiasm or the press of need would suffice to build partnership ditches, but friction would disrupt their subsequent operation. Human selfishness would then assert itself. The man whose land was near the ditch did not need to keep it in repair; so long as water for others had run past his lateral, the people below him would have to attend to this or do without. The irrigator having this fortunate location showed equal ingenuity in manipulating his head gates so as to take more than his share of the water, while the unfortunate irrigator at the lower end of the ditch found himself doing more work and getting less for it than the other members of the partnership. Until farmers learned that they must place the control of the ditch in the hands of one individual, there was either murder or suicide in the heart of every member of the partnership. (Bretsen and Hill 2006, 311–12)

The Mormon pioneer irrigators addressed the free-rider problem ecclesiastically. As Mormon historian Leonard Arrington writes in *Great Basin Kingdom*:

> When a group of families found themselves in need of water (or additional water) to irrigate their farms and gardens, the bishop [the local religious leader] arranged for

> a survey and organized the men into a construction crew. Each man was required to furnish labor in proportion to the amount of land he had to water. Upon completion of the project the water would be distributed by a ward water-master in proportion to the labor. The labor necessary to keep the canal in good repair was handled in the same way, in accordance with assignments made in regular Sunday services. (Arrington 1958, 53)

Mutual irrigation associations did not have ecclesiastical authority, but they addressed free riders by hiring a watermaster, whose job was to patrol the ditch and manage conflict. And conflict is real. In 1966 my father owned a 400-acre farm at the end of an irrigation ditch. We went out one morning to change sprinklers and none of them were turning. We drove up the hill to the reservoir and found it empty; no water was flowing in the ditch. But we could see upstream that sprinklers were active. It turned out that the ditch had broken between us and upstream users. Those users were getting their water and were not concerned with the downstream break. Arguments became heated, but the irrigation company chose three men to walk the ditch for the next 24 hours while a backhoe operator repaired the break. In the meantime, upstream users had to reduce their withdrawals so a small stream could get by the break and serve those of us downstream. The three men, including my father and the watermaster, patrolled the ditch *with shotguns!* No one even considered calling the county sheriff. The problem was internal to the company and they handled it. There is a lot of truth to the statement, "In the West, whisky is for drinking, water is for fighting."

Some people wonder why a small group of farmers cannot cooperate without a watermaster to enforce their rules. It turns out that any sustainable system for managing a common pool resource requires a means of enforcing the agreed-upon rules. Elinor Ostrom studied successful common-pool resource management across the world and found eight common traits, which she called design principles. Her fifth principle is "Develop a system, carried out by community members, for monitoring members' behavior" (Ostrom 1990). My own experience is anecdotal but mirrors Ostrom's findings. My city (Providence, Utah) is the majority owner of shares in a water canal that passes through a neighboring town of about 5,000 people. While I was mayor, only a small amount of water was reaching my city. I contacted the ditch company president and asked why. His response was that they had not hired a watermaster for the other city and people were just opening their head gates whenever they wanted, not when it was their turn. As soon as the city hired a watermaster, our share of the water reached us.

Because everyone who owns shares in the company is assessed an annual fee, the problem of upstream users not paying for downstream maintenance and improvements is solved. The fee also covers the costs of the watermaster. Decisions are made at an annual meeting where corporation officers are chosen. With the company owning all the water rights, no cost is imposed on junior users by senior users. Everyone has a right to a share of the flow. Thus, in low water years, even those at the end of the ditch get their share of the low flow. The companies are formed under the laws of the state, but are, for the most part, self-governing.

Mutual irrigation companies all have some features in common: they are voluntary organizations; they make cooperation possible by establishing collective decision-making mechanisms; they place the ownership of the irrigation works in the hands of a single entity that serves several farms; and the farmers own shares in the water right, which was owned by the company.[8]

Toward the beginning of the 20th century, irrigators began to form new, larger, public/private organizations, known as irrigation districts. Irrigation districts had many of the features of mutual irrigation companies, but states granted them added powers that included "eminent domain, the power of taxation, the power to issue bonds, and exemptions from state and federal income taxes" (Hill and Meiners 1998, 316). As the federal Bureau of Reclamation began constructing large irrigation projects, including dams and pipelines, it contracted with irrigation districts that gained exclusive distribution rights to the bureau's water. Today, irrigation districts deliver water to both individual water users and to irrigation companies, which then reallocate the water to their members.

Transaction costs are reduced even more by irrigation districts than by mutual irrigation companies because the districts have the police power of the state behind them. They can condemn private property in order to build a canal across land, so they are not subject to holdout problems.[9] They are not voluntary since, although state laws vary about the sizes of the required majority, a vote by a majority of landowners forces all landowners within a district's boundaries to join, and they can issue bonds backed by assessments of the district's land values. Like mutual irrigation districts, they provide a way to make collective decisions and to enforce those decisions.

Irrigation districts are a far cry from the initial pioneer ditch companies or the mutual irrigation association in which I own shares. They control vast amounts of water. The Imperial Irrigation District in Southern California, for example, annually diverts 2.5 million acre feet of water from the Colorado River (nearly two-thirds of California's legal share), serves over 5,000 farms totaling 520,000 acres, and has more than 3,000 miles of canals and drains in an area that receives just three inches of rainfall per year (Imperial Irrigation District n.d.). Besides becoming powerful economic interests, irrigation districts have become powerful political interests, lobbying state legislatures for, among other things, more taxing powers.

Why Doesn't Water Move from Agriculture to Urban Uses?

The water management institutions that developed, based on clear property rights and reducing transaction costs, have made it very difficult to transfer water from one use to another, even when the marginal value of water to agriculture is far below its value for municipal or environmental uses. The irony is that transaction costs, which were reduced for irrigators trading within a company, are very high for trading from agriculture to municipal or industrial uses. Majoritarian decision rules keep farmers from contracting individually outside the association. Owning a share in a water company or association does not include the right to sell or transfer one's shares to nonmembers. If one's share of a water right is in an association involved with the Bureau of Reclamation, the transaction costs of moving water across uses are even more difficult.

Irrigation institutions were not organized to transfer water for uses outside the mutual association or the district. Their purpose was and continues to be entirely internal. Water share markets are active within mutual associations and districts, but little trading takes place outside the district. I, for example, own three and a half shares in Spring Creek Water Company, a mutual irrigation company. I recently purchased two of those shares from a fellow company member. The company then adjusted the times at which I access those shares in order not to adversely affect downstream users who need "carry water" in the ditch to make sure they receive their full shares. I did not contact the water company, the state, or anyone else about whether or not I could purchase those shares. The previous owner and I just agreed on a price and he signed his share certificates saying he had sold them to me. Our ditch also has an active informal system for trading rights and sharing excess water that does not need to be approved by anyone but ourselves. But if I wanted to sell my shares to someone who would use them outside our company, the process would be difficult. The board of directors would have to agree. The state water engineer would have to approve the sale. Other interested parties could appeal the sale; the rules for being an interested party are extremely lax.

The process for transforming an irrigation right into a municipal right can be Byzantine. While I was mayor, we (the city) purchased water rights from an individual whose point of diversion was 15 miles away on a source that did not flow even close to our city. The purchase was not from someone owning shares in a mutual or irrigation company, so we did not have to get the board of directors' approval. The right was a tertiary right, so it was very junior. We applied to the state engineer to transfer the point of diversion from its historical site to a new well we would develop in our city. The engineer approved and the appeals started. Transferring the right cost thousands of dollars in attorney fees, engineering witness fees, fees for expert witnesses who presented data about the effects on downstream users (in our case aquifer users), and took two years. What might have been a simple exchange became a long, contentious process. After going to the state's First District Court twice and holding numerous hearings, we finally made the purchase. The focus of the review by the state water engineer was to ensure that no other water rights were injured by the transaction. He decided that no one would be harmed. We had to go to court because other interested parties disagreed. See figure 5.1 for a description of the process.

Some of the difficulties of moving water from agriculture are illustrated by the lengthy process involving the Imperial Irrigation District and the Metropolitan Water District of Southern California. Negotiations for long-term water leases began in 1984, and concluded in 2003. Agreements were reached during that time, but collapsed after challenges by opponents. The US Department of the Interior, which administers Colorado River water, intervened and a transfer of 30 million acre feet to urban users over 75 years finally was agreed to. The initial plan was to idle some agricultural lands, but opposition was so intense that the final agreement was that water for the transfer would be provided by lining ditches to reduce seepage, even though it is likely that fallowing would have been cheaper.

Prior appropriation is partially at fault for the difficulty of transferring water across alternative uses. Because the property rights are for specific amounts of water, junior rights holders are likely to be harmed if the senior rights holders sell their rights. Thus, junior rights holders are likely to protest and litigate. If, however, rights were specified as shares of the annual flow, then junior rights holders would be protected.

Figure 5.1. Utah Water Transfer Application Process

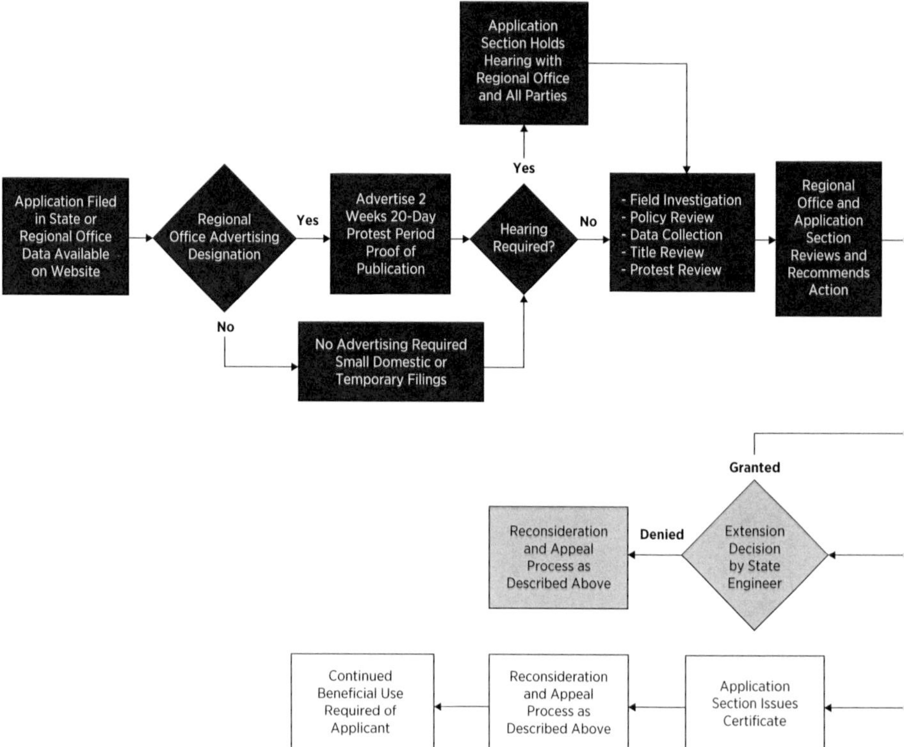

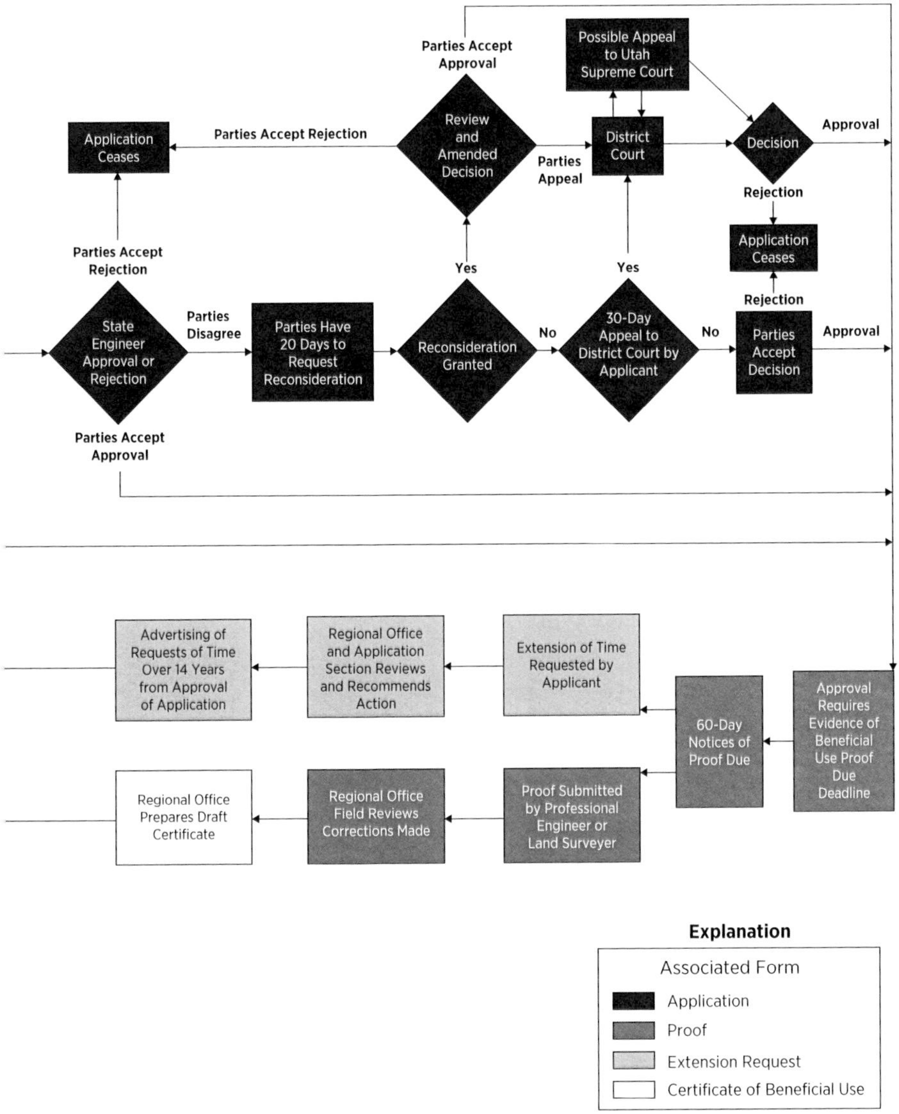

Parties Accept Approval
Possible Appeal to Utah Supreme Court
Application Ceases
Parties Accept Rejection
Review and Amended Decision
Parties Appeal
District Court
Decision
Approval
Rejection
Application Ceases
Rejection
Parties Accept Rejection
Yes
Yes
State Engineer Approval or Rejection
Parties Disagree
Parties Have 20 Days to Request Reconsideration
Reconsideration Granted
No
30-Day Appeal to District Court by Applicant
No
Parties Accept Decision
Approval
Parties Accept Approval
Advertising of Requests of Time Over 14 Years from Approval of Application
Regional Office and Application Section Reviews and Recommends Action
Extension of Time Requested by Applicant
60-Day Notices of Proof Due
Approval Requires Evidence of Beneficial Use Proof Due Deadline
Regional Office Prepares Draft Certificate
Regional Office Field Reviews Corrections Made
Proof Submitted by Professional Engineer or Land Surveyer
Explanation
Associated Form
Application
Proof
Extension Request
Certificate of Beneficial Use

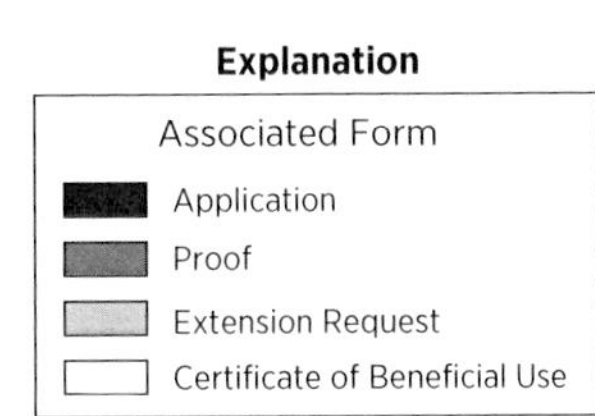

What about Transferring to Environmental Uses?

Transferring water from agricultural uses to environmental uses faces the same difficulties as transferring it to urban uses. The water management institutions that served the development of agriculture so well get in the way of seemingly simple trades. Again, the problem is one of externalities and transaction costs.

A dewatered streambed would seem to qualify as an externality demanding government intervention. A Coasean perspective might be to ask who owns the water right—the fish that will be killed if the stream is dewatered or the farmer. It turns out that fish do not own water rights, farmers do, but only if they divert water from the stream. The farmers' appropriative right may allow them to divert the entire stream, leaving the fish and other aquatic species high and dry, literally. Given that the right to divert is clear, it ought to be relatively simple for friends of fish to purchase some of the diversion rights and leave the water in the stream. The problem is that under the prior appropriation doctrine and state legislation, water has to be diverted in order for a property right to exist and be enforced. Water rights are only for "beneficial uses," as defined by state law; until relatively recently, leaving water in the stream was not considered to be a beneficial use in most western states.

Beneficial use was intended to prevent wasteful water use by requiring that all diverted water is used in a beneficial way. If appropriators fail to put water to such use, the state can revoke the water right. Utah's statute is typical: "[W]hen an appropriator or the appropriator's successor in interest abandons or ceases to use all or a portion of a water right for a period of seven years, the water right or the unused portion of that water right is subject to forfeiture."[10]

Water rights owners must put their appropriated allocation of water to beneficial use or risk forfeiting all or a portion of that right to the state or to those with junior rights. The beneficial use doctrine discourages conservation because it slows the discovery of new beneficial uses and forces water rights owners to use their full share of water or lose their right without compensation.

Commonly accepted beneficial uses include agriculture, industry, domestic use, and recreation, but do not include uses like conservation or instream flows, which is leaving water in the stream rather than diverting it. Utah water law, for example, "allows for current water rights to be converted to an instream flow only by the Division of Wildlife Resources or the Division of Parks, Lands and Recreation."

Over the last 25 years, most western states have legally recognized instream flows as a beneficial use, but with significant diversity in implementation. Thus, large differences exist between states in allowing the sale or lease of appropriative rights for instream uses. Oregon and Washington have approved hundreds of leases and other transfers, while Wyoming, Arizona, and New Mexico have approved almost none.

Montana's chapter of Trout Unlimited has an impressive record of converting water rights to instream flows, whether through purchase or lease. As might be expected, given that only selected state agencies can own an instream flow in Utah, the Utah Trout Unlimited chapter has not had similar success. And the transaction costs of working around the state's rules are very high. They have had, however, one significant success on the headwaters of the Bear River, a 350-mile-long river that starts in the Uinta Mountains in Utah, travels through parts of Wyoming, Idaho, and Utah, and empties into the Great Salt Lake. Two different irrigation companies own rights to divert water near the river's headwaters. Until recently, each spring the companies hired a D9 Caterpillar to drive up 15 miles of streambed and create a "push-up dam at the diversion point." The dam completely dewatered the next several miles until smaller streams joined the streambed. Utah's chapter of Trout Unlimited spent three years negotiating with the irrigation companies and the state to move the diversion point of the irrigation water several miles downstream and build new distribution canals. Changing the diversion point meant more water in the river than at the previous diversion point, meaning that the irrigation companies could not take all of the water and dewater the river. Trout Unlimited successfully raised the money, got the blessing of the state water engineer, and reached agreement with the canal companies. They had to develop such a roundabout way to get an instream flow because they were not allowed to purchase and hold an instream flow outright under Utah's beneficial use rules.

CONCLUSION

I started by asserting that irrigation is an art. Designing institutions also is an art, but it is one that few are able to master. That is probably why the best institutions often are those that emerge from human experiences as opposed to being created consciously. The prior appropriation doctrine and the organizations that developed to manage water and water users are ones that emerged in the American West.

Water rights in the American West (by and large) are clear. They are not fee simple rights, but are usufructuary, meaning that they represent rights to use water, but the state retains ownership of the water. Emerging out of mining camps and pioneer irrigation experiments, the use rights are well established and are recognized by the states, courts, and even banks. Where extensive irrigation infrastructure was required to move water to irrigable lands, irrigators developed ways to minimize transaction costs by creating mutual irrigation companies and irrigation districts.

Those same institutions, however, make transferring water across alternative uses difficult. That is, they create transaction costs and rules that get in the way of potential markets in water. Sometimes people can find clever, if costly, ways around the existing system, as did the Utah chapter of Trout Unlimited. At other times and in other places, the process is so drawn out and complicated that a central authority is needed to break the logjam, as was the case with the Imperial Irrigation District.

Yandle suggests some hope for those of us interested in systems evolving that will allow more flexible water markets when he notes at the end of his chapter that:

> New institutions for protecting environmental assets that emerge from the market encounter the raw forces of politics and an entrenched bureaucracy. Each day, a new world emerges from these encounters. Part of the outcome we observe is Coasean; another part is Pigouvian. Underlying it all is a system of property rights that continues to evolve. Both Coase and Pigou help us to understand the evolutionary process that generates an ever-changing definition of environmental rights. (Hill and Meiners 1998, 149)

NOTES

1. This is not a fanciful statement. Private individuals and associations in the United Kingdom, for example, have long held water quality rights. The most famous court case on the topic was *Pride of Derby and Derbyshire Angling Association Ltd. v. British Celanese Ltd.*, 1953, ruling that the plaintiffs could seek relief under the Public Health Act of 1936. https://swarb.co.uk/pride-of-derby-and-derbyshire-angling-association-ltd-v-british-celanese-ltd-ca-1953/, accessed July 19, 2018.
2. Transaction costs are the costs of defining, enforcing, and exchanging property rights. See Eggertson (1990).
3. But see Cheung's "Fable of the Bees" for examples counter to this claim (Cheung 1973).
4. Being able to separate water rights from land rights was not always the case. In Utah, for example, water could not be sold separately from land until 1880, when the territorial legislature passed An Act for Recording Vested Rights to the Use of Water and Regulating Their Exercise. The law allowed individual users to buy and sell water rights. In addition, most of the shares of common stock issued by the early mutual irrigation companies were considered appurtenant to the land irrigated by those shares of water.

5. $27,316,210 in 2018 dollars. $1,766,959 in 1865 → 2018. "Inflation Calculator," US Official Inflation Data, Alioth Finance, https://www.officialdata.org/1865-dollars-in-2018?amount=1766959, accessed August 8, 2018.
6. $186 in 2018 dollars. $12 in 1865 → 2018. "Inflation Calculator," US Official Inflation Data, Alioth Finance, https://www.officialdata.org/1865-dollars-in-2018?amount=12, accessed August 8, 2018.
7. A central part of Wallace Stegner's novel *Angle of Repose* (2000) has to do with the enthusiasm for and then failure of a commercial irrigation company.
8. Remember that, according to each western state's constitution, the state owns the water. Water rights are usufructuary rights—rights to use the water.
9. Courts have decided that this exercise of eminent domain is not an unconstitutional Fifth or Fourteenth Amendment taking because irrigation is a public purpose.
10. Utah Code, title 73, chapter 1, section 4, "Reversion to the Public by Abandonment or Forfeiture for Nonuse within Seven Years—Nonuse Application," http://le.utah.gov/xcode/Title73/Chapter1/73-1-S4.htm, accessed November 21, 2018.

REFERENCES

Anderson, T. L. 2004. "Viewing Land Conservation through Coase-Colored Glasses." *Natural Resources Journal* 44, no. 2: 361–81.

Arrington, L. J. 1958. *Great Basin Kingdom: An Economic History of the Latter-Day Saints, 1830–1900*. Lincoln: University of Nebraska Press.

Bretsen, S. N., and P. J. Hill. 2006. "Irrigation Institutions in the American West." *UCLA Journal of Environmental Law and Policy* 25, no. 2: 283–331.

Cheung, S. N. S. 1973. "The Fable of the Bees: An Economic Investigation." *Journal of Law & Economics* 16, no. 1: 11–33.

Coase, R. H. 1960. "The Problem of Social Cost." *Journal of Law & Economics* 3: 1–44.

——. 1988. "Notes on the Problem of Social Cost." In *The Firm, the Law, and the Market*. Chicago: University of Chicago Press.

Eggertson, T. 1990. *Economic Behavior and Institutions: Principles of Neoinstitutional Economics*. Cambridge: Cambridge University Press.

Hill, P. J., and R. E. Meiners, eds. 1998. *Who Owns the Environment?* Lanham, MD: Rowman & Littlefield.

Imperial Irrigation District. n.d. "About IID Water." https://www.iid.com/water/about-iid-water, accessed November 21, 2018.

Ostrom, E. 1990. *Governing the Commons: The Evolution of Institutions for Collective Action*. Cambridge: Cambridge University Press.

Pigou, A. C. 1920. *The Economics of Welfare*. London: Macmillan.

Stegner, W. 2000. *Angle of Repose*. New York: Penguin.

Widtsoe, J. A. 1928. *Success on Irrigation Projects*. New York: John Wiley & Sons.

Yandle, B. 2010. "Much Ado about Pigou." *Regulation* 33, no. 2: 2–4.

CHAPTER 6
Moralists, Moonshiners, and Monitors

SEAN E. MULHOLLAND

Every winter, tens of thousands of drivers replace their summer or all-season tires with winter tires. Owners often do so by mounting winter tires on a second set of wheels. Having two sets of wheels allows owners to swap summer and winter wheels and tires without having to mount and balance two sets of tires on a single set of wheels twice a year. Winter tires provide better traction in all road conditions when temperatures are below 45 degrees because the rubber compound is softer than all-season tires and the tread is designed to grip ice (Edmunds 2009). Yet in 2008, the federal government raised the cost of owning and maintaining additional sets of wheels and tires. Passed in 2000 and finalized in 2005 as part of the TREAD Act, tire pressure warning systems, later called tire pressure monitoring systems (TPMS), require each vehicle sold after 2007 to be equipped with a system that alerts the driver when one or more of the vehicle's tires are underinflated.

AUTOMOTIVE SAFETY

However, the TPMS story begins many decades before the TREAD Act of 2000. In some sense, it began in the United States when Henry Bliss, a 68-year-old real estate agent, became the first pedestrian to be struck and killed by a taxi in New York City on September 14, 1899. From that date on, manufacturers voluntarily introduced many safety improvements. These include emergency brakes, safety glass, and padded dashboards. But this evolutionary and voluntary nature of safety designs came to a screeching halt with the introduction of General Motors' Chevy Corvair and Ralph Nader's critique of automobile safety, *Unsafe at Any Speed* (Nader 1965).

In the 1950s, almost all domestic vehicles were large: the 1957 Chevy Bel Air was 200 inches long, or about seven inches longer than a 2018 Toyota Camry. Many foreign automobiles in the US market at that time were small. For instance, the 1951 Volkswagen Beetle was only 161 inches long, and the 1962 BMW 1500 was 180 inches long. In response, General Motors (GM) introduced a smaller vehicle of its own in 1960: the Corvair. At only 180 inches long, the Corvair was innovative and unique in many ways. It was GM's first unibody vehicle that lacked an independent frame. Unlike most domestic cars at the time, which had front engine placement on a steel chassis with solid beam rear axles, the Corvair's engine was placed in the rear, which required an independent rear suspension. It was this rear engine placement and the initial design of its independent rear swing axle suspension that Nader and others most often criticized.

Most vehicles of the era had solid rear beam axles. With solid rear beams, the wheels and tires remain parallel to each other. When one wheel on a solid rear axle traverses over a ridge or dip, the opposing wheel must remain parallel to the wheel traversing the ridge. This means that the contact point of the tire not traversing the ridge or dip will rotate outward on a ridge and inward on a dip. Or, stated another way, the angle of contact with the ground or camber will change, but the distance between the two tires and their parallel relationship remain fixed. While this reduces the contact area of the nontraversing tire, it enables the traversing tire to maintain a high level of contact. However, with an independent suspension, the non-ridge tire and wheel will remain perpendicular to the ground when the opposing wheel and tire traverses a ridge or dip. Or, stated another way, the non-ridge or dip-traversing tire remains perpendicular to the road and maintains a high level of contact with the terrain, but the angle and distance between the tires will change. Independence of movement is achieved by connecting the left and right drive shafts to the center differential with universal joints that can transmit rotation while also allowing the axles to move up and down independently of each other.

The rear engine and rear wheel drive design of the Corvair did not allow enough space for a solid rear axle and thus necessitated an independent rear suspension. The initial design used in the 1960–1964 Corvair was a swing axle that used universal joints between the differential and drive shaft but did not include a universal joint between the drive shaft and the wheel. The benefits promoted by GM were that the design enables the non-ridge or dip-traversing tire to remain perpendicular to the road and that it reduced unsprung weight.

However, as pointed out by Ralph Nader in his book *Unsafe at Any Speed* (1965), the design had several drawbacks. The one most concerning to Nader was the loss in cornering force due to changes in camber. When cornering, a vehicle's body tends to roll toward the outside of the turn. With enough cornering force, a Corvair's independent rear suspension would experience inside wheel lift, altering the camber and reducing the inside tire's contact patch and traction. The loss of inside traction placed more force on the outer wheel than a traditional solid beam rear axle, increasing the outer tire traction required to negotiate the turn successfully. The result was a vehicle that oversteered so that the rear had a greater tendency to come around when negotiating a turn. The faster the cornering speed, the larger the oversteer, and, ultimately, an ever-increasing likelihood that the vehicle would spin out.

When initially introduced, General Motors sought to offset this tendency by recommending low tire pressure for the front tires and high tire pressures for the rear tires. By using tire pressure to produce understeer, GM sought to overcome the mechanical tendency of the swing axle to oversteer. Nader and others criticized this method because most other vehicles recommended the same pressure in all four tires, and thus many Corvair owners mistakenly inflated all four tires to the same pressure. Driving with equalized tire pressures increased the risk of crashes because the Corvair's rear suspension tended to oversteer. Others noted that underinflated tires experience additional stress and often lead to uneven wear. Repeated use while underinflated increases the likelihood of tread separation and sudden failure as well. Moreover, in hot summer months, underinflated tires experience additional stress because more surface area of the tire contacts the hot pavement and there is less air within the tire to dissipate the heat (*Tires-Easy.com* 2017).

Nader lobbied for numerous design changes and additional safety equipment, including tire pressure monitors, to reduce the number of accidents and of injuries and fatalities (Williams 2015). His book and congressional testimony persuaded Congress to establish the National Highway Transportation Safety Administration and grant it the authority to regulate passenger vehicle safety and design. Many of Nader's safety equipment demands, such as two-piece steering columns (Standard no. 204, 1968), safety belts (Standard no. 208, 1968), and door bars (Standard no. 214, 1973), were put into law. However, others, like Nader's demand for tire pressure sensors, were not.

WHAT IS NEEDED TO BECOME A REGULATION?

To investigate why tire pressure monitoring systems were not required in the late 1960s or early 1970s, while other safety measures were, requires an understanding of why some regulatory proposals are successful and others are not. Luckily, Bruce Yandle's (1983) "Bootleggers and Baptists" theory of regulation provides such insight. Building on earlier theories of regulation, most notably public interest theory and Stigler's (1971) "The Theory Economic of Regulation," Yandle (1983) ponders why some types of regulatory proposals become a reality while others do not. His theory also provides insight on why particular types of regulation are used more often.

He notes that regulatory bodies have several ways to generate a preferred outcome. These methods can be categorized into two broad categories:

1. Command-and-Control Methods: Agencies tell firms and individuals exactly how to behave. To meet this standard, a person or firm is required to use a specific technology or a specific method. No ifs, ands, or buts.
2. Performance Standard: Agencies create a standard. Individuals and firms must meet this standard. Any legal method that meets the standard is acceptable. However, groups or individuals will be punished if they fail to meet the standard.

Categorizing regulatory proposals in this manner, Yandle puzzles over why a large swath of regulatory actions used command-and-control methods, which often result in much higher costs than performance standards. That is, given the goal, the performance standards are often cheaper, yet agencies regularly chose the higher-cost command-and-control methods.

To answer his question, Yandle developed his Bootleggers and Baptists theory of regulation (Yandle 1983; Smith and Yandle 2014). It straddles the public interest theory and the economic theory of regulation. The name, Bootleggers and Baptists, has much to do with Yandle's experience living in the rural South. In many small, rural, southern towns, moral Baptists want no, or at least little, consumption of alcohol. They seek to prohibit the sale of alcohol, especially on Sunday. They do so for moral reasons. They lobby the state or county council to prohibit all alcohol sales or at least alcohol sales on Sunday.

However, closing stores on Sunday does not eliminate demand. Those seeking alcohol will find alternative sources. Entrepreneurial community members will meet this demand. In the rural South, these suppliers were often called bootleggers. These bootleggers would sell illegally produced beverages from moonshiners or otherwise legal booze on Sunday to private drinking houses or private customers.

The result: bootleggers and moonshiners gain the market one day a week and the Baptists can feel better because they have prohibited the legal sale of alcohol on Sunday. When this type of legislation is proposed, it is unlikely that we will see bootleggers at the county courthouses with placards saying, "Help your good neighbor bootlegger keep his dishonest living, keep alcohol sales illegal." Yet both parties reach the ends that they desire even though we would never imagine them being a part of a collusive effort or forming the "Bootleggers and Baptists for America" coalition.

Thus, the theory's name is based on a regulatory story which is common in many localities. Yandle's theory combines the economic theory of regulation that explains why some parties are involved for their narrow economic interest and the public interest theory of those who are morally motivated. Yandle explains why politicians often claim to support a regulation for moral reasons but may also be willing to vote for a proposed rule because of moonshiners' support.

The upshot is that government regulation works out in complicated ways. Not only does the theory suggest whether a proposed rule is likely to become law; it also explains why particular types of regulations are enacted, when they are enacted, and the form they take. The reason: because every detail of the rule will affect special interests in different ways.

Furthermore, Yandle (1983) notes that firms often lobby for new regulatory rules that require a specific technology or process in which the lobbying firm has a comparative advantage. Once enacted, the lobbying firm can effectively raise its rivals' costs.

Yandle's Bootleggers and Baptists theory has been used to explain many unlikely bedfellows, such as anti-smoking organizations and cigarette makers seeking ways to limit the use of electronic cigarettes (Adler et al. 2016); the combined efforts of clean air advocates and General Motors in requiring all cars to use catalytic converters (Yandle 2007); Archer Daniels Midland and environmentalists seeking subsidies for biofuels (Vanderkam 2007); and the promotion of accountable care organizations as part of the Affordable Care Act by physicians, hospitals, and other medical providers along with health rights advocates (see chapter 10 in this volume by Smith).

To comply with such regulations, firms must employ additional compliance officers or hire higher-skilled employees to operate and maintain the new, specific technology. Therefore, regulation may be biased in favor of high-skilled workers. Moreover, as firms comply with ever-increasing regulatory complexity, skill-biased regulation likely results in a relative increase in the demand for higher-skilled workers, both across and, more importantly, within occupations, at the expense of lower-skilled workers.

Yandle concludes that bootleggers and moonshiners are essential and moral Baptists are influential and necessary. And thus, if we investigate passenger vehicle regulatory proposals using Yandle's lens, we see that many of the successful vehicle design and safety proposals offered by moralists, like seat belts and two-piece steering columns, were already being produced by some moonshining manufacturers with an economic interest. However, in the 1960s, TPMS were not. That is, moonshiners could profit from requiring seat belts and two-piece steering columns, but TPMS had not yet been invented, and thus no moonshiners with TPMS were ready for the profit opportunity. At least, not yet.

INTRODUCTION OF THE TPMS

By the late 1970s, a few moonshiners began viewing tire underinflation as an economic opportunity. In 1978, the Society of Automotive Engineers investigated real-world tire inflation and discovered that 27 percent of the vehicles they analyzed had tires that were underinflated by 4 to 16 pounds (Viergutz, Wakeley, and Dowers 1978). Seeking to require low-pressure warning systems, the Society of Automotive Engineers submitted their report to the National Highway Traffic Safety Administration (NHTSA). Initially, the NHTSA said it was going to require low-pressure warning systems, but it decided against this under the Reagan administration (US House of Representatives 2000).

Furthermore, retail outlets like Brookstone began producing warning systems that could be placed on the end of each tire's valve stem so that drivers could quickly and easily see if a tire was underinflated before entering the vehicle. In 1981, *Consumer Reports* found Brookstone's pressure warning device to be accurate and reliable (US Environmental Protection Agency 1981). Unfortunately for these moonshiners, by the late 1970s and early 1980s, Ralph Nader and many moralists had moved on to corporate accountability, nuclear energy, and the environment, and thus the burgeoning moonshiners were no longer actively supported by a large, focused group of moralists.

But the moonshiners continued to slowly grow. By the mid-1980s, TPMS that alerted drivers via dash lights were ready for retail customers. Tire pressure monitoring systems were first installed in Porsche 959s in 1986. In 1991, Corvettes became the first US vehicle equipped with TPMS. The system coincided with run-flat tires that could be safely driven for a limited number of miles without inflation. Because the handling characteristics of run-flat tires change little with the loss of pressure, General Motors included TPMS on Corvettes so drivers would be alerted if their run-flat tires had deflated.

In 1998, companies such as Bartec began selling tools that enabled tire shops to read and test TPMS systems (Bartec 2018). In 2000, Renault launched the first high-volume passenger vehicle to include TPMS: the Laguna II. As the number of moonshiners increased, the variety of warning systems increased. Over time, two systems became the most prevalent: the direct systems and the indirect systems. Direct systems require a pressure sensor to be placed inside the wheel at the base of the valve stem. The sensor periodically measures the tire pressure and sends a wireless signal to the vehicle's electronic control unit (ECU). If the tire pressure falls below a prescribed level, the sensor alerts the vehicle's ECU, which triggers a light on the dash. Indirect systems do not directly measure tire pressure. Instead, they measure the speed of tire rotation. When a tire is underinflated, its circumference is reduced, and thus the wheel must rotate faster than properly inflated tires. The indirect system makes use of the vehicle's stability control system to recognize when one or more wheel is rotating faster. If this takes place, the TPMS alerts the driver.

With many moonshiners present, a new, moral call to action was about to gain steam. Evidence began to mount that tread on BFGoodrich tires on Ford Explorers was abruptly failing and causing rollovers and fatalities. The concern began when State Farm employee Sam Boyden received an inquiry from a claims adjuster about sudden tread separation in July of 1998 (Spurgeon 2000). Boyden recognized that sudden tread separation—where the tire suddenly falls apart without warning—was not a result of common wear and tear and decided to investigate. He discovered that all 21 tread separation cases he investigated involved Bridgestone Corporation's Firestone ATX tires. He also found that 14 of these incidents affected Ford Explorers. He forwarded his findings to the NHTSA, but no action was taken. In 1999, Boyden counted and submitted 30 additional cases to the NHTSA (Spurgeon 2000).

In February of 2000, numerous complaints were submitted to regulators after Houston's KHOU TV station aired a segment on sudden tread separation (Tompkins 2002). In May 2000, after accumulating 90 complaints involving four deaths, the NHTSA opened a formal investigation (Pinedo, Seshadri, and Zemel 2002). On August 9, 2000, Bridgestone-Firestone announced a recall of 6.5 million Firestone Wilderness, AT, ATX, and ATX II P235/75R15 tires (15-inch tires). These tires were often, though not exclusively, standard equipment on many Ford Motor Company vehicles, including the Ford Explorer from 1991 to 2000. "By September 2000, there were 2,200 complaints involving 103 deaths and more than 400 injuries" (Pinedo, Seshadri, and Zemel 2002, 1).

In September, Congress held hearings on the Firestone recall and Ford Explorer. The hearings provided evidence that BFGoodrich tires experienced more failures than others. "For example, the 235/75R15 tire, which amounted to only 6 percent of Firestone production of these tires, nevertheless were 36 percent of the total separations in 1 year alone in 1999" (US House of Representatives 2000, 3). They also discovered that the Decatur plant, which produced 17 to 18 percent of the tires in question, accounted for 57 percent of the total separations in 1999 (US House of Representatives 2000). Ultimately, "[o]ne of every 400 tires produced in the Decatur, Illinois, plant in 1995 was returned under warranty because of a tread separation by 2000" (Krueger and Mas 2004, 254). Later investigations revealed that lower-quality tires were produced by the Decatur plant during contentious labor negotiations that involved many replacement workers and returning strikers working on the assembly line at the same time (Krueger and Mas 2004).

Much of the congressional discussion surrounded proper tire inflation and rollover risk. BFGoodrich had tested their tires at 32 pounds per square inch (psi), while Ford recommended 26 psi for its Explorer. Ford recommended the lower tire pressure for a number or reasons. First, because the Ford Explorer was based on a double I-beam truck frame, it required the engine to be mounted higher in the vehicle. This resulted in a higher center of gravity than most passenger vehicles. In addition, the vehicle was shorter and narrower than most trucks, resulting in a much smaller wheelbase than most trucks. The combination of a higher center of gravity and a smaller wheelbase made the Explorer more prone to rollover. By lowering the recommended tire pressure, Ford effectively lowered the ride height of the vehicle and the probability of rollover. However, the lower tire pressure increased tire stress and the risk of sudden failure. Moreover, because past research had shown that customers often fail to check tire pressures, real-world tire pressures may have been even lower than the recommended 26 psi.

TPMS REGULATIONS

The moralists were back on the scene. A vast number of articles were published decrying the risks of low tire pressure (Bradsher 2000a, 2000b; *CNN Money* 2000; Spurgeon 2000; Simison et al. 2000). Following the September 2000 hearings on BFGoodrich X tires and Ford Explorers, the federal government enacted legislation that ultimately required all new passenger vehicles after 2007 to be equipped with tire pressure monitoring sensors (H.R. 5164). Specifically, Section 13 of the TREAD Act 2000 stated:

> Not later than one year after the date of the enactment of this Act, the Secretary of Transportation shall complete a rulemaking for a regulation to require a warning system in new motor vehicles to indicate to the operator when a tire is significantly under-inflated. (H.R. 5164)

The goal was to provide drivers a quick way to ensure their tires were not underinflated and thus reduce tire failures. However, like any new regulation, the advent of TPMS had many effects.

First and foremost, the regulation increased the cost of vehicles. Second, the regulation raised the cost of wheel and tire maintenance and replacement. Third, it required tire service technicians to update their human capital so that they could service vehicles with TPMS. The new regulation likely increased inequality within the tire maintenance occupations as those with the human capital necessary to service TPMS vehicles received a wage premium, while those without slowly realized a decline in the number of vehicles they could legally service.

ESTIMATED COSTS AND BENEFITS BY EPA VERSUS REALITY

In 2002, the NHTSA issued an estimate of the costs and benefits of installing TPMS in passenger vehicles. The agency estimated the costs of alerting the driver when the pressure in one or more tires are 20 percent below recommended level (Alternative 1) and when one or more tires are 25 percent below recommended levels (Alternative 2) (US NHTSA 2002). The NHTSA assumed that a direct system was necessary to detect a tire 20 percent below its recommend levels, whereas it assumed an indirect system could recognize when a tire was 25 percent below the recommended levels (US NHTSA 2002). The NHTSA then estimated the benefits of maintaining proper tire inflation pressures: fewer fatalities, fewer injuries, improved fuel mileage, and reduced tread wear. For Alternative 1, the NHTSA estimated 79 fewer fatalities and 10,635 fewer injuries. Combining fatalities and injuries by estimated severity, the NHTSA estimated the number of equivalent fatalities to be reduced by 300 under Alternative 1 and 184 under Alternative 2 (US NHTSA 2002).

The NHTSA then estimated the cost of installing a TPMS in a new vehicle. The agency determined that Alternative 1 would cost $66.33 per automobile and Alternative 2 would cost $30.54 per vehicle (US NHTSA 2002). Assuming 16 million new cars and trucks sold annually, the NHTSA estimated $1,061 million (2001 dollars) in annual costs for Alternative 1 and $489 million in annual costs for Alternative 2 (US NHTSA 2002). Adjusting for improved fuel mileage and reduced tread wear, the NHTSA estimated $369 million annually for Alternative 1 or $1.9 million per equivalent life saved (at a 7 percent discount rate), and $138 million annually, or $1.1 million per equivalent life saved, for Alternative 2 (US NHTSA 2002). Assuming $3.5 million per statistical life, this results in a net benefit to society of $480 million (300 * $1.6 million) under Alternative 1 and $441.6 (184 * $2.4 million) under Alternative 2.

However, the NHTSA failed to include the maintenance costs that most direct systems, and some indirect systems, require:

> Furthermore, there is a battery in the sensor in most systems, which has a finite life of about ten years currently, that will have to be eventually replaced to keep the system functioning. The agency has not attempted to estimate these maintenance costs and requests comments. . . . These costs are real, but they will decrease as improvements keep being made to the systems. (US NHTSA 2002, VI-9)

When the NHTSA issued its proposed TPMS rule in July of 2001, it received extensive comments. The agency then issued its final rule on December 18, 2001. However, on February 12, 2002, OMB returned the rule to the NHTSA for reconsideration. Ultimately, the final rule and regulatory economic impact assessment (RIA) was issued in March of 2005. The updated 2005 RIA added a measure of maintenance costs, the cost of refilling tires, as well as the benefits of less property damage and reduced travel time from fewer accidents. The updated RIA also assumed 17 million vehicles sold annually instead of the 16 million assumed in the 2002 RIA (US NHTSA 2005).

In the 2005 RIA, the NHTSA investigated three compliance options: The first is a direct system that supplies a continuous readout of tire pressures. The second is a direct system that alerts the driver with a warning light if one or more tires are underinflated. The third option is a hybrid, with two direct sensors and an indirect system with a warning light for the driver. The updated assessment finds that installation of a direct system (option 2) is $66.08. This is slightly less than the $66.33 used in the 2002 assessment. However, because direct systems require sensors with batteries that will likely need to be replaced after eight years, the 2005 RIA notes that maintenance costs may be as high as $40.40 per vehicle. Table 6.1, row 1 replicates row 2 of table VII-4 (b) of the

Table 6.1. Total Annual Costs for 17 Million Vehicles at 7 Percent (millions of 2001 dollars)

Option	Source/ Construction	Vehicle Costs	Present Value of Maintenance Costs* (Range)	Present Value of Opportunity Costs of Refilling Tires	Present Value of Fuel Savings	Present Value of Tread Wear Savings	Present Value of Property Damage and Travel Delay Savings	Net Costs Range
2	NHTSA (2005) Table VII-4(b)	$1,123	$0 to $689	$114	$257	$85	$105	$791 to $1,479
2	NHTSA (2005) Table VII-4(b) with vehicle costs from Simons (2017) and maintenance costs from *Tirerack.com* (2018)	$2,129	$0 to $1,016	$114	$257	$85	$105	$1,797 to $2,813
2	NHTSA (2005) Table VII-4(b) with vehicle costs from Simons (2017) and maintenance costs from *Tirerack.com* (2018) adjusted for winter tire use	$2,248	$0 to $1,072	$114	$257	$85	$105	$1,915 to $2,987

Table 6.2. Net Cost per Equivalent Life Saved (millions of 2001 dollars)

Option	Source/Construction	7% Discount Rate
2	NHTSA (2005) Table VII-4(b)	$4.90 to $9.20
2	NHTSA (2005) Table VII-4(b) with vehicle costs from Simons (2017) and maintenance costs from *Tirerack.com* (2018)	$11.16 to $17.47
2	NHTSA (2005) Table VII-4(b) with vehicle costs from Simons (2017) and maintenance costs from *Tirerack.com* (2018) adjusted for winter tire use	$11.89 to $18.56

Table 6.3. Net Benefits with a Value of $3.5 Million per Statistical Life (millions of 2001 dollars)

Option	Source/Construction	7% Discount Rate
2	NHTSA (2005) Table VII-4(b)	–$226 to –$915
2	NHTSA (2005) Table VII-4(b) with vehicle costs from Simons (2017) and maintenance costs from *Tirerack.com* (2018)	–$1,233 to –$2,249
2	NHTSA (2005) Table VII-4(b) with vehicle costs from Simons (2017) and maintenance costs from *Tirerack.com* (2018) adjusted for winter tire use	–$1,352 to –$2,424

2005 RIA to show the total annual cost for 17 million cars and trucks (in millions of 2001 dollars at a 7 percent discount rate). Notably, the 2005 assessment finds that the annual cost of a direct system (option 2), including the cost of sensor/battery maintenance and tire inflation minus the benefits of improved fuel mileage, less tire wear, less time in traffic, and less property damage is between $791 and $1,479 million (2001 dollars).

The NHTSA estimates that 161 equivalent lives will be saved using option 2. Table 6.2, row 1 shows the cost per adjusted life saved to be between $4.91 and $9.2 million (2001 dollars). Assuming a statistical life is valued at $3.5 million, the NHTSA reversed its positive net benefit finding from its 2002 report. Instead of the $441.6 to $480 million in benefits found in the 2002 RIA, table 6.3, row 1 shows that the NHTSA's 2005 RIA finds a net benefit of –$226 to –$915 million.

Using current real-world values reveals that the NHTSA's 2005 report was overly optimistic about the cost of installing and maintaining a direct TPMS. First, the installation value of $66.08 is much lower than the teardown cost found by Simons (2017) on behalf of the NHSTA. Simons (2017) finds that the cost of TPMS required by rule FMVSS 138 is $162.13 (2012 dollars) for passenger vehicles, or $125.25 in 2001 dollars. This is $59.17 (2001 dollars) higher than the $66.08 (2001 dollars) used in the final 2005 RIA.

Second, the NHTSA assumes that each replacement sensor, save installation costs, will cost the owner $22.50 (2001 dollars). However, using the July 20, 2018, retail prices of the 159 sensors listed for sale on Tirerack.com, the largest online supplier of tires and tire accessories, I find that the median price of a sensor is $49 each (*Tirerack.com* 2018). Following the NHTSA 2005 methodology but replacing their estimated price of a sensor of $22.50 ($7.50 each times 3 for retail markup) with the current median price on Tirerack.com of $49 (2018 dollars) adjusted to 2001 dollars, $34.61, the maintenance cost for a direct system with one sensor for each wheel increases to $59.76.[1]

Table 6.1, row 2 shows the annual cost of 17 million vehicles with the updated installation cost from Simons (2017) and maintenance costs from Tirerack.com (2018). These more realistic estimates raise the annual cost from the $1,479 million (2001 dollars) reported in the NHTSA final 2005 RIA to $2,813 million. Table 6.2, row 2 shows that these higher costs translate to $11.16 to $17.47 million per equivalent life saved. If I use the NHTSA's value of $3.5 million per statistical life, table 6.3, row 2 shows that the net *cost* to society increases from $226 to $915 million to $1,233 to $2,249 million.

Not only are maintenance costs underestimated, but the NHTSA failed to note the increased cost of winter tire use. Many owners in northern states use winter tires when temperatures dip below freezing. To avoid the cost and hassle of mounting and balancing two sets of tires on one set of wheels twice a year, most owners permanently mount their winter tires on a second set of wheels. This necessitates a second set of sensors as well. If we assume that winter wheel sensors or their batteries must also be replaced after eight years, the installation and maintenance costs are double for those who use winter tires.

According to a Harris Interactive survey commissioned by Bridgestone Americas, 25 percent of households in snowbelt states planned to use winter tires in 2014 (*Tire Business* 2014).[2] According to the Auto Alliance, the number of new vehicles purchased in these snowbelt states was 944,541 for 2017 (Auto Alliance 2018). If 25 percent of these owners use winter tires, their costs will be twice as high as those estimated above. Table 6.1, row 3 includes these higher costs for 25 percent of the 944,541 vehicles sold in the snowbelt states in 2017. This results in $1,915 to $2,987 million in costs. Table 6.2, row 3 reveals that the cost is $11.89 to $18.56 million (2001 dollars) per equivalent life saved. This results in an annual net *cost* to society of $1,352 to $2,424 million (2001 dollars), or 2.5 times higher costs than those estimated by the final rule's 2005

RIA. Or, put another way, the moonshiners and bootleggers benefit from the lobbying moralists, but car owners and lessees are, on net, worse off.

WAGE INEQUALITY

Regulations require more sophisticated technology and the human capital to monitor, maintain, and repair the new technology properly. Therefore, those with the skills necessary to service these new TPMS will likely witness an increase in their wages relative to those who do not. This may increase wage inequality within occupations that repair and replace tires. One way to investigate this is by using the Bureau of Labor Statistics's (BLS's) Occupational Employment Statistics (OES) survey, which contains employer-provided data on establishment characteristics and wages by occupation and industry for the millions of employees in the 400,000 establishments surveyed in May and November of each year. The BLS classifies occupations according to its Standard Occupational Classification (SOC) system. The SOC groups occupations using a tiered, hierarchal system with four levels. The bottom-most disaggregated level is a detailed level consisting of approximately 840 categories. For each occupation, the OES provides salaries at the 10th, 25th, 50th, 75th, and 90th percentiles as well as the mean salary and total employment.

Although the OES began in 1996, I use data only from 2001 to 2017 for two important reasons: First, the OES was not designed to study the time series of wage inequality. As such, the BLS has updated its methodology many times since its inception in 1996, with little concern for comparability across time. The changes include adding establishments with fewer than five employees in 1997, altering weights in 1998, and adding a 12th income category in 1999. Second, the OES moved from the Standard Industrial Classification (SIC) to the North American Industry Classification System (NAICS) in 2001. Therefore, I use the wage data from 2001 through 2017 to investigate income inequality within industries.

The BLS OES survey contains information on four detailed occupations that involve auto repair: automotive body and related repairers, automotive glass installers and repairers, automotive service technicians and mechanics, and tire repairers and changers. I focus on the category most likely affected by the installation of TPMS: tire repairers and changers.

I use the ratio of the hourly wage at the 90th and 10th percentiles to estimate the degree to which tire repairers and changers experienced an increase or decrease in inequality after the introduction the TPMS regulation. Figure 6.1 shows the evolution of the 90/10 Tire Repairers and Changers ratio from 2001

Figure 6.1. Ratio of 90/10 Hourly Wages for Tire Repairers and Changers

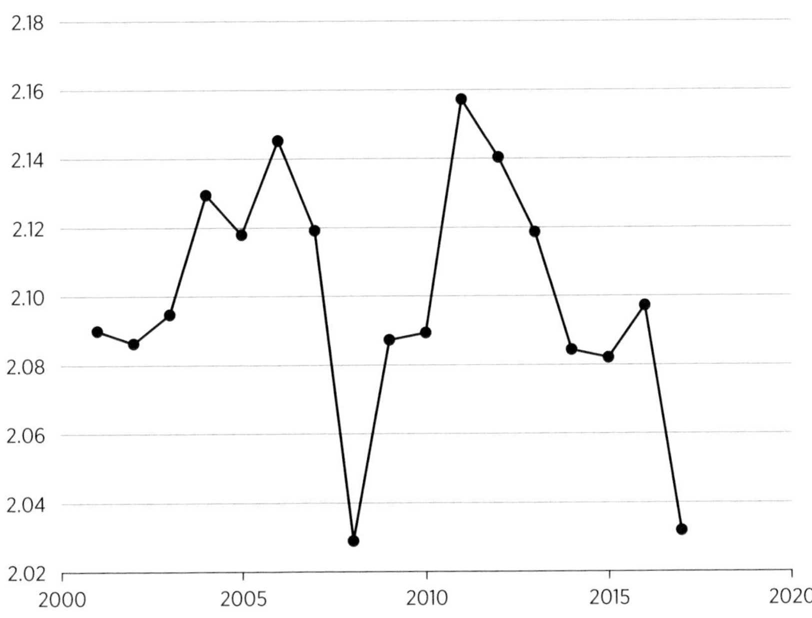

through 2017. Tire repairers and changers experienced an increase in hourly wage inequality from 2002 when the proposed rule was announced until the year after the final rule was issued in 2006. This is consistent with chapter 8 in this volume by Lipford, who finds that regulations via occupational licensure and land use restrictions contribute to the widening income gap in the United States, and with Mulholland (2018), who shows that within-occupation inequality tended to increase when final regulations are issued. However, in 2008, when the Great Recession was in its early stages, inequality within the occupation fell substantially.

This large decline during the Great Recession reveals that investigating the change in the inequality witnessed by tire repairers and changers alone fails to account for potential changes in the overall economy. Furthermore, the wage movements in auto-repair occupations may be the result of automotive industry–specific shocks. Therefore, to account for labor market shocks and those specific to the automotive industry, I construct a ratio of the 90/10 ratios using the two automobile repair occupations that are most similar to tire repairers and changers: automotive body and related repairers and automotive service technicians and mechanics. The ratio of these 90/10 ratios gives me an estimate of the change in inequality experienced by tire repairers and changers

Figure 6.2. Increase in Hourly Wage Inequality of Tire Repairers and Changers

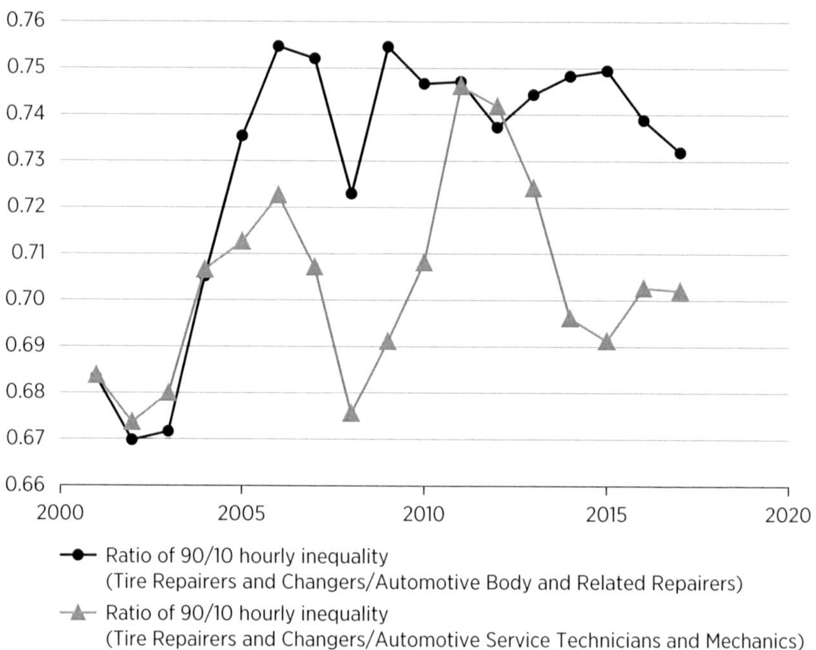

relative to other workers in the automotive industry. Figure 6.2 shows the evolution of these ratios from 2001 through 2017. Both reveal that tire repairers and changers witnessed a larger increase in inequality from 2002 through 2006 relative to the two other automotive repair occupations. Much of the increase took place between 2002, when the rule was first proposed, and 2005, when the rule was finalized. This suggests that the TPMS regulation had a stratification effect on those in the tire repairers and changers occupation. Auto technicians may also need to know how to assess, repair, and replace TPMS components, which may be why the relative effect is smaller when comparing tire repairers and changers with auto technicians.

CONCLUSION

The TPMS saga follows the Bootleggers and Baptists theory of regulation. In the 1960s, many were calling for tire pressure warning systems for moral reasons, but no bootleggers or moonshiners were active. In the 1980s and 1990s, moonshiners like the Society of Engineers were pushing for TPMS, and bootleggers like GM and others were producing TPMS, but few moral activists were pushing for TPMS. Only with the Firestone-Explorer rollover controversy in 2000 did moralists return and, along with profit-seeking moonshiners, successfully enact the TREAD Act of 2000 requiring TPMS. Although both parties viewed this as a success, the net effect on society is negative. Moreover, the regulation is associated with increases in wage inequality for those who repair and replace tires relative to other types of automotive repair occupations.

NOTES

1. To construct the maintenance costs, I follow the NHTSA (2005), which assumes each sensor would be $22.50 or $7.50 * 3. "At the 7 percent discount rate, the estimated maintenance costs are $39.24 for passenger cars ($7.50 * 4 * .775 * .5626 * 3) and $43.39 for light trucks ($7.50 * 4 * .857 * .5626 * 3), making the average maintenance costs for a direct measurement system for all four wheels of $40.91" (NHTSA 2005, VI-9). "At the 7 percent discount rate, the average maintenance costs for a direct measurement system for all four wheels would be $40.50 (40.91 * .99)" (NHTSA 2005, VI-12). To construct my value, I replace $7.50 * 3 with $49 adjusted to 2001 dollars, $34.61, and then take this value and multiply times 4 * .775 * .5626. Then I follow the NHTSA and multiply by 0.99 to get a value of $59.76.
2. Snowbelt states included in the survey were New York, Pennsylvania, Ohio, Michigan, Minnesota, Wisconsin, Maine, New Hampshire, North Dakota, South Dakota, Montana, Wyoming, and Vermont.

REFERENCES

Adler, J. H., R. E. Meiners, A. P. Morriss, and B. Yandle. 2016. "Baptists, Bootleggers and Electronic Cigarettes." *Yale Journal on Regulation* 33, no. 2: 313–61.

Auto Alliance. 2018. "Every State Is an Auto State." https://autoalliance.org/in-your-state/.

Bartec. 2018. "TPMS Legislation." https://www.bartecusa.com/tpms-legislation, accessed July 7, 2018.

Bradsher, K. 2000a. "Explorer Tires Had to Carry a Heavy Load." *New York Times*, August 23.

——. 2000b. "Tire Deaths Are Linked to Rollovers." *New York Times*, August 16.

CNN Money. 2000. "Ford Explorer Scrutinized." September 20. https://money.cnn.com/2000/09/20/companies/ford/index.htm.

Edmunds, D. 2009. "Tire Test: All-Season vs. Snow vs. Summer: Will It Grip or Will It Slip?" *Edmunds.com*. https://www.edmunds.com/car-reviews/features/tire-test-all-season-vs-snow-vs-summer.html.

Krueger, A. B., and A. Mas. 2004. "Strikes, Scabs, and Tread Separations: Labor Strife and the Production of Defective Bridgestone/Firestone Tires." *Journal of Political Economy* 112, no. 2: 253–89.

Mulholland, S. E. 2019. "Stratification by Regulation: Are Bootleggers and Baptists Biased?" *Public Choice* 180, nos. 1–2: 105–30.

Nader, R. 1965. *Unsafe at Any Speed*. New York: Grossman.

Pinedo, M., S. Seshadri, and E. Zemel. 2002. "The Ford-Firestone Case." New York: Leonard N. Stern School of Business, New York University.

Simison, R. L., K. Lundegaard, N. Shirouzu, and J. Heller. 2000. "How a Tire Problem Became a Crisis for Firestone, Ford." *Wall Street Journal*, August 10. https://www.wsj.com/articles/SB965870212891028108.

Simons, J. F. 2017. "Cost and Weight Added by the Federal Motor Vehicle Safety Standards for MY 1968–2012 Passenger Cars and LTVs." Report no. DOT HS 812 354. Washington, DC: National Highway Traffic Safety Administration.

Smith, A., and Yandle, B. 2014. *Bootleggers and Baptists: How Economic Forces and Moral Persuasion Interact to Shape Regulatory Politics*. Washington, DC: Cato Institute.

Spurgeon, D. 2000. "State Farm Researcher's Sleuthing Helped Prompt Firestone Recall." *Wall Street Journal*, September 1. https://www.wsj.com/articles/SB967764514906874559.

Stigler, G. J. 1971. "The Theory of Economic Regulation." *Bell Journal of Economics and Management Science* 2: 3–21.

Tire Business. 2014. "U.S. Drivers Eschew Winter Tires." November 26. http://www.tirebusiness.com/article/20141126/NEWS/141129902/us-drivers-eschew-winter-tires.

Tirerack.com. 2018. "All Tire Pressure Sensors Listed for Sale." https://www.tirerack.com/tpms/category.jsp?category=Sensor.

Tires-Easy.com. 2017. "Top Ten Causes of Tire Failure . . . and Manufacturer Defect Is Not One of Them!" January 26. https://www.tires-easy.com/blog/top-causes-of-tire-failure/.

Tompkins, A. 2002. "Breaking the Big One." *Poynter*, August 2. https://www.poynter.org/news/breaking-big-one, accessed July 15, 2018.

US Environmental Protection Agency. 1981. "Costs, Benefits, and Methods of Including Tire Inflation in State Vehicle Inspection Programs." Motor Vehicle Emissions Lab, September. EPA-460/3-81-022.

US House of Representatives. 2000. "The Recent Firestone Tire Recall Action, Focusing on the Action as It Pertains to Relevant Ford Vehicles." Hearings before the Subcommittee on Telecommunications, Trade, and Consumer Protection and the Subcommittee on Oversight and Investigations of the Committee on Commerce, September 6 and 21. Serial no. 106-165.

US National Highway Traffic Safety Administration. 2002. "Tire Pressure Monitoring System FMVSS no. 138. Preliminary Economic Assessment."

——. 2005. "Tire Pressure Monitoring System FMVSS no. 138. Final Regulatory Impact Analysis."

Vanderkam, L. 2007. "Biofuels or Bio-Fools?" *American.com*, May/June. http://www.aei.org/publication/biofuels-or-bio-fools/.

Viergutz, O., H. Wakeley, and L. Dowers. 1978. "Automobile In-Use Tire Inflation Survey." Society of Automotive Engineers, February.

Williams, C. 2015. "Nader Talks Car Safety on 50th Anniversary of 'Unsafe at Any Speed.'" *Chicago Tribune*, July 3. https://www.chicagotribune.com/classified/automotive/sc-cons-0702-autocover-unsafe-nader-50-20150626-story.html.

Yandle, B. 1983. "Bootleggers and Baptists: The Education of a Regulatory Economist." *Regulation* 7, no. 3: 12–15.

——. 2007. "Bruce Yandle on Bootleggers and Baptists." *Econtalk.com*, January 15. Interview by Russ Roberts. http://www.econtalk.org/bruce-yandle-on-bootleggers-and-baptists.

CHAPTER 7
Bootleggers and Baptists
The Experience of Another Regulatory Economist

SUSAN E. DUDLEY

Over the last 60 years, the number and scope of federal regulations has grown dramatically. In 1960, the Code of Federal Regulations occupied around 70,000 pages; today it is more than 178,000. In 1960, 57,000 full-time federal regulators worked to develop and enforce regulations; in 2019 their numbers exceeded 280,000 (Dudley and Warren 2018). Concern over the continuously changing and progressively intrusive nature of the administrative state may have been one contributor to the surprise election of Donald Trump in November 2016. Voters were increasingly concerned that regulations were serving well-connected interests at the expense of everyday Americans.

This chapter examines some recent trends in regulation through the lens of Bruce Yandle's "Bootleggers and Baptists" (B&B) theory of regulation. Illustrations from my own experience in government and a review of regulatory and deregulatory activity during the first two years of the Trump administration suggest that, while Baptist arguments may change from one

I am grateful for the research and analysis of Julianna Balla, graduate research assistant with the Regulatory Studies Center, and feedback from my colleagues Bridget Dooling and Brian Mannix, as well as participants in the Mercatus Festschrift symposium, "Reflecting on the Work of Bruce Yandle," September 2018.

administration to the next, the combination of moral and economic forces continues to influence regulatory policy.

ORIGINS OF THE BOOTLEGGERS AND BAPTISTS THEORY

Why do we regulate and when? Normative approaches to regulation call for government intervention when competitive conditions are not met, and markets fail to allocate resources efficiently (Office of Management and Budget 2003). Positive approaches, on the other hand, focus not on when regulation "should" occur, but on theories explaining observations of "when" it occurs and "why." One theory of regulation, the "public interest" theory or "normative-analysis-as-positive theory" (Joskow and Noll 1981; Viscusi, Vernon, and Harrington 2005) assumes that regulators are sufficiently informed and publicly motivated to serve the public interest by regulating only when necessary to correct "market failures"—intervening to internalize externalities, clarify property rights, regulate monopolists, or provide information (Dudley and Brito 2012).

However, the public interest theory offers no mechanism by which the optimal regulations will occur and fails to explain real-world evidence. Observing that laws and regulations do not necessarily correspond to industries characterized by market failures, and that many regulations seem to subvert the public interest and favor private interests, political scientists and economists in the 1960s offered an alternative hypothesis. They suggested that politicians and regulators are often "captured" by special interests, usually the producers whom they regulate. As a result, laws and regulations serve, not the public interest, but those special interests.

While the capture theory better explains the occurrence of regulation than the public interest theory, it too is incomplete. Many regulations do not appear to serve the industry being regulated. The capture theory fails to explain *why* regulators would get captured and by *whom*.

George Stigler's 1971 article "The Theory of Economic Regulation" offered a clear, testable theory that explained the presence of regulation in different industries (Stigler 1971). It also raised awareness of the incentives and wealth-redistribution consequences of economic regulation. Stigler started with the basic premises that the government's main resource is the power to coerce. Thus, a rational, utility-maximizing interest group that could convince the government to use its coercive power to the group's benefit could improve its well-being at the expense of others.

With this foundation, Stigler hypothesized that regulation is supplied in response to the demands of interest groups acting to maximize their own well-being. He observed that legislators' behavior is driven by their desire to stay in office, which requires that they maximize political support. Regulation is one way to redistribute wealth, and interest groups compete for that wealth by offering political support in exchange for favorable legislation.

This theory implies that regulation (and enabling legislation) is likely to be biased toward benefiting interest groups that are well organized and that stand to gain from the wealth redistribution. Hence, regulation is likely to benefit small interest groups with strongly felt preferences at the expense of large interest groups with weakly felt preferences.

The economic theory of regulation has proven better at explaining why and when regulation occurs than either the public interest or simple capture theory, but it raises two questions. First, why do politicians and interest groups resort to regulation to transfer wealth from the general public to private interests when direct cash transfers would be less costly to all concerned? Second, why do politicians often rely on public interest rhetoric when imposing regulations that transfer wealth to a small group?

Here is where Bruce Yandle's colorfully named Bootleggers and Baptists theory comes in (Yandle 1983). Yandle observed that special interest groups cannot expect politicians to push through legislation that simply raises prices on a few products so that the protected group can get rich at the expense of consumers. Like bootleggers in the early 20th century South who benefited from laws that banned the sale of liquor on Sundays, special interests need to camouflage their efforts to obtain special favors by advancing public interest stories. In the case of Sunday liquor sales, the Baptists, who supported the Sunday ban on moral grounds, provided that public interest support. While they vocally endorsed the ban on Sunday sales, the bootleggers worked behind the scenes and quietly rewarded the politicians with a portion of their Sunday liquor sale profits (Dudley and Brito 2012, 19). As a result, Yandle concluded, "durable social regulation evolves when it is demanded by both of two distinctly different groups" (Yandle 1999).

THE EDUCATION OF A REGULATORY ECONOMIST

Yandle conceived of his B&B theory while working as a young economist in the federal government, first on the staff of President Jimmy Carter's Council on Wage and Price Stability in 1977 and then as executive director of the US Federal Trade Commission in 1983 (Yandle 2011). This was a time when old forms of "economic" regulation (that established controls on prices, quantities, etc.) were being removed,[1] but new forms of "social" regulation (aimed at environmental, health, and safety goals)[2] were in ascendance. Yandle asked himself:

> Why was command-and-control, technology-based regulation the dominant form of regulation preferred by the new social regulators? Why not economic incentives, taxes, and market processes? Why did most social regulation require less stringent rules of existing firms than for new ones? Why were environmental regulations generally more rigorous for newly developing regions than for older regions? (Yandle 2011, 6)

He concluded that "successful lobbying efforts and durable regulation emerge when one interest group, labeled the Baptists, takes the moral high ground while another group, the bootleggers, use the Baptists for cover as they pursue a narrow economic end" (Yandle 2011, 10). He noted that while both parties seek the same outcome, they do not necessarily cooperate.

Reflecting on his theory 16 years later, he wrote:

> It is worth noting that it is the details of a regulation that usually win the endorsement of bootleggers, not just the broader principle that may matter most to Baptists. Thus, for instance, bootleggers would not support restrictions on the Sunday *consumption* of alcoholic beverages, although Baptists might. Bootleggers want to limit competition, not intake. Important to the theory is the notion that bootleggers can rely on Baptists to monitor enforcement of the restrictions that benefit bootleggers. (Yandle 1999)

Yandle and his grandson, Adam Smith, extended the theory in 2014, identifying different modes of interaction that make for successful coalitions, including a "covert" mode, where bootleggers make Baptist arguments; a "noncooperative" mode, where bootleggers and Baptists operate independently but toward the same end; a "cooperative" mode, where the bootleggers support the Baptists; and a "coordinated" mode, where the government operates to coordinate the players (Smith and Yandle 2014).

ANOTHER REGULATORY ECONOMIST GETS AN EDUCATION

I arrived in Washington in the mid-1980s as an idealistic recent graduate with a passion for the environment. I got my education at the Environmental Protection Agency (EPA) and the Office of Information and Regulatory Affairs (OIRA) in the Office of Management and Budget.

In those days, the Hazardous Waste Treatment Council (HWTC) was an influential organization. Congress passed the Hazardous and Solid Waste Amendments to the Resource Conservation and Recovery Act in 1984, and, according to a Senate staffer who worked on hazardous waste issues at the time, "the staffers who were the most instrumental in writing the bill were extremists who relied on the environmental lobbies and the Hazardous Waste Treatment Council for most of their information" (Bovard 1989). The HWTC, which represented waste-treatment companies, was also actively involved in the regulations EPA issued under the act. It successfully argued for technology-based standards over risk-based standards, "pushing the EPA to impose the most stringent treatment standards," and denouncing "the agency to the press when its regulations [were] less than draconian" (Bovard 1989). Its members were frequent witnesses at hearings held on EPA's restrictions on waste disposal on land, and were cited often in the press as representing "the good industry" that supported more regulation. Rarely did legislators or the media acknowledge that regulations requiring the incineration of waste directly benefited HWTC members (Bovard 1989).[3]

The HWTC worked with environmental organizations in what Yandle and Smith might call a "cooperative mode," including collaborating with the Natural Resources Defense Council (NRDC) to bring a lawsuit against EPA over its decision not to list used oil as a hazardous waste. EPA had based its decision on analysis that suggested such a listing would have discouraged the recycling of used oil, which offered environmental benefits; but, siding with the HWTC and NRDC, the DC Circuit Court remanded the rule to EPA.[4]

My years working on the waste-related regulations opened my eyes to the rent-seeking involved. I had expected analysis of costs and public benefits (environmental and health risk reductions) to drive policy decisions and was surprised by the regulatory outcome—an absolute ban on the land disposal of hazardous waste. I had not heard of Yandle's theory at the time, but true to the B&B prediction, the form of the regulation mattered to HWTC; a risk-based performance standard for waste disposal would not have ensured that all wastes would require treatment.[5] For HWTC, an absolute ban, which environmentalists also supported and EPA eventually issued (US Environmental Protection Agency 2016), was necessary to funnel business to its members' companies.

BOOTLEGGERS AND BAPTISTS AT "MIDNIGHT"

Fast forward to 2007, when I became the administrator of OIRA, the office responsible for reviewing all significant regulations of executive branch agencies before they are published. With less than two years remaining in the George W. Bush administration, I was the presidential appointee in charge of overseeing the completion of President Bush's regulatory priorities. I knew it was too late to initiate new regulatory policies, and I was fully aware that the approaching end of a presidency magnifies the pressure to regulate (Dudley 2001). Historically, the regulatory activity between Election Day and Inauguration Day—dubbed the "midnight regulation" period—is 17 percent greater, on average, than during those calendar days in non-election years (Dudley 2009a; Miller and Pérez 2016). Determined to resist this tendency, the OIRA staff and I worked closely with agencies starting in early 2007, reminding them that issuing a regulation from start to finish takes more than a year, and encouraging them to focus on completing their regulatory priorities, rather than commencing new ones. In May 2008, President Bush's chief of staff, Josh Bolten, supported our efforts in a memorandum to agencies admonishing them to "resist the historical tendency of administrations to increase regulatory activity in their final months" and setting a November 1, 2008, deadline for completing rules except in extraordinary circumstances (Bolten 2008).

As I have recounted elsewhere (Dudley 2009a), these actions had mixed success. While the Bush 43 administration succeeded in issuing significantly fewer regulations during the November to January postelection quarter than previous administrations (100 vs. 143 significant final rules and 21,000 vs. 27,000 *Federal Register* pages compared to the Clinton administration), the final year of regulatory activity was 7 percent higher than the previous year (Dudley 2009a).

As Smith and Yandle say in their 2014 book, "When the pace of regulation accelerates, Bootleggers and Baptists are sure to barbecue while the political fire pits are hot" (Smith and Yandle 2014, 170). OIRA reviewed more than 650 final rules during the last two years of the Bush administration when I was administrator; 121 of them were expected to have impacts of $100 million or more in a year.[6] Below are a few B&B stories from that time with which I had firsthand experience.

GENETICALLY ENGINEERED ANIMALS

On January 15, 2009 (five days before "midnight"), FDA published guidelines defining genetically engineered (GE) animals with heritable recombinant DNA (rDNA) constructs as "new animal drugs" under the Food, Drug, and

Cosmetic Act. Biotechnology companies had been using rDNA techniques to breed animals that are leaner, produce less waste, are more resistant to disease, or reach maturity more quickly than their traditional counterparts. The promising AquAdvantage salmon, for example, grew more quickly (using fewer resources) than farm-raised Atlantic salmon due to the insertion of genetic sequences from the Chinook salmon and ocean pout (US Food and Drug Administration 2017).

In reviewing the guidance, OIRA analysts objected that defining each animal so engineered as a "new animal drug" was not only a contrived interpretation of FDA's statutory authority, but also that the evidence was too thin to justify subjecting these animals to extensive premarket regulation and examination. We argued for a risk-based approach focused on the potential risk of the modified animal, rather than imposing regulations based on the process by which it was produced.[7] We understood that anti-GMO activists objected to any process that would allow genetically modified animals to be marketed. However, it was representatives from the Biotechnology Industry Organization[8] (BIO) who called for a meeting to convince me that FDA's proposed approach was necessary. Their argument was that, while their products did not pose risks that differed from traditional products, consumers would be reassured by FDA oversight. BIO generally represented larger firms, which tend to have the experience and capacity to deal with FDA regulations, whereas smaller and start-up firms do not. As Yandle's theory predicted, they supported increased barriers to entry in the form of premarket regulatory approval rather than performance-based regulation. They were the bootleggers operating in what Smith and Yandle might call a "non-cooperative" mode with support from the anti-GMO activists' Baptist arguments.

PRODUCT SELF-CERTIFICATION VERSUS CERTIFICATION BY NATIONAL TESTING LABORATORY

During my OIRA tenure, I served as the US lead of the EU-US High Level Regulatory Cooperation Council, seeking to find ways to reduce regulatory barriers to trade. A European priority for these negotiations was that the US Occupational Safety and Health Administration (OSHA) reopen its rulemaking that required low-risk workplace electrical equipment to be certified by a "nationally recognized testing laboratory." The EU allowed manufacturers to self-certify that their products complied with regulations, and the US third-party testing requirement added an additional burden for any products sold in US markets. OSHA was reluctant to revisit a settled rule even though the risks of the European approach were not higher than theirs. OSHA's position was supported by the US testing laboratories (Underwriter Laboratories 2009), which argued aggressively on safety grounds against self-certification. It was a classic illustration of Smith and Yandle's "covert" mode, where self-interested actors use Baptist language to obscure their bootlegger motive. To my knowledge, no workplace safety advocates raised concerns with the European approach. To this day, OSHA requires third-party certification.

TOBACCO, FOOD, TOY, AND ENERGY BOOTLEGGERS

Although it did not reach the point of regulation during my tenure at OIRA, I observed other rent-seeking behavior camouflaged in public interest rhetoric. Tobacco companies endorsed legislation (also supported by anti-smoking advocates) that would have required cigarettes to obtain FDA approval before they could be marketed, which would make it harder for new brands to enter the market. Food and toy companies lobbied for more regulation to ensure their products' safety, thereby keeping out foreign competitors who may not be as able to demonstrate that their products meet the same standards. Energy companies joined with national environmental organizations to push for carbon cap-and-trade (Yandle 2010), which would confer financial benefits on the holders of grandfathered emission allowances.[9]

PUSHBACK AGAINST BOOTLEGGERS AND BAPTISTS ARGUMENTS

OIRA was able to claim some small victories against B&B pressures during those midnight years. We resisted entreaties from a domestic cruise line and the US Merchant Marine to restrict foreign-owned cruise line activities at American ports. Their covert Baptist argument was twofold: that US-flagged ships were inherently safer (not supported by evidence) and that restricting foreign-flagged ships would protect American jobs (an argument that might have more salience in the current administration).

Despite strong lobbying from the pesticide industry, I returned a draft regulation that would have mandated recycling of used pesticide containers (Dudley 2008). The Ag Container Recycling Council (ACRC), an initiative of the pesticide manufacturing industry, had established a network of designated drop-off locations to facilitate recycling of used pesticide containers. Supported by the council's manufacturers, the program was free to farmers and retailers, but the ACRC was dissatisfied with participation rates. Rather than rely on market incentives to encourage greater participation, it lobbied EPA to require retailers of pesticides to recycle certain plastic pesticide containers, and EPA obliged. EPA's draft proposed rule also would have required pesticide container recycling programs to meet the American National Standards Institute and American Society of Agricultural and Biological Engineers Standard S569 for "Recycling Plastic Containers from Pesticides and Pesticide-Related Products," a standard the ACRC's recycling centers presumably met. This might meet the Smith and Yandle definition of "coordinated" mode, with EPA taking a supportive role. In announcing its plan to propose the regulation, EPA said it was "intended to protect human health and the environment by reducing the risk of unreasonable adverse effects to public health and the environment that may be associated with the improper disposal of certain nonrefillable pesticide containers and their associated residues" (US Environmental Protection Agency 2008). Yet, as my letter returning the rule indicated, the claims of health and environmental benefits were unsubstantiated, yet the costs were real (Dudley 2008).

IMPORTANCE OF INSTITUTIONS IN COUNTERING OR AMPLIFYING BOOTLEGGERS AND BAPTISTS BEHAVIOR

As these few successes illustrate, the value of an institution like OIRA lies in its cross-cutting perspective and its focus on understanding trade-offs and consequences, intended and unintended. It is less susceptible to pressure from both bootleggers and Baptists than single-mission agencies (Dudley 2009b). Other White House offices, like the National Economic Council or the Domestic Policy Council, which are headed by directors with the title of assistant to the president, have typically had similar cross-cutting missions and serve as a check against agencies and political appointees that may be captured by well-organized groups. But presidents sometimes add specialized "czars" with narrowly focused, issue-oriented missions to the White House staff. Not only are these presidential advisers not accountable to Congress and the public (they do not require Senate confirmation and are not expected to testify before congressional oversight committees), but the advice they offer the president can be heavily influenced by special interests.

In the Bush administration, the Homeland Security Council became a focal point for interests involved in security; it generally aligned with the Department of Homeland Security in policy disputes and prioritized preventing and deterring terrorist attacks over other goals (such as privacy, welcoming lawful immigrants, etc.). President Obama abolished the Homeland Security Council and created a White House Office of Energy and Climate Change

Policy, which attracted B&B interests of its own (Yandle 2017). President Trump has created an Office of Trade and Manufacturing Policy, headed by anti-trade economist Peter Navarro. These czars are well positioned to coordinate bootleggers and Baptists in support of their preferred policies, as the Trump administration's tariffs (to protect American jobs), followed by subsidies to farmers hurt by the tariffs, illustrate.

BOOTLEGGERS AND BAPTISTS IN A DEREGULATORY WORLD

The eight years following my tenure as OIRA administrator witnessed a sharp increase in regulatory activity. During President Obama's two terms, executive branch agencies issued 503 economically significant final regulations, compared to 362 and 358 issued during the tenures of Presidents Bush and Clinton, respectively.[10] See figure 7.1. The inauguration of President Trump in January 2017 brought an abrupt change to the pace of regulation, however. During his second week in office, Trump signed Executive Order 13771 (White House 2017a), requiring agencies to offset the costs of new regulations by removing existing burdens and to eliminate two regulations for every new one they issue. At the end of February, he issued Executive Order 13777

Figure 7.1. Economically Significant Final Regulations by Presidential Year

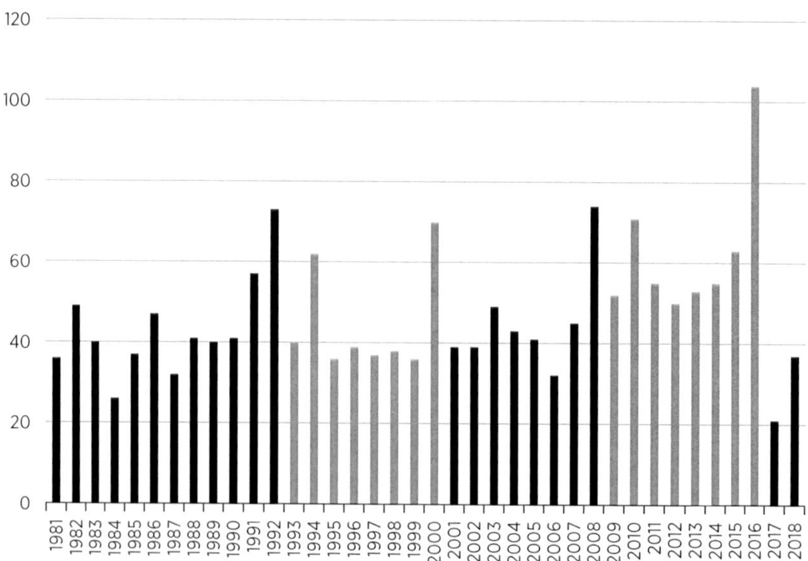

Source: Author's analysis of data available at RegInfo.gov. "Presidential years" run from January 20th to January 19th.

Figure 7.2. Classification of Economically Significant Final Rules: First Two Years of Trump Administration

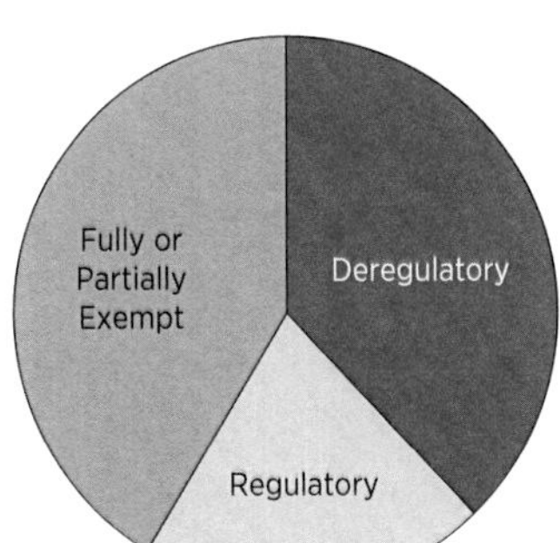

(White House 2017b), requiring regulatory agencies to designate an agency official to be the regulatory reform officer overseeing implementation of regulatory reform initiatives and to form a regulatory reform task force to make recommendations for agency regulatory reforms (Dudley 2017a).

These actions have resulted in a dramatic slowdown in the pace of new regulations (figure 7.1). In Trump's first two years in office, OIRA cleared 58 economically significant final rules for publication, dramatically less than the 123 and 78 economically significant rules concluded over the same period in the Obama and Bush administrations, respectively. Economically significant rules are those with annual impacts (costs or benefits) of $100 million or more.

The Trump administration has, for the first time, classified each regulatory action as to whether it is regulatory or deregulatory. Of the 58 economically significant rules OIRA reviewed in the first two years of the administration, agencies claim that only 12 added new regulatory burdens. They classify 22 as deregulatory, and the remaining 24 as at least partially exempt from the order (see figure 7.2). At least four of these actions offer insights into the influence of B&B coalitions in a deregulatory environment.

PRACTICES REQUIRED TO LABEL MEAT, POULTRY, AND EGGS AS "ORGANIC"

The Department of Agriculture's (USDA) regulation regarding organic livestock and poultry practices rescinds a final rule issued on the last day of the Obama administration (82 FR 10775). That rule had imposed animal welfare practices as a condition of labeling meat and eggs as "organic." In rescinding that rule, USDA pointed to the lack of statutory authority, "the high degree of uncertainty and subjectivity in evaluating the benefits . . . , the lack of any market failure to justify intervention, and the clear potential for additional regulation to distort the market or drive away consumers" (82 FR 59988). Supporters of retaining the Obama rule, mostly organic producers operating in what Smith and Yandle would likely call a "covert" mode, made public interest arguments to suggest that the requirements would result in healthier animals, meat, and eggs.

Interestingly, this Baptist argument was insufficient to persuade the new USDA team; the preamble to the final rule disputes those claims in what reads as a direct rebuke to the bootleggers:

> AMS [Agricultural Marketing Service—a unit of USDA] will not regulate when statutory authority is insufficient and potential costs do not justify potential benefits, whether there is a pro-regulatory "consensus" or not. As a matter of USDA regulatory policy, AMS should not regulate simply because some industry players believe that more regulations will help their competitive position. (83 FR 10780)

How was this possible? Perhaps the incentives the regulatory budget requirement provided were strong enough to embolden reformers in USDA to stand up to the B&B elements (inside the agency as well as commenters). It may also be relevant that the rule was issued so late in the Obama administration that organic bootleggers were not speaking with one voice. Had the rule been in place for a few years, all organic farms would have either converted to compliant practices or gone out of business, which would have left no support for rescinding the regulation.

REVISING THE DEFINITION OF AN "EMPLOYER" UNDER ERISA FOR ESTABLISHING ASSOCIATION HEALTH PLANS

The Department of Labor (DOL) issued a particularly controversial rule in June 2018 allowing employers to group together to form association health plans (AHPs). Under the Affordable Care Act, "individual" and "small group" health insurance markets face more stringent requirements regarding the coverage they must offer their employees than "large group" markets do. As a result, the Trump DOL expressed concern that insurance premiums in the individual and small group markets were significantly higher than the large group market. To address this concern, the rule revises the criteria under the Employee

Retirement Income Security Act (ERISA) for determining "when employers may join together in a group or association of employers that will be treated as the 'employer' sponsor" (83 FR 28912) of a health plan. In issuing this rule, the department argued that it "will promote broader availability of group health coverage for these small business owners and self-employed people, and help alleviate their problems of limited or non-existent affordable healthcare options for these small businesses and self-employed people" (83 FR 28915).

The department received more than 900 comments on its proposal, and the final rule reports that small business owners "were very supportive of the Proposed Rule as a way to expand the options they have to obtain more affordable healthcare coverage for themselves and their employees" (83 FR 28915). However, other commenters "believed that a proliferation of groups or associations established for the exclusive purpose of sponsoring an AHP could oversaturate the market, diminishing the value of existing trade and professional groups or associations which, for decades, have focused on building and maintaining relationships with their members and serving their members' needs on a multitude of issues well beyond health benefits" (83 FR 28917). These commenters expressed concern that the rule "could invite unscrupulous promoters to enter the market with mismanaged and thinly funded AHPs and could increase the prevalence of fraudulent and abusive practices" (83 FR 28917).

Arguments about "unscrupulous promoters," "fly-by-night operators," and similar villainous characters are a pretty reliable indication that someone is attempting a B&B swindle of the regulators. The rule, issued in July 2018, will likely face legal challenge.[11]

FEDERAL ACQUISITION REGULATION (FAR): FAR CASE 2017-015, REMOVAL OF FAIR PAY AND SAFE WORKPLACES RULE

On July 31, 2014, President Obama signed Executive Order 13673 "to promote economy and efficiency in procurement by contracting with responsible sources who comply with labor laws" (White House 2014). Several agencies[12] and the Federal Acquisition Regulation Council issued regulations to implement the order, arguing that "ensuring compliance with labor laws drives economy and efficiency by promoting 'safe, healthy, fair, and effective workplaces.'" The joint final rule issued on August 25, 2016, had three elements. It (1) created "new paycheck transparency protections"; (2) required contractors to "disclose decisions regarding violations of certain labor laws," which could affect a decision on eligibility for future awards; and (3) limited "the use of predispute arbitration clauses in employment agreements on covered Federal contracts" (81 FR 58565). The latter two elements proved very controversial.[13]

In October 2016, in response to an emergency motion for a temporary restraining order and preliminary injunction brought by several associations whose members contract with the federal government, a district court enjoined the government from implementing the requirements to report and disclose labor law violations and from enforcing the restriction on arbitration agreements (81 FR 58668). On March 27, 2017, Congress passed, and the president signed, a joint resolution disapproving the rules in their entirety.[14] Following that resolution, the agencies issued a five-page final rule rescinding the 2016 rule (and President Trump rescinded President Obama's order).

While the Obama administration had support for its executive order and implementing regulations, these appeared to be "coordinated" actions initiated by the government, rather than by a concerted coalition of B&B advocates. The fact that supporters of the rule did not file briefs opposing the October 2016 lawsuit brought by contractors may indicate that their preferences were not as strongly felt as the opponents'. The tepidity of the B&B support for the 2016 rule apparently made it unsustainable in the face of opposition from the directly affected parties.

RENEWABLE FUEL AND BIOMASS-BASED DIESEL VOLUME STANDARDS

The 2007 Energy Independence and Security Act directs EPA to set annual levels of renewable fuels that refiners must blend into transportation fuel, such as gasoline and diesel. The Baptist argument for the renewable fuel standard (RFS) is that it improves the environment by shifting consumption from fossil fuels to renewable fuels, such as corn-based ethanol and soy-based biomass diesel.[15] However, research indicates that RFS's environmental benefits are modest at best and are likely overshadowed by the environmental costs, including polluting water bodies via nitrogen fertilizer runoff and potentially larger CO_2 emissions than gasoline (Miller 2016). They also increase consumer costs, not only for transportation fuel but for food. Yet they persist because they benefit a narrow group of special interests: corn and soy farmers (Miller and Dudley 2017).

In two separate notices in 2017, EPA proposed modest changes to reduce the statutory RFS volume targets for 2018 and 2019. These proposals brought the immediate ire of corn state farmers and threats from a bipartisan group of senators led by Senator Chuck Grassley (R-IA) to delay confirmation of President Trump's EPA nominees. President Trump and EPA Administrator Pruitt responded to assure midwestern states of their commitment to the RFS program, and in December 2017, EPA issued final standards higher than those proposed.

The growing evidence of the negative environmental and consumer consequences of mandatory biofuel use has led to the unraveling of the once "cooperative" support for RFS from environmentalists (Bordestsky et al. 2007). Yet the bootlegger pressure remains very powerful, especially given the outsized influence of the state of Iowa in the presidential nomination process. The more "covert" mode of action is evident in the emergence of a new Baptist argument—protection of rural America and the small farmer.

Similar to the Trump administration's bailout of farmers harmed by tariffs, EPA grants hardship waivers from the RFS to small refiners. This may dampen influential petroleum companies' opposition to the standards, but it also dilutes the benefits to the corn lobby. According to reports in 2018, EPA granted dozens of waivers to large as well as small refiners, which has incensed the corn lobby.

OBSERVATIONS: THE NATURE OF BAPTIST ARGUMENTS VARIES BY ADMINISTRATION

Once you start looking for them, bootleggers and Baptists are everywhere. Different Baptist arguments may hold more sway in different administrations, however. As Smith and Yandle observe, "fervent environmentalists make good Baptists" (Smith and Yandle 2014, 109), and their voices carried a lot of weight in the Obama administration, especially regarding efforts to combat climate change.[16] True to B&B predictions, Obama's EPA issued regulations that constrained certain industries (coal) to the benefit of others (natural gas and alternative energy sources). But the Trump administration is much less receptive to environmental concerns; it is more persuaded by Baptist arguments about protecting American jobs, enhancing security, and "winning!" As a result, not only is Trump's EPA working to reverse the Obama-era Clean Power Plan (citing coal jobs, among other things), but his energy secretary is considering subsidies to keep coal plants operating (citing electric grid security), using a little-used provision of the Federal Power Act aimed at responding to electricity reliability emergencies.

INSTITUTIONS MATTER

Institutions matter. My own experience convinces me that OIRA is quite resistant to B&B influences; its small staff of analysts see a variety of regulatory requests across agencies and have no ties to particular industries or interest groups. Furthermore, its culture values and rewards objective analysis of benefits, costs, and other metrics, rather than more rhetorical, emotional, or anecdotal policy justifications. Regulatory agencies are more susceptible to both bootlegger and Baptist arguments; they are compelled to respond to crises or issues that are publicly salient, and, because they focus on a narrow mission, tend to succumb to what Justice Breyer called "tunnel vision" (Breyer 1995).

How the White House is organized can influence the opportunities for B&B coalitions to thrive. Many White House policy offices provide the president the cross-cutting perspective that OIRA does, such as the Council of Economic Advisors or the Domestic Policy Council. But narrowly targeted policy offices, such as Bush's Homeland Security Council, Obama's Office of Energy and Climate Change Policy, and Trump's Office of Trade and Manufacturing Policy, behave quite differently. They are led by czars with narrow missions who are well-positioned to coordinate bootleggers and Baptists in support of their preferred policies. When they hold sway in an administration, without checks from more cross-cutting offices, they can steer policies that benefit bootleggers under the cover of Baptist support.

DEREGULATORY EFFORTS FACE RESISTANCE FROM BOOTLEGGERS AS WELL AS BAPTISTS

Interestingly, B&B activity appears to be less evident in the 20 deregulatory actions agencies completed during the first two years of the Trump administration. This may not be surprising. Bootlegger activity usually occurs behind the scenes, and in a deregulatory environment may be even less visible because it influences the rules *not* chosen for review. In identifying regulations for removal or modification, agency officials seek input from affected companies, which are unlikely to nominate rules for which they have already made investments, or which protect them from potential competition. Opposition to any change from interest groups that support the goal of existing regulations (e.g., consumer financial protection) combined with behind-the-scenes pushback from affected industry (e.g., larger banks)[17] make existing regulations "durable," as Yandle predicts, and less likely to be targeted for removal.[18]

To date, most of the claimed deregulatory actions are either recently issued rules (for which regulated parties have not yet invested in compliance) or minor changes (streamlining reporting requirements, extending compliance deadlines, etc.) (Dudley 2018). This experience is similar to that in the UK, which has implemented a three-in-one-out policy for regulations (Kohli 2017).

Once a regulation is in place, efforts to remove it often get little support because firms have either complied or gone out of business, and advocates oppose anything perceived as backtracking on goals they support. The renewable fuel standard is an interesting exception in that environmental advocates have generally abandoned support for ethanol fuels. In this case, the bootleggers have been successful at changing the Baptist argument for the regulations (protect farming communities and jobs) and have maintained political support.

Note that, generally, the business community has been supportive of Trump's regulatory policies because they have dramatically slowed the *pace of new* regulations (Dudley 2018). Regulatory uncertainty is frequently cited as a major concern for companies of all sizes, so efforts to reduce regulatory churn appear to have been welcome, despite concerns raised by Baptists. Nevertheless, when it comes to taking individual deregulatory actions, incumbents are more likely to resist, and they welcome the backing of Baptist arguments.

NOTES

1. This was due, in part, to acceptance of the economic theory of regulation, and bipartisan recognition across all branches of government that economic regulation tended to benefit incumbent firms at the expense of consumers. See Dudley (2015).
2. For discussion on the development and rationale of US regulation, see Weidenbaum (1999).
3. The *Washington Post* and other major news organizations have gobbled up the council's statements as if they were gospel. Reporters rarely, if ever, note that the group is about as objective as an agricultural lobby calling for more farm subsidies.
4. *Hazardous Waste Treatment Council v. U.S. EPA*, 861 F.2d 270, 1988 U.S. App. LEXIS 13909, 274 U.S. App. D.C. 37, 19 ELR 20059, 28 ERC (BNA) 1305 (D.C. Cir. October 7, 1988). The American Petroleum Institute also joined in the lawsuit, presumably because used oil provided competition to its products.
5. Both the composition of the waste and the characteristics of the site in which it is disposed affect the potential for human exposure and the hazard if exposed.
6. Data available through RegInfo.gov search function.
7. Equivalent products produced by breeding are exempt from regulation.
8. Now renamed the Biotechnology Innovation Organization. https://www.bio.org/.
9. While cap-and-trade regulation is superior to command-and-control regulation, well-organized incumbent firms generally have an advantage in how caps are set and who is entitled to the tradable permits. See Mannix (2018).
10. Economic significance is defined as having "an annual effect on the economy of $100 million or more" (White House 1993).
11. Two state attorneys general announced their intent to "sue to safeguard the protections under the Affordable Care Act and ensure that all families and small businesses have access to quality, affordable health care" (Hellmann 2018).
12. The Department of Defense, the General Services Administration, and the National Aeronautics and Space Administration.

13. Violations to be disclosed would have included "non-final administrative merits determinations, regardless of the severity of the alleged violation, or whether a government contract was involved, and without regard to whether a hearing has been held or an enforceable decision issued." Order referencing 81 FR 58668, "Memorandum and Order Granting Preliminary Injunction: Fair Pay and Safe Workplaces" from the Eastern District of Texas in 2016.

14. Yea and nay votes were largely along party lines. "H.J.Res. 37—Disapproving the Rule Submitted by the Department of Defense, the General Services Administration, and the National Aeronautics and Space Administration Telating to the Federal Acquisition Regulation," 115th Congress, March 27, 2017, https://www.congress.gov/bill/115th-congress/house-joint-resolution/37/all-actions?q=%7B%22roll-call-vote%22%3A%22all%22%7D.

15. Yandle (1999) has some fun with earlier incarnations of these subsidies and mandates. "On hearing the siren call of environmentalism, Secretary of Agriculture Dan Glickman donned Baptist clothing and indicated his strong support for extending the ethanol subsidy, exclaiming that 'renewable fuels provide an important opportunity . . . to lower greenhouse gas emissions.'"

16. Todd Zywicki's chapter in this volume (chapter 4) may offer insights into why different Baptist arguments hold sway in different administrations.

17. Larger banks have reportedly raised concerns about proposed changes to the Volcker rule. https://www.wsj.com/articles/banks-say-no-thanks-to-volcker-rule-changes-1534353932.

18. Indeed, conversations with the regulatory reform officers responsible for identifying and reforming regulations confirm that they do not pursue deregulatory actions without the endorsement of affected industries. For example, officials expressed surprise that banks did not support major changes to the Dodd-Frank regulations. However, with both bank bootleggers and consumer finance Baptists supporting the existing rules, they are unlikely to be revised in ways that might benefit smaller banks or consumers.

REFERENCES

Bolten, J. B. 2008. "Issuance of Agency Regulations at the End of the Administration." White House, May 9. https://obamawhitehouse.archives.gov/sites/default/files/omb/assets/omb/inforeg/cos_memo_5_9_08.pdf.

Bordestsky, A., S. Casey-Lefkowitz, D. Lovaas, E. Martin-Perera, M. Nakagawa, B. Randall, and D. Woynilowicz. 2007. "Driving It Home: Choosing the Right Path for Fueling North America's Transportation Future." Natural Resources Defense Council, June. https://www.nrdc.org/sites/default/files/drivingithome.pdf.

Bovard, J. 1989. "A Hazardous Waste," *Reason*, November 1. http://reason.com/archives/1989/11/01/a-hazardous-waste/print.

Breyer, S. 1995. *Breaking the Vicious Circle: Toward Effective Risk Regulation*. Cambridge, MA: Harvard University Press.

Dudley, S. 2001. "Reversing Midnight Regulations." *Regulation* 24: 9.

——. 2004. "The Bush Administration's Regulatory Record." *Regulation* 27, no. 4: 4–9.

——. 2008. "Letter to the Environmental Protection Agency on 'Pesticide Container Recycling.'" Office of Information and Regulatory Affairs, July 3. https://www.reginfo.gov/public/return/Epa_Return_letter_7_03.pdf.

——. 2009a. "Administrative Law & Regulation: Regulatory Activity in the Bush Administration at the Stroke of Midnight." *Engage* 10, no. 2: 27–29.

——. 2009b. "Lessons Learned, Challenges Ahead." *Regulation* 32, no. 2: 6–11.

——. 2015. "Improving Regulatory Accountability: Lessons from the Past and Prospects for the Future." *Case Western Reserve Law Review* 65, no. 4: 1027–57.

——. 2017a. "Putting a Cap on Regulation." *Administrative and Regulatory Law News* 42, no. 3: 4–6.

——. 2017b. "Report Card on Trump's Deregulatory Activity." *Forbes*, October 17. https://www.forbes.com/sites/susandudley/2018/10/17/report-card-on-trumps-deregulatory-activity/.

——. 2018. "Documenting Deregulation." *Forbes*, August 14. https://www.forbes.com/sites/susandudley/2018/08/14/documenting-deregulation/.

Dudley, S., and J. Brito. 2012. *Regulation: A Primer*. Arlington, VA: Mercatus Center and the George Washington University Regulatory Studies Center.

Dudley, S., and M. Warren. 2018. "FY 2019 Regulators' Budget: More for Homeland Security, Less for Environmental Regulation." George Washington University Regulatory Studies Center and Weidenbaum Center at Washington University in St. Louis.

Geman, B. 2014. "Tom Steyer Takes a Side in Environmentalists' Ethanol Fight." *The Atlantic*, August 19. https://www.theatlantic.com/politics/archive/2014/08/tom-steyer-takes-a-side-in-environmentalists-ethanol-fight/447000/.

Hellmann, J. 2018. "NY, Mass. to Sue over Trump Health Plans Skirting ObamaCare Requirements." *The Hill*, June 20.

Joskow, P. L., and R. G. Noll. 1981. "Regulation in Theory and Practice: An Overview." In *Studies in Public Regulation*, edited by Gary Fromm, 1–65, Cambridge, MA: MIT Press.

Kohli, J. 2017. "What President Trump Can Learn from the UK about Reducing Regulations." *Forbes*, January 27. https://www.forbes.com/sites/realspin/2017/01/27/what-president-trump-can-learn-about-reducing-regulations-from-the-uk/#706b83ec4c3a.

Mannix, B. 2018. "Comments on EPA's Notice, 'State Guidelines for Greenhouse Gas Emissions from Existing Electric Utility Generating Units.'" George Washington University Regulatory Studies Center. https://regulatorystudies.columbian.gwu.edu/sites/g/files/zaxdzs1866/f/downloads/Mannix-EPA-CPP-Replacement-w-Appendices.pdf.

Miller, S. E. 2016. "Oversight of the Renewable Fuel Standard." George Washington University Regulatory Studies Center, March 2. https://regulatorystudies.columbian.gwu.edu/oversight-renewable-fuel-standard.

Miller, S. E., and S. Dudley. 2017. "'Drain the Swamp?' Trump Opts for Politics as Usual When It Comes to Ethanol." *Forbes*, October 27. https://www.forbes.com/sites/susandudley/2017/10/27/drain-the-swamp-trump-opts-for-politics-as-usual-when-it-comes-to-ethanol/.

Miller, S. E., and D. R. Pérez. 2016. "The Final Countdown: Projecting Midnight Regulations." George Washington University Regulatory Studies Center. https://regulatorystudies.columbian.gwu.edu/sites/g/files/zaxdzs1866/f/downloads/Midnight_The-Final-Countdown-2016_Miller_P%C3%A9rez.pdf.

Office of Management and Budget. 2003. "Circular A-4." September 17. www.whitehouse.gov/sites/whitehouse.gov/files/omb/circulars/A4/a-4.pdf.

Smith, A., and B. Yandle. 2014. *Bootleggers and Baptists*. Washington, DC: Cato Institute.

Stigler, G. 1971. "The Theory of Economic Regulation." *Bell Journal of Economic and Management Science* 2: 3–21.

Underwriter Laboratories. 2009. "On Docket no. OSHA-2008-0032." January 20. https://www.regulations.gov/contentStreamer?documentId=OSHA-2008-0032-0072&attachmentNumber=1&contentType=msw8.

US Environmental Protection Agency. 2008. "Pesticide Agricultural Container Recycling Program." RIN 2070-AJ29. https://www.reginfo.gov/public/do/eAgendaViewRule?pubId=200810&RIN=2070-AJ29.

——. 2016. "Land Disposal Restrictions for Hazardous Waste." https://www.epa.gov/hw/land-disposal-restrictions-hazardous-waste#keys. https://www.epa.gov/sites/production/files/2016-02/documents/ldr_rules_and_regulations_pre.pdf.

US Food and Drug Administration. 2017. "AquAdvantage Fact Sheet." December. https://www.fda.gov/AnimalVeterinary/DevelopmentApprovalProcess/GeneticEngineering/GeneticallyEngineeredAnimals/ucm473238.htm.

Viscusi, W. K., J. M. Vernon, and J. E. Harrington Jr. 2005. *Economics of Regulation and Antitrust*. Cambridge, MA: MIT Press.

Weidenbaum, M. L. 1999. *Business and Government in the Global Marketplace*, 6th ed. Upper Saddle River, NJ: Prentice Hall.

White House. 1993. "Executive Order 12866: Regulatory Planning and Review, Section 3(f)(1)." 58, no. 190 (October 4). https://www.reginfo.gov/public/jsp/Utilities/EO_12866.pdf.

——. 2014. "Executive Order—Fair Pay and Safe Workplaces." July 31. https://obamawhitehouse.archives.gov/the-press-office/2014/07/31/executive-order-fair-pay-and-safe-workplaces.

——. 2017a. "Presidential Executive Order on Reducing Regulation and Controlling Regulatory Costs." January 30. https://www.whitehouse.gov/the-press-office/2017/01/30/presidential-executive-order-reducing-regulation-and-controlling.

——. 2017b. "Executive Order 13777: Enforcing the Regulatory Reform Agenda." 82, no. 12287: 12285–87. https://www.federalregister.gov/documents/2017/03/01/2017-04107/enforcing-the-regulatory-reform-agenda.

Yandle, B. 1983. "Viewpoint: Bootleggers and Baptists: The Education of a Regulatory Economist." *Regulation* 7, no. 3: 12–15.

——. 1999. "Bootleggers and Baptists in Retrospect." *Regulation* 22, no. 3. https://www.cato.org/sites/cato.org/files/serials/files/regulation/1999/10/bootleggers.pdf.

——. 2010. "Bootleggers, Baptists, and Global Warming." *Retrospect PERC Reports* 28, no. 2. https://www.perc.org/2010/06/01/bootleggers-baptists-and-global-warming-in-retrospect/.

——. 2011. "Bootleggers and Baptists in the Theory of Regulation." *Jerusalem Papers in Regulation and Governance*, Working Paper no. 9, May.

——. 2017. "When Industries Love Regulation." *PERC Reports* 36, no. 1. https://www.perc.org/2017/07/27/when-industries-love-regulation/.

CHAPTER 8
Income Inequality in the US States
Do Regulations Play a Role?

JODY W. LIPFORD

Rising income inequality in the United States has become a recurrent theme in political and public discourse and in academic research. President Barack Obama used his position and office to draw attention to the issue throughout his administration. In a 2013 speech before the Center for American Progress, Obama traced the rise in income inequality from the late 1970s to the present, asserting that the share of income earned by the top 10 percent has risen from one-third to one-half, and that this imbalance has left the country with "a dangerous and growing inequality and lack of upward mobility" that threatens the country's economy, families, democracy, and even the American dream itself (Obama 2013). In Obama's final State of the Union address, he raised the issue again, identifying it as one of the country's biggest problems (Luhby 2016).

The political uproar over income inequality has resonated well with a public that believes incomes have grown more unequal and that this inequality

This paper is a contribution to the Festschrift for Bruce Yandle, sponsored by the F. A. Hayek Program for the Advanced Study in Philosophy, Politics, and Economics at the Mercatus Center at George Mason University. Much of this research was conducted while I was a visiting scholar at the Center for the Study of Free Enterprise at Western Carolina University in the spring of 2018. I thank all of the conference participants for helpful comments on an earlier draft. I am responsible for any remaining errors.

is a problem. A Pew Research Center poll released in January 2014 stated that there is "broad public agreement that economic inequality has grown over the past decade," and that this agreement is shared across the political spectrum, with nearly an equal share of Republicans and Democrats believing the income gap has risen between the rich and the rest (Pew Research Center 2014). The American Enterprise Institute (2015) cautioned that jobs and the economy, along with terrorism, education, health care, and illegal immigration, were more important issues to Americans than the income gap, but like the Pew Research Center, it reported that a substantial majority of Americans from across the political spectrum believe the income gap is widening.

In the academy, French economist Thomas Piketty has been at the forefront of the analytical work on this issue. His work with Saez (2003) provides evidence that the share of income of the top decile in the United States fell precipitously during the early 1940s, remained flat for decades, and then turned up in the 1970s to levels nearly as high as before the Second World War. The pattern across the 20th century in the US is profoundly U-shaped, in contrast to the inverted U-shape postulated by Kuznets (1955).

Of course, documenting rising income inequality does not explain its causes, elaborate its consequences, or recommend what, if anything, government should do about it. Nonetheless, here too political and public voices have spoken loudly, but the widespread agreement that income has grown more unequal is not accompanied by widespread assessments of the causes of inequality or of support for policy changes. President Obama blamed a long list of factors for rising income inequality, ranging from technology and outsourcing to weaker unions and deteriorated infrastructure. He went on to argue that government should play a vital role in reducing inequality through policies to increase growth, expand education, raise the minimum wage, strengthen unions, and expand the social safety net.

The American public may agree that the distribution of income has grown more unequal, but they show less agreement on the reasons why or what to do about it. According to a Pew Research Center poll, an increasing share of Americans believe hard work does not guarantee success, but partisan differences are striking. Democrats are far more likely than Republicans to believe that circumstances rather than work effort determine economic outcomes and that the economic playing field is tilted toward the wealthy. Democrats are also twice as likely as Republicans to say government should do something to reduce the income gap through policies to redistribute more income, raise the minimum wage, and extend unemployment benefits. The American Enterprise

Institute (2015) survey found similar partisan differences on questions of the fairness of the US economic system and the role government should play in reducing income inequality. A 2015 Gallup poll revealed a long, steady rise in the share of Americans who favor redistribution of wealth through higher taxes on the rich. The share now exceeds 50 percent, but the majority opinion conceals stark fissures in society's viewpoints, as these policies are much more favored by Democrats, liberals, the young, and those with lower incomes, trends that repeat when survey respondents are asked about whether the distribution of income is fair (Newport 2015).

Piketty's (2013) later landmark work argued that the rate of return to capital exceeds the rate of growth of the economy, leading to vast concentrations of wealth that can only be reduced by state redistributive policies. Gregory Mankiw (2013), however, takes a more nuanced view, stressing our limits on understanding the causes of income inequality and the efficacy of policies to address it. Mankiw asks, for example, if rising inequality is the result of government policies, such as monopoly and regulation, or if it results from skill-based technological change. If the former policies are to blame, they should be redressed, but if the latter are the cause, Mankiw argues it is not clear what, if anything, government should do.

The contrast in viewpoints on income redistribution fits well within the larger context of US political perspectives expounded by Kling (2017). As Kling explains, progressives understand political issues along an "axis" of the oppressed versus the oppressors. Those who hold this view see individual effort as having little relation to economic outcomes and blame income inequality on an economy where the rules are rigged in favor of the rich. At the other end of the spectrum, libertarians think in terms of freedom versus coercion and are more likely to oppose government programs that force income from the pockets of some to put it into the pockets of others. Conservatives use a lens of civilization versus barbarism and are likely to lean toward the libertarians in their attitudes on income inequality and the policies to lessen it.

Against this backdrop, Brink Lindsey, a libertarian, and Steven M. Teles, a progressive, have written a book, *The Captured Economy: How the Powerful Enrich Themselves, Slow Down Growth, and Increase Inequality*, on a topic on which they both agree: rising income inequality in the United States—and the pessimism and frustration that flow from it—are, in part, the result of a rigged economy marred by regressive regulation and upward redistribution. The political left that sees markets as always unjust and the state as the bearer of economic justice has missed the point, as has the political right, which sees economic outcomes as the result of fair market processes and the state as little more than the lead actor in an ongoing drama of rent-seeking (Lindsey and Teles 2017). In the language of Kling, there is both oppression and coercion.

This paper examines the Lindsey-Teles hypothesis empirically, using data on US states from 2006 to 2014 (even years). Specifically, I examine state income inequality, as measured by the ratio of the wage rate of the 90th percentile of workers to the wage rate of the 10th percentile of workers, and states' regulatory climates, as measured by the Cato Institute's measures of economic freedom (Ruger and Sorens 2016). The empirical analysis broadly supports the hypothesis set forth by Lindsey and Teles by finding that greater regulatory freedom (or a less stringent regulatory burden) is associated with a narrower gap between wages of the 90th percentile of workers and wages of the 10th percentile of workers.

In the following section, I explain why this topic is especially relevant to Bruce Yandle and his decades of work as an economist. I then present, in the third section, data on income inequality in the United States over the years of my empirical analysis. The fourth section provides a brief review of related literature on the broader link between income inequality, economic freedom, and regulation. With this background in place, I discuss the Lindsey-Teles hypothesis in greater detail in the fifth section. I examine the data and present the results of the empirical estimates in the sixth section. In section seven, I consider the implications and conclusions derived from the work presented.

INCOME INEQUALITY, REGULATION, AND BRUCE YANDLE'S CONTRIBUTION TO ECONOMICS

A paper examining income inequality and regulation's contribution to it is suitable for this volume of papers because Bruce has always been, foremost, a regulatory economist. In government, he is perhaps best known for serving for two years as the executive director of the Federal Trade Commission, and among his academic colleagues, he is best known for his regulatory theory of "Bootleggers and Baptists" (Yandle 1983). At a personal level, my first graduate-level class was Bruce's course on government regulation, where Bruce taught his students the public interest, capture, and economic theories of regulation, aided by warm drinks and coffee cakes on cold mornings.

An empirical analysis is also fitting. Bruce always encouraged his students to read, ponder, and then test the ideas using data. Much of my work with Bruce has been empirical. We would talk through an entire project and then utilize division of labor, with Bruce writing the literature and theory sections while I would crunch the numbers and write the empirical sections.

Further, the catalyst for this paper, the Lindsey-Teles book, is one I read along with Bruce in our Clemson economics reading group, a small group of scholars who have met in Clemson monthly for over 25 years to discuss books from economics and other disciplines. Bruce's direction of and participation in our reading group has contributed directly to this work.

Last, I utilize data on regulation that has long been a project of the Mercatus Center, where Bruce currently serves as a Distinguished Adjunct Fellow.

INCOME INEQUALITY IN THE US, 2006 TO 2014

To set the stage for the forthcoming empirical work, I present figure 8.1, which charts the ratio of wages for the 90th percentile of workers to the wages of the 10th percentile of workers for the US over the period of my empirical analysis. The pattern is clearly upward, although it took a slight dip in the aftermath of the Great Recession. On the whole, the ratio has risen from a value of 4.71 in 2006 to 4.91 in 2014, a rise of over 4 percent.[1] Although this rise may not be much, it continues the longer-term trend analyzed by many others. The more

Figure 8.1. U.S. Hourly Wage Ratio: 90th Percentile to 10th Percentile

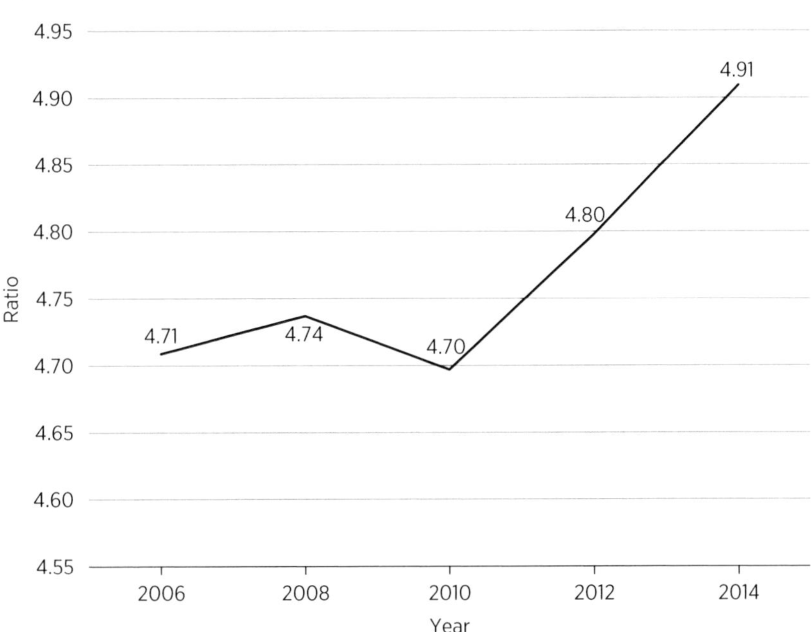

Source: Bureau of Labor Statistics, Occupational Employment Statistics, 2006, 2008, 2010, 2012, 2014.

telling question is why this trend has been rising for so long. This research hopes to shed some light on this question through a cross section–time series analysis that may have implications for the national trend.

INCOME INEQUALITY, ECONOMIC FREEDOM, AND REGULATION: A REVIEW OF THE LITERATURE

Many market-oriented economists, such as the contributors to this volume, have shown little interest in income inequality. If economic outcomes such as income are the result of market processes, many market-leaning economists are content to leave well enough alone, arguing that government attempts to alter these (and other) market outcomes will at best accomplish little and will at worst distort incentives in ways that undermine productivity and slow economic growth.

Nonetheless, many economists, including some with a pro-market bent, have delved into the economics of income inequality in an effort to peel back the layers and shed some light on why the distribution of income is what it is. In this section, I provide a brief overview of literature that proceeds along two strands. First, I look at literature that investigates the link between income inequality and economic freedom: Do countries or states within a country where markets are relatively free have wider or narrower distributions of income? Second, I turn to literature more closely aligned with Lindsey and Teles and this paper in which researchers examine whether regulations differentially benefit workers at the upper end of the income distribution and harm workers at the lower end of the income distribution.

Income Inequality and Economic Freedom

Economists' work on economic freedom focused initially on the relationships between economic freedom and per capita income and its growth, but the research agenda expanded quickly to include the effects of economic freedom on health, education, environmental quality, and a host of other factors including poverty and income inequality.

In an early work utilizing international data on Gini coefficients and the Fraser Institute's Economic Freedom of the World measure of economic freedom, Scully (2002) found that economic freedom reduced income inequality, a finding that Carter (2007) questioned on the basis of misreported data and his own work, in which he found that economic freedom increased inequality for the majority of countries in his sample. Using a different sample of countries,

Clark and Lawson (2008) looked at marginal tax rates specifically, as well as economic freedom in general, to determine their effects on income inequality. They found that higher marginal tax rates and higher economic freedom ratings led to reduced income inequality.

Later work using Gini coefficients and international data call all prior work into question. In an analysis stressing policy, economic systems, and ethnolinguistic fractionalization, Strum and De Hann (2015) found that higher per capita GDP, globalization, and higher stocks of foreign direct investment increased income inequality, but that economic freedom had no effect. In addition, they found that countries with high values of ethnolinguistic fractionalization redistribute less income. Given the contradictory results across studies, it is not surprising that Bennet and Nikolaev (2017), in a thorough review of the literature that includes their attempts to replicate two prior studies, found that results are sensitive to country sample, time period, and measures of inequality. Further, they pointed out that the relationship between income inequality and economic freedom may be bidirectional.

In a change of emphasis, Ashby and Sobel (2008) shifted the focus of study to the 50 US states and used the Fraser Institute's Economic Freedom of North America measure of economic freedom. They recognized that the results of prior work were ambiguous and, like Carter, pointed out that theory gives limited guidance. Economic freedom provides greater opportunity, leading to greater income equality, but it also reduces income redistribution that may curb income inequality. Ashby and Sobel examined state income in terms of levels, growth rates, shares of total income, and ratios of highest to lowest quintiles and found consistently that gains in economic freedom reduced income inequality.

Later work supports the Ashby-Sobel findings. Bennett and Vedder (2013) found that increases in economic freedom reduced income inequality and went on to extend the analysis by estimating and constructing a Kuznets-like curve between the level of economic freedom and income inequality. They found that beyond an economic freedom rating somewhat above 7, increased economic freedom reduced income inequality. Webster (2013) also found corroborative evidence supporting Ashby and Sobel. Wiseman (2017) approached the task somewhat differently, focusing on which segments of the income distribution benefit most from the higher rates of economic growth that economic freedom engenders. On the whole, he found that the bottom 90 percent of the income distribution benefits more from economic freedom and the growth it brings than the top 10 percent, and so concluded that increased economic freedom leads to income convergence.

As with prior state-level work, Apergis, Dincer, and Payne (2014) found that economic freedom reduced income inequality. However, they also took up the challenge to investigate the possibility of bidirectional causality between economic freedom and income inequality and found evidence suggestive of a disturbing "vicious cycle." Utilizing Granger causality tests, they found that higher income inequality led to reduced economic freedom, which in turn led to higher income inequality.

Nonetheless, not all of the evidence points to a negative relationship between economic freedom and income inequality among the US states. In a multi-equation model examining economic freedom, per capita income, the employment–population ratio, and the Gini coefficient, Lipford and Yandle (2015) found that higher values of economic freedom increased economic inequality.

Income Inequality and Regulation

Other economists have followed the pathway set so clearly by Stigler (1971), arguing that regulation, whatever its form, has little to do with the "public interest" and much to do with legislator- and regulator-provided benefits to special interests who gain from policies that concentrate benefits among the few and disperse costs across the many.[2] Whether economists (or anyone else for that matter) consider income equality a public interest or not, the fact remains that regulations may alter the distribution of income, in particular in ways that favor high-income earners who may be politically connected and who favor public regulation of negligible risks that costs them only a small share of their incomes. For low-income earners, the cost of risk reduction through regulations is almost surely more than the cost of private risk-reduction strategies (Thomas 2012).

Using the banking industry as a case study, Black and Strahan (2001) examined the effects of banking deregulation on employees' wages. They argued that banking deregulation, especially the fall of legislation that prohibited interstate banking, led to more competition in the industry, which, in turn, would reduce wages. Their empirical findings were consistent with this line of reasoning: banking deregulation led to lower wages in the industry, in particular for men, who apparently captured a disproportionate share of regulatory rents relative to women.

Mulholland (2018) takes rising income inequality head-on, arguing that the conventional explanation of skill-biased technological change isn't wholly satisfactory, because of timing and a deceleration in educational wage premiums.

Using occupational wage data, Mulholland finds evidence that regulation is a significant part of the explanation for rising income inequality.

Similarly, Bailey, Thomas, and Anderson (2018) examine occupational wages and regulation and find that although regulation reduces wages overall, the effects are regressive in that wage earners at the bottom of the income distribution experience larger negative wage effects. Further, the authors find that regulations raise wages for occupations tied to regulatory compliance, such as managers, accountants, and workers in the legal field.

Taken together, these strands of literature point to evidence that economic opportunity benefits all, but especially those at the bottom of the income distribution, and that regulation reduces the wages of all, but mostly those of workers at the bottom of the income distribution. These findings are consistent with the hypothesis of Lindsey and Teles, to which I now turn.

IS THE US ECONOMY CAPTURED? THE LINDSEY-TELES HYPOTHESIS

Lindsey and Teles acknowledge from the outset of their book that slow growth and rising income inequality in the United States have fueled pessimism and frustration among a wide swath of the country's population. Advances in information technology and globalization have increased income inequality, but the authors argue that regulations are important determinants of both economic maladies. Regulations lead to slower growth because they raise the return to rent-seeking in lieu of innovation and raise income inequality because they enhance opportunity for some, especially those already earning high incomes, and deny opportunity to others, especially those at the lower end of the income distribution.

A first regulatory culprit is the financial sector, which Lindsey and Teles regard as "a big piece of the puzzle" (2017, 36). Subsidies from the Federal Reserve System and the Federal Deposit Insurance Corporation, along with a policy of too-big-to-fail, have weakened the link between risk and the interest rates that creditors demand, infusing moral hazard into the entire financial system. As a result, the financial sector has grown larger than it should have, and the rents earned have been concentrated among upper managers and professionals, leading to greater income inequality. Lindsey and Teles conclude that a "less-subsidized financial sector would be a smaller financial sector, and a healthier one" (63).

Occupational licensure is a second culprit in the rise of income inequality. Occupational licensure is extensive and growing, with requirements that are variable and arbitrary. Barriers to entry in numerous fields, from cosmetology to health care to the legal professions, enrich those with the license while thwarting opportunity for aspiring workers at the bottom of the income distribution.[3]

Land-use regulations are a third major contributor to regulation-induced income inequality. Higher population densities in urban areas raise the marginal product and income of labor in those locations, but in-migration to urban areas should reduce the wage differential between urban and rural areas. However, this migration is blocked by a plethora of zoning and land-use regulations. The result is urban areas that are filled with skilled, educated, high-income workers and rural areas that are filled with low-skilled, less-educated, low-income workers, an outcome Lindsey and Teles aptly refer to as "geographic inequality" (115). With land-use restrictions in place, the rural poor cannot afford to move into high-rent urban areas, even to offer low-wage services to the more affluent.

As the contributors to this volume well recognize, Bruce's theory of Bootleggers and Baptists regulation explains the appeal and resilience of these regulations. Regulations that serve narrow, private interests are all the more potent when cloaked in a public interest argument. The public interest theory of regulation need not be discarded; it merely needs to be modified to show its usefulness to the economic theory. The examples highlighted by Lindsey and Teles are permeated with Bootleggers and Baptists force: regulation of the financial sector insures against the collapse of financial intermediation so vital for economic well-being; occupational licensure protects an unsuspecting public from unscrupulous charlatans; and land-use regulations provide aesthetically appealing green spaces and raise property values.

The cumulative effects of these regulations, however, are to widen the distribution of income for reasons on which even libertarians and progressives can agree. Libertarians object to the rent-seeking policies that deprive people of opportunity: the widening income gap should not be the result of artificial and coercive government policies. Progressives object to a widening income gap on principle or on philosophical grounds, but if the root of the inequality is the oppression of those with low incomes by those with high incomes, the inequality is all the more distasteful.[4]

DATA, MODELS, AND EMPIRICAL TESTS

In this section, I present empirical tests of the Lindsey-Teles hypothesis that regulation has widened the income gap by estimating empirical models of wage inequality and regulation across the US states. Before presenting the model and results, I provide a brief discussion of the data.

Data Descriptions and Sources

To measure income inequality, I use the ratio of the hourly wage of workers at the 90th percentile to the hourly wage of workers at the 10th percentile for each of the 50 states across the years of analysis. These data are taken from the Bureau of Labor Statistics Occupational Employment Statistics. Higher ratios indicate greater inequality.

For the regulatory variables, I use two sources. For data on employment in the finance and insurance industries, I use the Bureau of Economic Analysis Regional Data on Total Full-Time and Part-Time Employment by Industry for each state and year. The data on occupational licensure and land-use regulations, as well as more comprehensive measures of the regulatory burden and economic freedom across the states, come from the Cato Institute's database, *Freedom in the 50 States* (Ruger and Sorens 2016).[5] Higher values indicate greater freedom or less regulation. Unlike the Fraser Institute's Economic Freedom of North America measure of economic freedom used in previous studies, the Cato Institute does not weigh variables equally. Instead, weights are determined "according to the value of the freedom affected by a particular policy to those people whose freedoms are at stake."

In addition, I use per capita income, the employment–population ratio, the percent of the adult population with at least a high school diploma, and minimum wage rates as control variables. State per capita income measures and state minimum wages are taken from the Bureau of Economic Analysis and Department of Labor, respectively, and are adjusted to 2014 dollars using the Consumer Price Index. The employment–population ratio is taken from the Bureau of Labor Statistics, and the share of state adult population with at least a high school diploma is taken from the *Statistical Abstract of the United States, 2012* for 2006 and 2008 and from the Census Bureau for the remaining years.

Although most data are available annually, the sample includes only even-numbered years from 2006 to 2014 because of limits on the availability of the regulatory variables.[6] Table 8.1 presents the descriptive statistics for each variable used in the empirical tests.

The Models and Empirical Results

In accordance with the precedence established by prior researchers, I estimate three models: one using levels with current values for all variables, one using levels with lagged values for the regulatory variables, and one with changes in the dependent and independent variables. Further, I estimate first a generalized

Table 8.1. Descriptive Statistics

Variable	Mean	Std. Dev.	Minimum	Maximum
Hourly wage ratio: 90th percentile to 10th percentile	4.386	0.492	3.386	5.714
Per capita personal income (2014 dollars)	44,124	6,988	32,542	67,443
Employment rate (%)	61.41	4.72	49.60	72.00
High school graduation rate (%)	86.72	3.50	77.90	92.40
Minimum wage (2014 dollars)	7.47	0.81	6.05	9.32
Employment in finance and insurance (%)	4.988	1.375	2.365	9.965
Occupational freedom	−0.004	0.022	−0.058	0.054
Land-use freedom	−0.00098	0.0773	−0.2607	0.0581
Regulatory policy freedom	−0.0095	0.1645	−0.4728	0.2730
Economic freedom	−0.0069	0.2607	−1.0343	0.4839

least squares (GLS) or random effects (RE) model, followed by a model that utilizes fixed effects (FE) for the states.

Models in Levels Using Current Values

The first model is shown in the equation below:

$$\begin{aligned}&\text{Hourly Wage Ratio, 90th to 10th Percentile}_{i,t}\\&= \alpha_0 + \alpha_1 * \text{Per Capita Personal Income}_{i,t}\\&+ \alpha_2 * \text{Employment Rate}_{i,t} + \alpha_3 * \text{Percent of Adult}\\&\quad \text{Population with a High School Diploma}_{i,t}\\&+ \alpha_4 * \text{Minimum Wage}_{i,t}\\&+ \alpha_5 * \text{Regulation Variables}_{i,t} + \varepsilon_{i,t}.\end{aligned}$$

The fixed effects models include the state dummy variables.

Regression results are shown in table 8.2 for the even years including and between 2006 and 2014, giving a total of 250 observations. All estimates are statistically significant, as shown by the chi-square and F statistics, and tests of the joint significance of the state dummy variables are significant in the fixed-effects estimates.

Columns (1) through (5) show the GLS estimates. The control variables perform as expected. Per capita personal income has a positive sign and is sta-

Table 8.2. Income Inequality and Regulation: All Variables Expressed as Current Levels

	Dependent Variable: Wage Ratio: 90th Percentile Divided by 10th Percentile									
	GLS/RE	*GLS/RE*	*GLS/RE*	*GLS/RE*	*GLS/RE*	*FE*	*FE*	*FE*	*FE*	*FE*
Variable	**Coeff./ *z*-stat (1)**	**Coeff./ *z*-stat (2)**	**Coeff./ *z*-stat (3)**	**Coeff./ *z*-stat (4)**	**Coeff./ *z*-stat (5)**	**Coeff./ *t*-stat (6)**	**Coeff./ *t*-stat (7)**	**Coeff./ *t*-stat (8)**	**Coeff./ *t*-stat (9)**	**Coeff./ *t*-stat (10)**
PC personal income	2.31*e–05/ (5.06)***	2.29*e–05/ (4.98)***	1.51*e–05/ (3.37)***	1.82*e–05/ (3.64)***	1.82*e–05/ (3.90)***	7.39*e–06 (1.39)	7.02*e–06 (1.32)	5.45*e–06 (1.12)	6.50*e–06 (1.18)	6.01*e–06 (1.13)
Employment rate	–0.028/ (–5.45)***	–0.028/ (–5.27)***	–0.026/ (–5.19)***	–0.021/ (–3.47)***	–0.022/ (–4.02)***	–0.025/ (–3.71)***	–0.025/ (–3.68)***	–0.015/ (–2.37)**	–0.024/ (–3.40)***	–0.021/ (–3.07)***
Pct. HS graduates	–0.001/ (–0.07)	–0.0001/ (–0.01)	0.005/ (0.54)	–0.011 (–1.01)	–0.002/ (–0.20)	0.033/ (2.35)**	0.036/ (2.52)**	0.024/ (1.84)*	0.029/ (1.83)*	0.030/ (2.10)**
Minimum wage	–0.123 (–6.41)***	–0.123/ (–6.40)***	–0.125/ (–6.99)***	–0.113/ (–5.79)***	–0.110/ (–5.80)***	–0.122/ (–6.36)***	–0.124/ (–6.44)***	–0.115/ (–6.51)***	–0.120/ (–6.09)***	–0.114/ (–5.81)***
Pct. fin. and ins. empl.	0.067/ (2.27)**	0.066/ (2.20)**	0.048/ (1.69)*	0.070/ (2.44)**	0.070/ (2.47)**	0.002/ (0.05)	0.013/ (0.28)	–0.026/ (–0.63)	0.002/ (0.04)	0.008/ (0.18)
Occupation freedom		–0.432/ (–0.29)					2.12/ (1.22)			
Land-use freedom			–3.836/ (–5.79)***					–14.748/ (–6.34)***		

(continued)

Table 8.2. *(continued)*

	Dependent Variable: Wage Ratio: 90th Percentile Divided by 10th Percentile									
	GLS/RE	*GLS/RE*	*GLS/RE*	*GLS/RE*	*GLS/RE*	*FE*	*FE*	*FE*	*FE*	*FE*
Variable	Coeff./ *z*-stat (1)	Coeff./ *z*-stat (2)	Coeff./ *z*-stat (3)	Coeff./ *z*-stat (4)	Coeff./ *z*-stat (5)	Coeff./ *t*-stat (6)	Coeff./ *t*-stat (7)	Coeff./ *t*-stat (8)	Coeff./ *t*-stat (9)	Coeff./ *t*-stat (10)
Regulatory policy				–0.491/ (–2.78)***					–0.119/ (–0.60)	
Economic freedom					–0.481/ (–3.93)***					–0.272/ (–1.87)*
Constant	5.76/ (6.05)***	5.70/ (5.90)***	5.52/ (6.10)***	6.24/ (6.74)***	5.55/ (6.05)***	3.61/ (2.59)***	3.34/ (2.37)**	3.97/ (3.12)***	3.93/ (2.63)***	3.65/ (2.64)***
Wald χ^2	77.33***	76.98***	120.32***	88.70***	97.97***					
F statistic						13.08***	11.17***	19.78***	10.92***	11.62***
F statistic: state dummy variables						42.12***	41.67***	44.21***	36.12***	38.23
N	250	250	250	250	250	250	250	250	250	250

Significance levels (two-tailed tests): * 10%. ** 5%, *** 1%.

tistically significant, indicating that high-income states tend to be states with higher wage inequality, a finding consistent with the notion that a concentration of relatively high-wage earners raises state average incomes and widens the income dispersion of a state. Employment proves an equalizer, as a higher share of a state's population being employed reduces the wage ratio at statistically significant levels, as would be the case if the increased share of employment is in jobs that pay wages between upper and lower extremes. A high school education may also be an equalizer if it provides higher wages at the lower end of the income spectrum. However, the sign on a state's share of the adult population with a high school diploma is negative and insignificant in all of the GLS estimates. The evidence on the minimum wage strongly supports arguments made by its supporters that a high minimum wage reduces wage inequality. Although the share of workers nationally who earn the minimum wage is in the single digits throughout this period of study,[7] the argument that a higher minimum wage puts upward pressure on the wages of all low-wage workers may have merit.

Turning to the regulatory variables, these estimates provide consistent support for the Lindsey-Teles hypothesis that employees in the financial services industry earn unduly high incomes because of government subsidies. The wage gap is higher in states with a larger share of employees in the finance and insurance sector, a finding in all of the GLS estimates. The other regulatory variables are also generally supportive of Lindsey and Teles. Land-use freedom, regulatory freedom, and economic freedom as a whole are negatively associated with the wage gap at high levels of statistical significance. Land-use restrictions evidently segregate workers by education and skill and so protect the earnings of residents in urban areas and limit the earnings of those in rural areas. The regulatory policy variable includes not only measures of occupational and land-use freedom, but also components that measure health insurance freedom, labor-market freedom, lawsuit freedom, cable and telecommunications, and various other miscellaneous regulatory freedom measures, and its negative and significant sign indicates that regulatory freedom, broadly defined, reduces wage inequality. The measure of overall economic freedom sums the measure of regulatory policy with a measure of fiscal policy that includes components for state and local taxes, government subsidies, and government debt. As shown in estimate (5), this variable too reduces wage inequality. The occupational freedom variable is not statistically significant, although its sign is negative.

The fixed effects estimates given in columns (6) through (10) are less supportive of the hypothesis advanced by Lindsey and Teles. For the control variables, the employment rate and minimum wage remain negative and highly significant. The share of state adult population with a high school diploma has a positive sign and is significant in each of these estimates, a finding at odds with the idea that a high school education raises wages at the lower end of the income distribution. Per capita personal income is not statistically significant in these estimates.

For the regulatory variables, the outcome is mixed. In these estimates, the share of state employment in the financial sector is not correlated with the wage gap, and neither are occupational freedom or regulatory policy as whole. On the other hand, the land-use freedom and economic freedom variables are consistent in sign and significance across all estimates: greater land-use and economic freedom are associated with narrower wage gaps across the states.

Models in Levels Using Lagged Regulatory Variables

In the second model, shown in the equation below, I follow a practice of other researchers and lag the regulatory variables.

$$\begin{aligned}&\text{Hourly Wage Ratio, 90th to 10th Percentile}_{i,t}\\&\quad = \alpha_0 + \alpha_1 * \text{Per Capita Personal Income}_{i,t}\\&\quad + \alpha_2 * \text{Employment Rate}_{i,t} + \alpha_3 * \text{Percent of Adult}\\&\qquad \text{Population with a High School Diploma}_{i,t}\\&\quad + \alpha_4 * \text{Minimum Wage}_{i,t}\\&\quad + \alpha_5 * \text{Regulation Variables}_{i,t-4} + \varepsilon_{i,t}.\end{aligned}$$

The fixed effects models include the state dummy variables.

The rationale for the lagged variables is that regulatory policies may not have immediate effects on the distribution of wages. For this estimate, I have lagged the regulatory variables four years (e.g., 2014 values of the wage ratio are regressed on 2010 values of the regulatory variables), reducing the number of observations to 150. The results are shown in table 8.3.

Each of the estimates is again statistically significant. An examination of the regulatory variables yields results that are often, though not always, supportive of the hypothesis set forth by Lindsey and Teles.

Looking first at the GLS estimates reveals that higher per capita incomes widen the wage gap and that higher minimum wages are associated with a lower wage ratio, at least in the fourth and fifth estimates, findings consistent with those reported in table 8.2. However, in the GLS estimates, there is no evidence that a higher share of state population employed reduces the wage

Table 8.3. Income Inequality and Regulation: Regulation Variables Expressed as Lagged Levels

	Dependent Variable: Wage Ratio: 90th Percentile Divided by 10th Percentile									
	GLS/RE	*GLS/RE*	*GLS/RE*	*GLS/RE*	*GLS/RE*	*FE*	*FE*	*FE*	*FE*	*FE*
Variable	**Coeff./ *z*-stat (1)**	**Coeff./ *z*-stat (2)**	**Coeff./ *z*-stat (3)**	**Coeff./ *z*-stat (4)**	**Coeff./ *z*-stat (5)**	**Coeff./ *t*-stat (6)**	**Coeff./ *t*-stat (7)**	**Coeff./ *t*-stat (8)**	**Coeff./ *t*-stat (9)**	**Coeff./ *t*-stat (10)**
PC personal income	2.57*e–05/ (5.12)***	2.48*e–05/ (4.99)***	1.98*e–05/ (4.07)***	1.90*e–05/ (3.84)***	2.39*e–05/ (4.89)***	8.83*e–06 (1.73)*	8.88*e–06 (1.72)*	9.32*e–06 (1.86)*	8.07*e–06 (1.61)	9.61*e–06 (1.87)*
Employment rate	–0.013/ (–1.30)	–0.010/ (–0.98)	–0.012/ (–1.26)	–0.002/ (–0.16)	–0.009/ (–095)	–0.002/ (–0.16)	–0.002/ (–0.16)	–0.003/ (–0.23)	0.004/ (0.33)	0.001/ (0.08)
Pct. HS graduates	0.028/ (2.01)**	0.033/ (2.34)**	0.024/ (1.86)*	0.028/ (2.15)**	0.032/ (2.36)**	0.058/ (3.63)***	0.058/ (3.57)***	0.049/ (3.03)***	0.058/ (3.69)***	0.062/ (3.84)***
Minimum wage	–0.033 (–0.93)	–0.026/ (–0.74)	–0.051/ (–1.52)	–0.063/ (–1.86)*	–0.075/ (–2.07)**	–0.026/ (–0.71)	–0.026/ (–0.70)	–0.025/ (–0.71)	–0.030/ (–0.85)	–0.034/ (–0.91)
Pct. fin. and ins. empl.	–0.030/ (–0.90)	–0.035/ (–1.04)	–0.031/ (–1.01)	–0.040/ (–1.28)	–0.014/ (–0.42)	–0.170/ (–3.63)***	–0.170/ (–3.32)***	–0.138/ (–2.69)***	–0.169/ (–3.44)***	–0.142/ (–2.62)***
Occupation freedom		–4.953/ (–2.17)**					–0.351/ (–0.11)			
Land-use freedom			–3.765/ (–5.10)***					–5.772/ (–2.28)**		

(continued)

Table 8.3. *(continued)*

	Dependent Variable: Wage Ratio: 90th Percentile Divided by 10th Percentile									
	GLS/RE	*GLS/RE*	*GLS/RE*	*GLS/RE*	*GLS/RE*	*FE*	*FE*	*FE*	*FE*	*FE*
Variable	**Coeff./ *z*-stat (1)**	**Coeff./ *z*-stat (2)**	**Coeff./ *z*-stat (3)**	**Coeff./ *z*-stat (4)**	**Coeff./ *z*-stat (5)**	**Coeff./ *t*-stat (6)**	**Coeff./ *t*-stat (7)**	**Coeff./ *t*-stat (8)**	**Coeff./ *t*-stat (9)**	**Coeff./ *t*-stat (10)**
Regulatory policy				−1.501/ (−4.86)***					−1.036/ (−2.38)**	
Economic freedom					−0.535/ (−3.62)***					−0.227/ (−1.31)
Constant	2.00/ (1.54)	1.40/ (1.07)	2.69/ (2.25)**	1.95/ (1.63)	1.78/ (1.43)	0.146/ (0.08)	1.63/ (0.09)	0.797/ (0.44)	−0.52/ (−0.03)	−0.53/ (−0.28)
Wald χ^2	88.00***	95.09***	126.23***	123.24***	107.24***					
F statistic						25.55***	21.07**	23.09***	23.27***	21.74***
F statistic: state dummy variables						94.28***	92.30***	82.42***	84.20***	87.29
N	150	150	150	150	150	150	150	150	150	150

Significance levels (two-tailed tests): * 10%. ** 5%, *** 1%.

ratio, and the share of a state's adult population with a high school diploma is positive and statistically significant, a finding inconsistent with expectations.

The regulatory variables are fully supportive of Lindsey and Teles. Greater occupational and land-use freedom are associated with a narrower wage gap, and the broader regulatory variables for regulatory policy and economic freedom are also negatively correlated with the wage ratio. Unlike the GLS estimates with all variables at current values, in these estimates, the share of state employment in the finance and insurance industries is not correlated with the wage ratio.

When state fixed effects are included, per capita personal income remains positively, albeit weakly, correlated with the wage ratio. Again, the employment rate is statistically insignificant. The share of adults with a high school education continues to be positive and significant. Higher minimum wages are statistically insignificant in all the fixed effects estimates. A most puzzling result is that the share of state population employed in the finance and insurance industries is negatively associated with the wage ratio in these estimates. Of the other regulatory variables, the land-use and regulatory freedom variables show again a negative correlation with the wage ratio, a finding that reinforces the Lindsey-Teles ideas in all of the estimates with lagged regulatory variables.

Models Using Changes in the Variables

As a final test, I estimated the model with all variables differenced over four years (e.g., $\Delta X_{\mathrm{i,t}} = X_{i,t} - X_{i,t-4}$) to test whether it is the changes in the variables that matter. The results of these models yield little of statistical significance. Because these estimates are so weak, I do not report them.

Conclusions from the Empirical Estimates

The estimates in this paper differ from prior estimates of income inequality across the US states in two important ways. First, they draw upon hypotheses spelled out in the work of Lindsey and Teles about how specific regulations are to blame, at least in part, for the widening distribution of income in the United States. Second, they use heretofore unused measures of regulation provided by the Cato Institute in its *Freedom in the 50 States*.

Focusing on the regulatory variables, the GLS estimates with current regulatory variables support the hypothesis that government regulation of the financial sector ("misregulation" in the terms of Lindsey and Teles) leads to greater dispersion of wages because this sector employs a disproportionate share of workers who are highly educated, skilled, and compensated.

The land-use freedom variable is negative and statistically significant in the GLS and FE estimates, whether the regulatory variables are current or lagged. Land-use restrictions are evidently an important factor leading to a less even distribution of income.

The aggregated measures of regulatory policy and economic freedom are also strongly supportive of regulations' role in increasing income inequality. The coefficients on regulatory policy are negative and significant in three of four estimates, and the coefficients on economic freedom are likewise negative and significant in three of four estimates, providing support for the hypothesis that economies with more regulatory and economic freedom also have more even distributions of income. However strong the arguments that occupational licensure matters to the distribution of income, the occupational freedom variable is negatively associated with a lower wage ratio in only the lagged GLS estimate.

IMPLICATIONS AND CONCLUSIONS

The evidence for rising income inequality in the United States has grown in recent decades, and the widening gap between the rich and poor has drawn increased attention and concern from the public, politicians, and academicians. With evidence for the growth of the trend, more researchers have questioned the factors behind this trend.

Although much rising income inequality is surely the result of natural market outcomes, such as skill-biased technological change, market explanations do not account for the whole of it. Regressive regulation has drawn the attention of many researchers of income inequality, and Brink Lindsey and Steven Teles, coming from opposite ends of the political spectrum, have argued that income inequality and regulation rise together. Specifically, they argue that regulations governing the financial sector, occupational licensing, and land use widen the income distribution by securing opportunity and high wages for some, while denying those benefits to those closed out of protected markets.

In this paper, I have sought to follow Bruce Yandle's contribution to the economics discipline by examining the effects of these regulations. As Bruce has often found, regulations can be detrimental, even and especially for those they are purported to help. Although further research on this topic will shed additional light on the extent of regulation's effect on relative wages, the evidence offered in this paper is, on the whole, consistent with the hypothesis that regulation widens the income distribution. To the author of the Bootleggers and Baptists theory of regulation, this finding can hardly be surprising. If future research buttresses these findings, those wanting to redress these problems may want to remember another point that Bruce and other public choice economists have found to be true: reforming government policy for the good is difficult and problematic. And this point reflects not only the results of academic studies but also the personal experiences of Bruce and countless other economists who have spent part of their careers in government.

NOTES

1. The Gini coefficient, a commonly used measure of income inequality, shows a similar trend, rising from a value of 0.464 in 2006 to a value of 0.480 in 2014. See the US Census Bureau, American Community Survey, various years.
2. For an overview of economists' theories of regulation, see Posner (1974).
3. For a detailed discussion of occupational licensure in the US, its prevalence, benefits, and costs, and recommendations for reform, see White House (2015).
4. Lindsey and Teles also argue that protection of intellectual property contributes to income inequality because it creates concentrated, highly profitable, winner-take-all markets. Because intellectual property laws are national in scope, I omit them from the discussion here and in the ensuing empirical analysis.
5. For components of the measures of Land Use Freedom, Occupational Freedom, Regulatory Policy, and overall Economic Freedom, see *Freedom in the 50 States*.
6. At the time I collected data and did the empirical work for this study, the Cato Institute had not issued the 2018 edition of *Freedom in the 50 States*. This edition improves on earlier editions by extending coverage through 2016 and including annual data back to year 2000. The 2016 edition used in this study only provided data for the even-numbered years 2006 through 2014.
7. See Bureau of Labor Statistics, Characteristics of Minimum Wage Workers, 2016, BLS Report 1067, April 2017.

REFERENCES

American Enterprise Institute. 2015. "Public Opinion on Income Inequality. AEI Political Report: A Monthly Poll Compilation." May.

Apergis, N., O. Dincer, and J. E. Payne. 2014. "Economic Freedom and Income Inequality Revisited: Evidence from a Panel Error Correction Model." *Contemporary Economic Policy* 32, no. 1: 67–75.

Ashby, N. J., and R. S. Sobel. 2008. "Income Inequality and Economic Freedom in the U.S. States." *Public Choice* 134, nos. 3/4: 329–46.

Bailey, J. B., D. W. Thomas, and J. R. Anderson. 2018. "Regressive Effects of Regulation on Wages." *Public Choice* 180, nos. 1/2: 91–103.

Bennett, D. L., and B. Nikolaev. 2017. "On the Ambiguous Economic Freedom-Inequality Relationship." *Empirical Economics* 53: 717–54.

Bennett, D. L., and R. K. Vedder. 2013. "A Dynamic Analysis of Economic Freedom and Income Inequality in the 50 U.S. States: Empirical Evidence of a Parabolic Relationship." *Journal of Regional Analysis & Policy* 43, no. 1: 42–55.

Black, S. E., and P. E. Strahan. 2001. "The Division of Spoils: Rent-Sharing and Discrimination in a Regulated Industry." *American Economic Review* 91, no. 4: 814–31.

Carter, J. R. 2007. "An Empirical Note on Economic Freedom and Income Inequality." *Public Choice* 130, nos. 1/2: 163–77.

Clark, J. R., and R. A. Lawson. 2008. "The Impact of Economic Growth, Tax Policy and Economic Freedom on Income Inequality." *Journal of Private Enterprise* 24, no. 1: 23–31.

Kling, A. 2017. *The Three Languages of Politics: Talking across the Political Divides*. Washington, DC: Cato Institute.

Kuznets, S. 1955. "Economic Growth and Economic Inequality." *American Economic Review* 45: 1–28.

Lindsey, B., and S. M. Teles. 2017. *The Captured Economy: How the Powerful Enrich Themselves, Slow Down Growth, and Increase Inequality*. New York: Oxford University Press.

Lipford, J. W., and B. Yandle. 2015. "Determining Economic Freedom: Democracy, Political Competition, and the Wealth Preservation Process." *Journal of Private Enterprise* 30, no. 3: 1–18.

Luhby, T. 2016. "Obama Decries Income Inequality in Final State of the Union Address." *CNN Money*, January 12.

Mankiw, G. N. 2013. "Defending the One Percent." *Journal of Economic Perspectives* 27, no. 3: 21–34.

Mulholland, S. E. 2018. "Stratification by Regulation: Are Bootleggers and Baptists Biased?" *Public Choice* 180, nos. 1/2: 105–30.

Newport, F. 2015. "Americans Continue to Say U.S. Wealth Distribution Is Unfair." *Gallup*, May 4.

Obama, B. 2013. "President Obama on Inequality (transcript)." *Politico*, December 4.

Pew Research Center. 2014. "Most See Inequality Growing, but Partisans Differ over Solutions." January 23.

Piketty, T. 2013. *Capital in the Twenty-First Century*. Cambridge, MA: Belknap Press.

Piketty, T., and E. Saez. 2003. "Income Inequality in the United States, 1913–1998." *Quarterly Journal of Economics* 118, no. 1: 1–39.

Posner, R. A. 1974. "Theories of Economic Regulation." *Bell Journal of Economics and Management Science* 5, no. 2: 335–58.

Ruger, W. P., and J. Sorens. 2016. *Freedom in the 50 States*. Washington, DC: Cato Institute.

Scully, G. W. 2002. "Economic Freedom, Government Policy and the Trade-Off between Equity and Economic Growth." *Public Choice* 113: 77–96.

Stigler, G. J. 1971. "The Theory of Economic Regulation." *Bell Journal of Economics and Management Science* 2, no. 1: 3–21.

Strum, J. E., and J. De Hann. 2015. "Income Inequality, Capitalism and Ethno-Linguistic Fractionalization." *American Economic Review Papers and Proceedings* 105: 593–97.

Thomas, D. 2012. "Regressive Effects of Regulation." Mercatus Center Working Paper, 12–35.

Webster, A. L. 2013. "The Relationship between Economic Freedom and Income Equality in the United States." *International Business & Economics Research Journal* 12, no. 5: 469–75.

White House. 2015. "Occupational Licensing: A Framework for Policymakers." July. https://obamawhitehouse.archives.gov/sites/default/files/docs/licensing_report_final_nonembargo.pdf.

Wiseman, T. 2017. "Economic Freedom and Growth in the U.S. State-Level Market Incomes at the Top and Bottom." *Contemporary Economic Policy* 35, no. 1: 93–112.

Yandle, B. 1983. "Viewpoint: Bootleggers and Baptists: The Education of a Regulatory Economist." *Regulation* 7, no. 3: 12–15.

CHAPTER 9
Which Bootleggers? Which Baptists?

ANDREW P. MORRISS

With characteristic modesty, Bruce Yandle claimed only to have offered "a footnote to the rich Stigler-Peltzman special-interest theory of regulation" (Yandle 1999, 7). As a longtime writer of law review articles, and so something of a footnote aficionado, I can only wish to produce at least one such momentous footnote in my career.

Yandle's contribution is much more than a footnote to another theory; it offers a critical connection between public interest rhetoric and special interest rent-seeking. That connection means that inefficient regulatory policies do not depend on regulators being economically ignorant, but instead allows us to understand such choices based on the mix of arguments presented in favor of rent-seeking policies. It allows us to abandon the pretense that regulators are naïve Jimmy Stewarts in a regulatory *Mr. Smith Goes to Washington* drama, hoodwinked from time to time by unscrupulous special interests. Instead, it permits us to make the realistic assumption that "[g]iven the voting rules, regulators must balance the political demands they sense, thus serving at least some part of the public interest" (Yandle 1999, 7). Public interest arguments are useful for regulators but are not enough: "rhetoric matters a lot in the

Thanks to Jack Manhire for helping refine the framework at a crucial moment—without his input, I'd be wandering in the wilderness still—and to Roger Meiners for helpful comments. Sara Murdock provided superb research assistance. Bruce Yandle has been an inspiration, a model, a terrific coauthor, and a good friend. All errors remain mine.

world of politics but that neither well-varnished moral prompting nor unvarnished campaign contributions can do the job alone. It takes both" (Yandle 1999, 7). Particularly important is Yandle's insight that "[d]urable social regulation evolves when it is demanded by both of two distinctly different groups" (Yandle 1999, 5). Yandle's model enriches economic discourse both by allowing us to incorporate the role of the language of politics[1] and by offering a means to predict where regulatory bargains will be durable.[2]

In this paper, I build on Yandle's insights—by standing on his tall shoulders—in an attempt to extend his theory to explore *which* Baptists are likely to be of use to *which* bootleggers in achieving bootlegger policy goals. Determining which types of Baptists can aid which types of bootleggers will help in identifying potential future bootlegger and Baptist coalitions.

Yandle developed his Bootleggers and Baptists theory of regulation in the context of regulatory measures within the US economy, and provided an explanation of why regulators made seemingly irrational choices of high-cost regulations over more cost-efficient alternatives. His theory solved a central mystery of regulation: Why do regulators keep doing things in inefficient ways when economists could easily offer them more efficient ways to accomplish their stated goals? A key part of Yandle's explanation is the recognition that economists were framing the problem incorrectly. As Yandle put it, "instead of assuming that regulators really intended to minimize costs but somehow proceeded to make crazy mistakes, I began to assume that they were not trying to minimize costs at all—at least not the costs I had been concerned with. They were trying to minimize their costs, just as most sensible people do" (Yandle 1983, 13).

Once we shift our focus to the regulators' and the parties' costs, rather than the societal cost, we understand more about what affects the relevant costs. Changes on both the demand (technological change, demographic change, significant changes in factor costs, new information) and supply (bureaucratic incentives and structure, political oversight) sides affect the supply of regulation (Yandle 1983, 14–15). Yandle described the two groups' roles:

> "Baptists" point to the moral high ground and give vital and vocal endorsement of laudable public benefits promised by a desired regulation. Baptists flourish when their moral message forms a visible foundation for political action. "Bootleggers" are much less visible but no less vital. Bootleggers, who expect to profit from the very regulatory restrictions desired by Baptists, grease the political

> machinery with some of their expected proceeds. They are simply in it for the money. (Yandle 1999, 5)

Crucially, "it is the details of a regulation that usually win the endorsement of bootleggers, not just the broader principle that may matter most to Baptists" (Yandle 1999, 5). Bootleggers want a policy that allows them to profit despite the adoption of a Baptist-pleasing policy that the Baptists believe will promote ends antithetical to the bootleggers' interests. As Yandle notes, "bootleggers would not support restrictions on the Sunday consumption of alcoholic beverages, although Baptists might. Bootleggers want to limit competition, not intake" (Yandle 1999, 5). Baptists have a further role to play as well. Bootleggers must be able to "rely on Baptists to monitor enforcement of the restrictions that benefit bootleggers" (Yandle 1999, 5). This puts a limit on the degree to which the policies implemented can contradict the Baptists' godly aims as well as a limit on which Baptist-promoted policies are useful to bootleggers. On the one hand, if a Baptist-promoted policy is too obviously favorable to the bootleggers, the Baptists will abandon their support of the policy. On the other hand, if the Baptists' rhetoric does not support a policy with enough wiggle room to enable the bootleggers to achieve their goals, the rhetoric will be of no use (or even be counterproductive) for the bootleggers.

This leaves us with two questions. First, *which Baptists* will be more useful to bootleggers? Not all Baptist arguments help bootleggers, as Yandle's example of a "no alcohol consumption on Sunday" rule illustrates. Further, some Baptists will be better than others at pointing to the moral high ground, providing the vital and vocal endorsement, and monitoring enforcement. I argue below that there is a distinguishing characteristic that makes some Baptists better implicit allies for bootleggers than others, which I label how "fundamentalist" the arguments are. Second, *which bootleggers* are more likely to need the Baptists' help? Not all bootleggers are identical. Their interests match up to different degrees with Baptist rhetoric, and different bootlegger-favored policies are more or less likely to align well with Baptist rhetoric. I argue below that more opaque bootlegger policies are better matches with Baptist rhetoric than clearer ones.

WHICH BAPTISTS ARE MOST USEFUL TO BOOTLEGGERS?

Baptists advocate for "godly" policies—that is, they make arguments designed to achieve their desired ends—regardless of their arguments' utility to any bootleggers. Even where bootleggers are not interested in these Baptist-promoted policies as political cover, the Baptists still make their arguments—they are just less likely to succeed without tacit support from the bootleggers. Sometimes Baptists need bootleggers' help to carry the day, although when there has been a political "great awakening," moral arguments alone may carry the day.[3]

There might be some corrupt Baptists willing to accept payoffs to mask a bootlegger-favorable argument in pious terms, but that's a different role than Yandle originally identified. In Yandle, Rotondi, Dorchak, and my 2008 article on tobacco regulation, we labeled state attorneys general and plaintiffs' lawyers (who we contended played this role) as "regulatory televangelists" since their feigning of faith masked their worldly ambitions (winning higher office, wealth) (Yandle et al. 2008).

Crucially, formation of a bootleggers and Baptists coalition occurs when the *bootleggers* choose to clothe themselves in Baptist raiment in an effort to attain their policy goals. Because these are implicit coalitions, the Baptists choose second—their choice is whether or not to disown the policies being proposed to further their professed goals. Because bootlegger support for politicians is by definition not publicly displayed and is often signaled behind closed doors, the Baptists are handicapped in ferreting out when they are being used as cover.

There are costs for bootleggers in using Baptist rhetoric (the rhetoric might lead to an uncomfortable degree of success achieving the Baptists' goals or require compromises from preferred positions). Hence, we need to focus on when Baptists' arguments are useful to bootleggers and how bootleggers can conceal their sinful goals within something that appears to Baptists as consistent with the Baptists' pious goals. Further, as some Baptist arguments will be more effective at providing cover for bootleggers' goals than others, we need to discover what makes them useful. Moreover, bootleggers have alternatives to forming implicit coalitions with Baptists. For example, they can resort to straightforward bribery,[4] use campaign contributions without attempting to claim the moral high ground,[5] or engage in logrolling.[6] We therefore need a theory that explains when bootleggers choose implicit coalition with Baptists over these alternatives.

We can separate Baptists' arguments according to the degree of what can be labeled "theological" sophistication, which I array on a spectrum from "fundamentalist" to "theologian" arguments. A fundamentalist argument is clear and straightforward. In theological terms, interpreting the Commandment "Thou shalt not kill" as requiring each of us to not murder another human being is an example of the type of argument I am labeling as "fundamentalist." It fits nicely on a bumper sticker, it is short and to the point, and it leads to clear policy prescriptions ("no war"). A theologian argument is more complicated. Interpreting "Thou shalt not kill" as the basis for a just war theory that reads the Commandment in conjunction with other texts and in light of historical practices from sources outside scripture to allow killing others in certain circumstances would be a "theologian" argument.[7] "No war" is a better political slogan than "no war except for just wars, and this one is a just war for all these reasons. . . ."

Fundamentalist arguments are more politically valuable to bootleggers than theologian arguments. A fundamentalist argument can be easily incorporated into a pressure group's voting scorecard, condensed into a 30-second political ad or a bumper sticker, and so on. It provides ready political cover for supporting a proposed policy. By contrast, theologian arguments require extended discourse to explain their nuances, using "rich, highly inflected language" (Charles and Corey 2012). They do not provide the political benefits of a simple, straightforward position. For low-information voters (e.g., those who are neither directly affected by a particular policy nor political junkies who get consumption value from reading about policy debates), theologian arguments are mostly noise to be screened out (Somin 1998).[8] Baptist arguments are thus more useful to bootleggers when they are fundamentalist arguments than when they are theologian arguments.

Examples of fundamentalist arguments include "save the bald eagle," "reduce oil imports," and "ban TV ads for tobacco products." These are clear, unambiguous propositions that flow directly from the relevant "theology": preserving biodiversity is good, depending on foreign energy producers is bad, and smoking is dangerous. By contrast, theologian arguments in these same policy spaces include "regulatory requirements aimed at species preservation need to consider the incentives they create for landowners to preserve habitat" (Morriss and Stroup 2000, 769), and "oil imported from Canada and Mexico is as secure as domestically produced oil and so should be treated by regulations as if it were domestically produced" (Morriss and Stewart 2006, 939), and "smokers switching from cigarettes to e-cigarettes or oral tobacco products is better than continuing to use cigarettes and so we should encourage substitution of less harmful forms of tobacco use" (Adler et al. 2016, 335–36). These are summarized in table 9.1. These theologian examples flow from the same underlying theological principles ("preservation of biodiversity," "enhancing energy security," and "smoking is dangerous") but are more complicated and harder to encapsulate in a slogan or sound bite. Theologian arguments are of less use to bootleggers in regulatory policy debates because fewer people understand them. Except with voters who are willing to invest in learning sophisticated policy analyses (and public choice analysis teaches us these tend to be those directly and significantly affected by the policy and so are likely to be bootleggers,

Table 9.1. Fundamentalist vs. Theologian Policies

Fundamentalist	Underlying Principle	Theologian
Save the bald eagle	Preservation of biodiversity	Regulatory requirements aimed at species preservation need to consider the incentives they create for landowners to preserve habitat.
Reduce oil imports	Enhancing energy security	Oil imported from Canada and Mexico is as secure as domestically produced oil and so should be treated by regulations as if it were domestically produced.
Ban TV ads of tobacco products	Smoking is dangerous	Smokers switching from cigarettes to e-cigarettes or oral tobacco products is better than continuing to use cigarettes, and so we should encourage substitution of less harmful forms of tobacco use.

professors, or policy wonks), these arguments are unlikely to buy much political support (Achen and Bartels 2017). As a result, when bootleggers are deciding whether or not to use an implicit coalition with Baptists in seeking a policy goal, they will be more likely to do so when the Baptists are making more fundamentalist arguments than when they are making more theologian arguments.

Consider the case of policies concerning e-cigarettes. The Baptists are the anti-tobacco groups that focus on public health arguments against tobacco (Adler et al. 2016, 344–47). The bootleggers are the cigarette companies, which found e-cigarettes to be unwelcome competition for their products, particularly because e-cigarettes were new competitors not burdened by the cost-increasing provisions of the Master Settlement Agreement that ended the state attorneys general litigation against the cigarette companies (Adler et al. 2016, 348). The cigarette companies supported efforts by anti-tobacco groups to impose regulatory constraints on competition via e-cigarettes from non-cigarette companies (Adler et al. 2016, 348–49). The arguments advanced by the anti-tobacco groups were "fundamentalist" ones: tobacco in any form is bad, smoking in any form is bad, and nicotine in any form is bad. (The counterargument is much more theologian in character: encouraging a less harmful form of nicotine consumption is a step in the right direction.) The tobacco bootleggers found the anti-tobacco Baptists useful in efforts to restrict competitors' e-cigarettes through regulation (Adler et al. 2016, 348).

Theologian arguments are less useful to bootleggers for two reasons. First, as noted, they are harder to convey. If the goal is to mobilize support outside of the community directly and significantly affected by a policy, the argument cannot be difficult to understand because those not directly affected are less likely to invest in figuring out a nuanced argument.[9] In some instances, this means bootleggers seek to use other methods (campaign contributions) to secure their goals. For example, in the classic public choice example of sugar tariffs and subsidies for the domestic sugar industry in the United States, consumers suffer an average annual loss of $2.4 billion, while US sugar producers reap $1.4 billion annually in benefits (Wohlgenant 2011, 2). As noted above, US sugar producers do not rely on Baptist arguments to gain their rents ("Eat American sugar" does not have much of a ring to it), they use old-fashioned lobbying and campaign contributions. Similarly, as noted previously, agricultural price support programs have traditionally rested on an alliance between rural and urban members of Congress, with rural members supporting nutrition programs that primarily serve urban members' constituents in return for their supporting the agriculture programs that primarily benefit rural members' constituents.[10] Old-fashioned political horse-trading and campaign contributions undergird the rent-creation of the agricultural subsidy programs.

Second, bootleggers need flexibility in crafting policy responses, so their interests are furthered by the resulting laws and regulations. It is easier to fit policies that serve their interests under the umbrella of a broad principle than into a more narrowly focused claim. For example, the mandate for oxygenating gasoline that underlies the US corn-based ethanol industry resulted in a complex policy environment in which the bootleggers were able to create significant rents. This required not only a mandate for oxygenating gasoline but also an effective mandate to do so in part with ethanol made from US corn (Adler 1992, 1996; Smith 2007). That this is wildly inefficient and likely counterproductive in achieving environmental goals is now broadly accepted (US Environmental Protection Agency 2012). Even if ethanol was the best choice for an additive (which is unlikely), corn-based ethanol is more environmentally damaging, has worse impacts on food prices, and is more expensive than sugar cane–based ethanol (Smith 2007, 3–4). But because a general ethanol requirement would benefit Brazilian sugar cane farmers and ethanol producers rather than US corn farmers and ethanol producers, the more efficient alternative had to be blocked and the less efficient domestic ethanol requirement imposed. Fortunately for the bootleggers, if not for food consumers, the Brazilian ethanol industry, or the environment, fundamentalist Baptist rhetoric about clean air allowed for development of a policy that created the rents the bootleggers sought.

WHICH BOOTLEGGER POLICIES CAN FIT WITHIN BAPTIST RHETORIC?

Bootleggers seek policies that advance their goals. The policies do so by including features that advance bootlegger interests but do not deter the Baptists from supporting the policy. These can span a wide range of provisions. As Yandle explained, "Things such as technology or specification standards, differential requirements for new and old sources, grandfather clauses, and procedures for new-source performance review are clues that bootleggers and Baptists are at work. Sometimes, though, a simple output restriction marks a B&B success story" (Yandle 1999, 6). What is important is that not every policy sought by bootleggers can fit within Baptist rhetoric, and so sometimes bootleggers have to resort to other tactics to obtain their preferred polices (as discussed earlier). In particular, straightforward creation of rents for bootleggers are harder to conceal beneath the cover of Baptist rhetoric. Furthermore, bootleggers have to live with the policies they gain under the cover of the Baptists' slogans, and so they are not interested in helping create policies that effectively thwart their more worldly goals. For example, while Baptists might be willing to advocate for total prohibition of alcohol and lengthy prison terms for those found in possession of alcohol, few bootleggers would support such policies if there was any chance they would be efficiently enforced.[11] Bootleggers thus need policies that provide sufficient regulatory space to achieve their goals.

Because bootleggers' policy goals are different from, and often antithetical to, the Baptists' policy goals, which are at least nominally embedded in the regulatory regime resulting from a bootleggers and Baptists coalition, the bootleggers need some degree of "nuance" in the policy's implementation within which to obtain desired outcomes while not driving the Baptists to denounce the policy. A policy with multiple dimensions, allowing for complicated rules that can incorporate special interest exemptions, technical details that can favor particular interests, and so on, can be a useful part of creating the opportunity for a bootleggers and Baptists coalition. So too are policies that block future competitors even if they raise incumbents' costs. Complexity is one way to make policy objectives opaque to public scrutiny. Another is for the policy's bootlegger-friendly impact to be unclear to low-information voters and Baptists alike, so they miss the connection. Bootleggers must avoid clear policies around which they would have difficulty navigating. For example, an effectively enforced complete ban on alcohol possession would be less conducive to bootleggers' interests than would a ban on Sunday sales, since under the latter bootleggers' customers would not need to worry about concealing their purchases but only conducting the purchase without attracting law enforcement attention. The opaqueness of the policy and its impacts thus influences the suitability of the policy for a bootleggers and Baptists coalition.

Compare the requirement for environmental impact statements (EIS) created by the National Environmental Policy Act (NEPA), the Clean Air Act Amendments of 1970 and 1977, and the Federal Water Pollution Control Act Amendments of 1972. NEPA is an example of a simple, clear policy goal: government policymakers will make better decisions if they have better information on the environmental impact of their decisions. The statute's requirements flow directly from this: decision makers are required to produce a comprehensive analysis of the policy's impact. These requirements dictate straightforward actions (every government agency must complete an EIS for significant actions), which are difficult for bootleggers to manipulate. We would therefore not expect a statute such as NEPA to be the result of a bootleggers and Baptists coalition, but rather a response to Baptist arguments alone. NEPA was just that; it came from the environmental "great awakening" in the late 1960s and early 1970s that produced strong political demand for Baptist measures, which passed without the need for bootlegger support.[12] In contrast, the more complex Clean Air Act Amendments of 1970 and 1977 and the Federal Water Pollution Control Act Amendments of 1972 married complex regulatory structures to fundamentalist Baptist arguments to produce an opaque policy environment. These statutes' length alone (respectively, 37,[13] 110,[14] and 87[15] pages in their printed form in Statutes at Large) suggests their opacity—few people not directly involved in drafting them would be familiar with their details. Even their drafters may not have understood their full impacts.[16] Environmentalists' (the Baptists) support for these statutes was fundamentalist: a vote for them was a vote for clean air or water, a vote against was a vote for polluters.

To see how opacity works in bootleggers' favor, consider the Clean Air Act's mobile source regulatory framework. In brief, since 1970, EPA must set multiple national ambient air quality standards (NAAQs) for certain pollutants and also determine emissions standards for automobiles, trucks, and other mobile sources that it believes will result in reaching the air quality levels in the various NAAQs (in concert with restrictions on stationary sources) (Morriss 2000, 285–87). The Baptist argument for federal mobile source regulation in 1970 was fundamentalist: emissions from cars and trucks damaged the environment and had to be controlled (Morriss 2000, 282–83). Because cars and trucks were mobile and so crossed state lines, they argued that this was best done by the federal government (Morriss, Yandle, and Dorchak 2004, 212–14).

The bootleggers' (car and truck manufacturers) goal was subtle. The bootleggers understood that regulation was inevitable: the environment had become a major political issue.[17] Moreover, President Richard Nixon saw Senator Edmund Muskie as a key rival in the upcoming 1972 presidential election; because Muskie positioned himself as a champion of environmental causes, Nixon was eager to undercut his claim (Morriss 2000, 283–84). The Nixon administration also had a keen appreciation for the value of threats of regulation in inducing campaign contributions (McGarity and Shapiro 1993). The vehicle manufacturers feared a series of inconsistent state regulations of automobiles and trucks that would lead to significantly higher regulatory costs (Morriss, Yandle, and Dorchak 2004, 412–15). They preferred national regulation—done from Washington, DC, where the US manufacturers had lobbyists and influence—to 50 potentially different state regulatory regimes created by regulators in 50 different jurisdictions, where the industry lacked as much lobbying infrastructure or influence (Morriss, Yandle, and Dorchak 2004, 412–15). The resulting compromise (national regulation with provision for California to have stricter requirements, which other states could opt to adopt as well) served their interests (Morriss 2000, 290). Their confidence that this was a good move was borne out in the series of postponements of various Clean Air Act requirements they obtained in the 1970s (disadvantaging Japanese automakers that had rushed to comply with new environmental standards on time) (Morriss 2000, 292–93).

But bootleggers do not need just a moral slogan to support their regulatory ends. They need sufficient leeway in the policy implemented to enable them to achieve their goals while allowing policy supporters to claim they are supporting it for Baptist reasons. Remember, because the bootleggers lack the high moral purpose of the Baptists, they often cannot openly advocate for their position—an Aid to the Bootleggers Act would likely draw little open political support.[18] Moreover, many Baptist-endorsed policies would prevent bootleggers from accomplishing their policy goals. For example, an effective blanket ban on all liquor would put bootleggers out of business. They need a less-effective-in-practice ban whose exceptions or work-arounds benefit them over competitors. Shutting down legitimate liquor stores on Sundays in Yandle's original example helps the literal bootleggers selling out of their car or backwoods still, particularly if they can persuade local law enforcement to turn a blind eye to the sales. Importantly, their customers are not at risk for possessing the alcohol the bootleggers sell to them, as they would be under a "no consumption on Sunday" rule.

Of course, special interests can sometimes win with a clear policy with no moral high ground in sight, as the US sugar producers have done. Bootleggers are more than just any special interest group—they are interest groups that benefit from regulatory policies that permit them to accomplish something indirectly that could not be accomplished directly. As Yandle described it:

> what do industry and labor want from the regulators? They want protection from competition, from technological change, and from losses that threaten profits and jobs. A carefully constructed regulation can accomplish all kinds of anticompetitive goals of this sort, while giving the citizenry the impression that the only goal is to serve the public interest. (Yandle 1983, 13)

Bootleggers thus are most interested in policies that can be "carefully constructed" to "accomplish . . . anticompetitive goals," not rules that express policy goals antithetical to their interests without providing the regulatory space to subvert those goals.[19] At the same time, bootleggers cannot be too blatant in their exploitation of their Baptist coalition partners. If the Baptists realize they are being used for cover, they may disown the deal the bootleggers constructed. For example, some environmentalists have disowned the corn-based ethanol mandate (Wolfgang 2018). Opaque policies are thus more likely to be served by a bootleggers and Baptists coalition.

WHERE BOOTLEGGER AND BAPTIST COALITIONS APPEAR

Combining the above analyses of bootleggers' preferences and Baptists' utility to bootleggers, Baptists are of the greatest use to the bootleggers in providing political support through fundamentalist arguments for opaque regulatory solutions that allow bootleggers room to maneuver while not exposing their efforts to sufficient scrutiny to reveal the conflict between Baptist rhetoric and bootlegger-friendly policy details. This is where an implicit coalition with Baptists is of the greatest utility to a group of bootleggers. Complex policy arguments, the sort where it takes a theologian to work out the preferred policy outcome for an interest group, offer chances for logrolling and backroom deals that obviate the need for Baptists' arguments. Clear policies do not allow for bootleggers and Baptists coalitions because their outcomes do not allow for the bootleggers to win substantively while leaving the Baptists believing that they have prevailed. Where opaque policies overlap with fundamentalist moral arguments is the sweet spot for a bootleggers and Baptists coalition.

The 1977 Clean Air Act Amendments' mandate of scrubber technology for coal-fired power plants is a classic example of bootlegger rent-seeking that benefited from Baptist rhetoric.[20] As Ackerman and Hassler explain in their account *Clean Coal/Dirty Air*, environmentalists sought a mandate for universal scrubber use by coal-fired power plants, rather than a policy that matched technological demands to emissions levels, because the scrubber mandates advanced their goal of tightening emissions controls on emissions from new sources (Ackerman and Hassler 1981, 29–33). Eastern coal interests, whose "dirty" coal was high in sulfur, broke with their prior allies, the coal-fired utilities who were their customers, and joined with environmentalists to support this policy. Western coal interests, whose "clean" coal was low in sulfur, and could be burned without the use of scrubbers, opposed the scrubber requirement, focusing instead on emissions levels. The eastern coal interests (mine owners and unions representing eastern coal workers) supported the scrubber policy because it shifted the cost of compliance with clean air regulations away from them and onto the utilities (Ackerman and Hassler 1981, 119–20). Environmentalists embraced the policy because it "promised additional protection to pristine areas in the West" by adding scrubbers to any power plants there even if they could meet the required emissions levels without the use of scrubbers (Ackerman and Hassler 1981, 59). Although Ackerman and Hassler described the result as "a fragile coalition" that was the result of the "peculiar conditions" existing in 1976 and 1977 when the amendments were adopted, the coalition achieved a durable regulatory bargain that aided the bootleggers and was blessed by the Baptists' advocacy (Ackerman and Hassler 1981, 116).

Opaque regulations often create barriers to entry for new firms or have differential impacts across firms within an industry. Where there are differences in impacts, there is potential for a bootleggers and Baptists coalition. For example, Maloney and McCormick found such effects using event studies of stock prices in OSHA's cotton dust regulations' impact on textile firms (which had smaller impacts on firms using lower proportions of cotton) and EPA's prevention of significant deterioration (PSD) regulations' impacts on copper, lead, and zinc smelters (which blocked new entrants) (Maloney and McCormick 1982). Although they did not explore whether or not the ultimate winners engaged in behind-the-scenes advocacy for the policies, their results indicate the potential for such gains and show where we should hunt for bootleggers and Baptists coalitions.

CONCLUSION

Using examples from domestic regulatory policy, this chapter offers an extension to Yandle's Bootleggers and Baptists theory. It showed when such coalitions are more likely to arise by detailing the types of Baptist "theology" most suitable to bootlegger ends and the type of bootlegger ends most suited to concealment within a Baptist argument.

As Yandle concluded, "Political action, which by definition always serves some interest groups, requires politicians to appeal to popular icons. By making a 'Baptist' appeal, the canny politician enables voters to feel better by endorsing socially accepted values in the voting booth. The same politician, if he is adroit, also can enjoy the support of appreciative bootleggers in the costly struggle to hold office. Bootleggers and Baptists are part of the glue that binds the body politic" (Yandle 1999, 7). Identifying when bootleggers and Baptists coalitions are likely to arise is an important step toward blocking their influence on regulatory policy.

NOTES

1. In some respects, Yandle's approach echoes Deirdre McCloskey's argument that choices about the language used to debate policies shapes outcomes in important ways. See McCloskey (1983). Also see Morriss and Meiners (2020).
2. Posner and Landes argue for the importance of an independent judiciary to ensure regulatory bargains are kept. See Landes and Posner (1975). Yandle's Baptists play a complementary role, sometimes through political pressure and sometimes by providing potential plaintiffs for lawsuits alleging breaches of the bargain.
3. For example, see US Environmental Protection Agency (2012).
4. ABSCAM is one of the more prominent, documented cases of outright bribery of members of Congress. See Greene (2013).
5. For example, US sugar producers provide campaign contributions to maintain barriers to sugar imports. There is no real moral high ground argument in favor of a blatantly protectionist barrier to trade that harms consumers. See Grabow (2018). Note that price stability is the primary justification, and that "[w]hile there is little doubt that price smoothing and reduced uncertainty are beneficial to sugar farmers and processors, it is much less clear why its pursuit is in the public interest, or why government resources should be committed to such a goal." As Senator Russell Long noted in 1971, "the distinction between a campaign contribution and a bribe is almost a hairline's difference. You can hardly tell one from the other" (Kaiser 2013).
6. The classic example is the alliance between urban and rural interests to swap support for food stamps and agricultural price supports. See Ferejohn (1986).
7. For example, see Charles and Corey (2012). "The just war tradition is the only framework that offers a rich, highly inflected language, a storehouse of categories, concepts, and commonplaces developed over centuries of reflection, in which moral particulars of war can be examined."
8. Somin (1998) describes the impact of voter ignorance on political discourse.
9. Those on whom a policy has a large impact are motivated by self-interest to understand the arguments for and against it, while those on whom a policy has only a small impact are not. See Wilson (1980).

10. P.L. 91-604, 84 Stat. 1676–1713 (December 31, 1970).

11. Bootleggers like Al Capone may have flourished in the United States during Prohibition, but we don't observe many Capones operating in Saudi Arabia or Iran, where alcohol prohibitions are more rigorously enforced than they were in Chicago in the 1920s.

12. See 42 U.S.C. §4321 and Bear (1995). As evidence of NEPA's origins within Baptist rhetoric, see Lazarus (2012, 1514): "Much of NEPA's greatness is reflected in the soaring rhetoric found in its first section, extolling the nation to move in bold new directions."

13. P.L. 91-604, 84 Stat. 1676–1713 (December 31, 1970).

14. P.L. 95-95, 91 Stat. 685–795 (August 7, 1977).

15. P.L. 92-500, 86 Stat. 816–903 (October 18, 1972).

16. P.L. 95-190, 91 Stat. 1399 (1977). Also see Morriss (2000).

17. Indeed, the idea of banning internal combustion engines was promoted by some environmentalists. See Mokhiber and Weissman (2000), noting the effort by California legislators to outlaw the internal combustion engine. See also Morriss (2000, 298), quoting a congressman that the internal combustion engine was the "most serious and dangerous source of air pollution in the Nation today."

18. This is why even the most blatant rent-seeking legislation must be wrapped in nontransparent packaging. For example, the Sonny Bono Copyright Term Extension Act of 1998 extended existing copyrights, an action difficult to justify under copyright's rationale of incentivizing the creation of new works. Opponents termed it the "Mickey Mouse Protection Act" in honor of the windfall it created for the Walt Disney Company by extending the copyright for Mickey Mouse. For example, see Lessig (2001). The arguments for the act focused on creating incentives for digitization of nondigital works and "maintaining a positive trade surplus by harmonizing the copyright term with the terms of European countries" (Liu 2002).

19. Richard Epstein argued for simple rules precisely to prevent the sort of rent-seeking bootleggers do, in *Simple Rules for a Complex World* (1995).

20. Yandle uses the scrubber mandate as an example of a capture theory of regulation rather than a bootleggers and Baptists coalition in a 2010 article (Yandle 2010). While I usually find that Bruce is right where we see things differently and so hesitate to disagree with him in print, I think his 2010 account understates the importance of the environmentalists in promoting the scrubber mandate. Given the closeness of the key roll call Senate vote on the requirement (45–44) just after Senator Howard Metzenbaum (D-OH) argued for the provision in the face of Senator Edmund Muskie's (D-ME) opposition by invoking the support for the amendment of "such prestigious groups who have concern with the whole question of clean air as the National Clean Air Coalition, the Environmental Policy Center, and the Sierra Club," I think the moral high ground from the environmentalists was critical to the policy's adoption. Ackerman and Hassler reach a similar conclusion: "Note the artful way Metzenbaum parried the concerns of Muskie, the principal architect of environmental legislation drafted in the past two decades. Rather than concede an assault on the integrity of the Clean Air Act, he beckoned his comrades to join hands with the National Clean Air Coalition in support of the fears of the United Mine Workers" (Ackerman and Hassler 1981).

REFERENCES

Achen, C. H., and L. M. Bartels. 2017. *Democracy for Realists: Why Elections Do Not Produce Responsive Government*, vol. 4. Princeton, NJ: Princeton University Press.

Ackerman, B., and W. T. Hassler. 1981. *Clean Coal/Dirty Air: Or How the Clean Air Act Became a Multibillion-Dollar Bail-Out for High-Sulfur Coal Producers.* New Haven, CT: Yale University Press.

Adler, J. H. 1992. "Clean Fuels, Dirty Air: How a (Bad) Bill Became Law." *Public Interest* 108: 116–32.

——. 1996. "Rent Seeking behind the Green Curtain." *Regulation* 19: 26–31.

Adler, J. H., R. E. Meiners, A. P. Morriss, and B. Yandle. 2016. "Baptists, Bootleggers and Electronic Cigarettes." *Yale Journal on Regulation* 33: 313–61.

Bear, D. 1995. "The National Environmental Policy Act: Its Origins and Evolutions." *Natural Resources & Environment* 10, no. 2: 3–73.

Charles, J. D., and D. D. Corey. 2012. *The Just War Tradition: An Introduction*. New York: Open Road Media.

Epstein, R. A. 1995. *Simple Rules for a Complex World*. Cambridge, MA: Harvard University Press.

Ferejohn, J. 1986. "Logrolling in an Institutional Context: A Case Study of Food Stamp Legislation." In *Congress and Policy Change*, edited by G. Wright, L. N. Rieselback, and L. C. Dodd, 224–25. New York: Agathon.

Grabow, C. 2018. "Candy-Coated Cartel: Time to Kill the U.S. Sugar Program." *Cato Institute Policy Analysis* 837.

Greene, R. W. 2013. *The Sting Man: Inside ABSCAM*. London: Penguin.

Kaiser, R. G. 2013. *Act of Congress: How America's Essential Institution Works, and How It Doesn't*. New York: Knopf.

Landes, W. M., and R. A. Posner. 1975. "The Independent Judiciary in an Interest-Group Perspective." *Journal of Law & Economics* 18, no. 3: 875–901.

Lazarus, R. 2012. "The National Environmental Policy Act in the US Supreme Court: A Reappraisal and a Peek behind the Curtains." *Georgetown Law Journal* 100, no. 5: 1507–87.

Lessig, L. 2001. "Copyright's First Amendment." *UCLA Law Review* 48: 1057–73.

Liu, J. P. 2002. "Copyright and Time: A Proposal." *Michigan Law Review* 101: 409–19.

Maloney, M. T., and R. E. McCormick. 1982. "A Positive Theory of Environmental Quality Regulation." *Journal of Law & Economics* 25, no. 1: 99–123.

McCloskey, D. N. 1983. "The Rhetoric of Economics." *Journal of Economic Literature* 21, no. 2: 481–517.

McGarity, T. O., and S. A. Shapiro. 1993. *Workers at Risk: The Failed Promise of the Occupational Safety and Health Administration*. Westport, CT: Praeger.

Mokhiber, R., and R. Weissman. 2000. "Conspiracy of Polluters." *Mother Jones*, July 28.

Morriss, A. P. 2000. "The Politics of the Clean Air Act." In *Political Environmentalism: Going Behind the Green Curtain*, edited by T. L. Anderson, 263–95. Stanford, CA: Hoover Institution Press.

Morriss, A. P., and R. E. Meiners. 2020. "The Language We Speak: Addressing Property Rights and Natural Resources Problem." Working Paper.

Morriss, A. P., and N. Stewart. 2006. "Market Fragmenting Regulation: Why Gasoline Costs So Much (And Why It's Going to Cost More)." *Illinois Public Law Research Paper* 06-11. http://ssrn.com/abstract=928503.

Morriss, A. P., and R. L. Stroup. 2000. "Quartering Species: The Living Constitution, the Third Amendment, and the Endangered Species Act." *Environmental. Law* 30: 769–809.

Morriss, A. P., B. Yandle, and A. Dorchak. 2004. "Regulating by Litigation: The EPA's Regulation of Heavy-Duty Diesel Engines." *Administrative Law Review* 56: 403–15.

Smith, F. B. 2007. "Corn-Based Ethanol: A Case Study in the Law of Unintended Consequences." Competitive Enterprise Institute, June.

Somin, I. 1998. "Voter Ignorance and the Democratic Ideal." *Critical Review* 12, no. 4: 413–58.

US Environmental Protection Agency and National Center for Environmental Assessment. 2012. *Biofuels and the Environment: First Triennial Report to Congress*. Washington, DC: Government Printing Office.

Wilson, J. Q. 1980. *The Politics of Regulation*. New York: Basic Books.

Wohlgenant, M. K. 2011. *Sweets for the Sweet: The Costly Benefits of the US Sugar Program*. Washington, DC: American Enterprise Institute.

Wolfgang, B. 2018. "Environmental Groups Back Ted Cruz, Republicans on Overhaul of the Renewable Fuel Standard." *Washington Times*, March 15. https://www.washingtontimes.com/news/2018/mar/15/renewable-fuel-standard-promoting-ethanol-shunned-/.

Yandle, B. 1983. "Bootleggers and Baptists: The Education of a Regulatory Economist." *Regulation* 7, no. 3: 12–15.

——. 1999. "Bootleggers and Baptists in Retrospect." *Regulation* 22, no. 3: 5–7.

——. 2010. "Bootleggers and Baptists in the Theory of Regulation." *Jerusalem Papers in Regulation and Governance*, Working Paper no. 9, May.

Yandle, B., J. Rotondi, A. P. Morriss, and A. Dorchak. 2008. "Bootleggers, Baptists and Televangelists: Regulating Tobacco by Litigation." *University of Illinois Law Review* 4: 1225–85.

CHAPTER 10

Bootleggers and Baptists Reconsidered

With Application to ACA and ACOs

ADAM C. SMITH

The theory of Bootleggers and Baptists is nearly as old as Adam Smith. I was born a few months before my grandfather's article appeared in Cato's *Regulation*. It is hard for me to think of politics without this perspective. Using public choice terminology, the theory stipulates that special interest groups attempting to rent-seek face the problem of packaging their desired outcome in a politically palatable manner. Yandle (1983, 1999) presents examples of "bootleggers" and "Baptists." The bootlegger is a special interest seeking to curry favor with political bodies to gain greater profits through desirable legislation. Baptists represent the moral component that may help convince decision makers that desired policies arise from a common value such as charity, morality, protection of the environment, or what might be broadly thought of as serving the public interest.

Legislative favors to private interests will be scrutinized, so a broader appeal to voters will help secure support. Self-interest legislation cloaked in moral clothing sells better. But what is it that creates benefits that are recognizable to the polity? What form does this output take? Consider the Affordable Care Act (ACA, aka Obamacare). It is hailed by many as a landmark achievement that serves the public interest. It was designed to deliver billions of dollars in revenue to private interest groups. The mandate that all Americans must have health insurance was construed at the time as a public benefit.[1] That is, requiring taxpayers to buy private health insurance was advertised as a public benefit. Why would (some) voters accept these legislative outcomes as beneficial to the public when private interests were the primary beneficiaries?

Yandle's theory provides context for this complex set of political interactions. Bootleggers (special interests) may benefit, but appeal to Baptist (moral) sentiment is crucial in persuading voters and their legislative representatives. Elected officials may have to explain votes to the folks back home, and none want to say "I did it so insurance companies and hospitals can make more money." Accordingly, the Obama administration touted health care as "not a privilege for the fortunate few, it is a right" (Wilson and Wiggins 2015). The additional benefits of broader insurance coverage would be offset by "bending the cost curve down" to reduce prices to consumers (*Economist* 2010a). Hence, the promise to bootleggers of new customers was balanced by an appeal to Baptist sentiment of greater coverage and reduced costs to make the overall package "morally desirable" (*Economist* 2010b).

With diverse support, the ACA enabled the federal government to gain control over how certain health services are provided. One particular delivery model, championed by ACA and the Department of Human and Health Services, accountable care organizations (ACOs), groups healthcare providers together so consumers are offered a bundle of services at a certain premium, as opposed to paying for services independently. While the structure was touted as reducing costs, its rollout under the ACA meant the appropriate incentives to balance cost and choice would not be in place, as market signals are manipulated by government agencies.

The ACO model fostered a cartelization of the industry by entangling the relationship between providers and insurers under bureaucratic management. This cartelization via the ACO model also increases market power for firms able to manipulate access to the network such as local hospitals. Hospitals account for about a third of total healthcare costs ($1.1 trillion in 2016) (US Center for Medicaid and Medicare Services 2017). *The Economist* reports the industry is rife with rent-seeking, with "health-care firms making excess profits of $65 billion a year" (*Economist* 2018). While the overall impact of the ACO model on consumer prices is difficult to discern, evidence indicates that cost reduction has not been encountered under the ACO model as advertised by promoters of the law (see Burns and Pauly 2018). This has encouraged greater regulation, further entangling market and government entities to the detriment of the consumer. This is an outcome predictable from the Bootleggers and Baptists theory.

Baptist groups seek direct control over political outcomes. Those representing moral interests want to influence legislation to address concerns of their stakeholders. Bootleggers, the industry interests, seek control over the market process itself. The direct legislative outcome may be of less interest than the amended process that emerges as a result.

Richard Wagner (2016) describes this process as the "peculiar business of politics," because the residual claimants of political economic activity cannot directly convert certain investments, such as lobbying, into economic profit. This interaction must be rendered through the legislative process. What emerges is not the effective allocation of scarce resources but the rearrangement of resources according to political agreements. The cartelization of health care under the ACA is a political outcome favored by Baptist crusaders intent on broadening healthcare coverage. But the new market process has less to do with those goals than the resourcefulness of the bootlegger firms dealing with the unavoidable political entanglement.

This paper uses the creation of government ACOs as a case study to expand upon Yandle's Bootleggers and Baptists theory. It first entails positioning the Baptist component itself as a "peculiar" transaction cost unique to the political process. Yandle's theory demonstrates how the observation that groups want political favors can be a starting point to the complexity our political structure imposes upon seekers of rents.

MIND READING, PUBLIC INTEREST, AND SOCIAL REGULATION

The theory of Bootleggers and Baptists is possibly the most southern-inspired contribution to public choice theory, next to James Buchanan's Samaritan's Dilemma (see Buchanan 1975). Like that theory, Yandle's argument balances the interest we have in others and that we have in ourselves. Each owes a lot to Adam Smith. Here I mean my namesake and author of *The Theory of Moral Sentiments* ([1759] 1982), where Smith outlined how the mind can conceive of itself in social relation to the actions of others. That is to say, in examining the actions of others, we may determine whether they are self-serving or not. Smith wisely recognized this as a gift of nature of the highest order. By being able to place the actions of others within a social context (to determine if the action is self-serving or not), the person can properly calibrate their own choices in a way that anticipates the likely responses of others.[2]

This positioning of the choices of others within a moral matrix converts us into what Nobel laureate Vernon Smith describes as "mind readers" (Hoffman, McCabe, and Smith 1998, 347). That is, humans are in a unique position to infer the intentions of others simply by observing their behavior. This invites cooperation even where incentives would otherwise motivate conflict. As Hoffman and colleagues explain, "a considerable body of research in experimental economics now identifies a number of environmental and institutional factors that promote cooperation even in the face of contrary individual incentives" (Hoffman, McCabe, and Smith 1998, 335–36). People are especially proficient at signaling cooperation when ongoing interactions are allowed.[3] Vernon Smith's experimental work demonstrates how subjects appreciate laboratory choices in ways that economists find difficult to provide game-theoretic context for (see Smith 2003).

Societies built around relationships of trust and reciprocity flourish when conflict is minimized. Government invariably involves itself by organizing this underlying need to appeal to the public interest. Whether government is necessary to organize society's relationships is beside the point.[4] The more relevant matter is how political authority is construed—that is, the form it takes before the polity. As Mulholland explains in "Moralists, Moonshiners, and Monitors" (chapter 6 of this volume), "Not only does the theory suggest whether a proposed rule is likely to become law; it also explains why particular types of regulations are enacted, when they are enacted, and the form they take. The reason: because every detail of the rule will affect special interests in different ways."

Baptists represent in this framing a transaction cost that must be undertaken if groups want to meet with political success. Michael Polanyi (1958, 212) offers his own take on this process within the context of group rituals:

> Since the passions expressed in a ritual affirm the value of group life, they declare that the group has a claim to the conformity of its members, and that the interests of group life may legitimately rival and sometimes overrule those of the individual. This acknowledges a common good for the sake of which deviation may be suppressed and individuals be required to make sacrifices for defending the group against subversion and destruction from the outside.

This observation fits remarkably well within the Bootleggers and Baptists framework. It is not that we simply want to see moral renderings of political action; it is that these must demonstrate genuine value to the public interest. Failure to do so invites inquiry that would reveal the deleterious effects of anti-group behavior such as cronyism.

Rituals of public sacrifice abound in the modern world. Glaeser and Shleifer (2001) argue that nonprofits offer entrepreneurs a credible commitment to not exploit donor gifts in the form of profit retention. This arrangement, the authors claim, is only suitable for transactions where donors want to invest substantial resources without dealing with the monitoring costs of ensuring these resources are not misused. This is not to say that nonprofit entrepreneurs are avoiding monetary returns, only that the form of entrepreneurship (e.g., profit vs. nonprofit) substantively reduces the available options for these returns. Hence, the appeal to nonprofit status can be seen as a form of genuine sacrifice to gain donors who would otherwise avoid these interactions.

Obtaining favorable legislation is similar in this respect in that groups need to credibly demonstrate public benefits. In this way, an effective Baptist serves not simply as flashy cover for political manipulation but as a genuine demonstration of sacrifice on behalf of those who would use the government to serve their purposes. Lobbying without this moral cover can be dangerous to special interest groups. Cases like Solyndra[5] illustrate how angry voters become when alerted to corporate influence within the political process. This public backlash can in turn negatively impact economic returns to the affected industry (National Public Radio 2012). This does not mean that business has no prospects for entering into lucrative transactions with government, only that these transactions are more acceptable when they demonstrate value to the public interest.

The Chicago school model is that economic gains are competed away by special interests through an efficient rent-seeking process (see Becker 1983, 1985). Appeal to the public interest is only possible from this perspective when these interests are organized to oppose legislation (see Peltzman 1976). Here the political outcome and subsequent new market process are collapsed into a set of economic benefits that accrue to one group or another. There is little need for moral persuasion in an environment dominated solely by economic interest. Bootlegger and Baptist theory goes beyond, positing that an effective way to motivate legislation is to appeal to values generally favored by the public.

Adam Smith, in *The Wealth of Nations* ([1776] 1982), stated that government services should be limited to a few basic (though by no means minimal) functions including national defense, preservation of law and order, and the provision of certain public goods (see Smith [1776] 1982, 687–88). All else, Smith reckoned, would fall outside the proper role government should take.

Lipford and Slice (2007) show how spending on social services overtook the traditional (Smithian) economic functions of government in the 1960s

Figure 10.1. Federal Government Spending on Smith's Duties and on Social Expenditures as a Percentage of Total Expenditures, 1962–2020

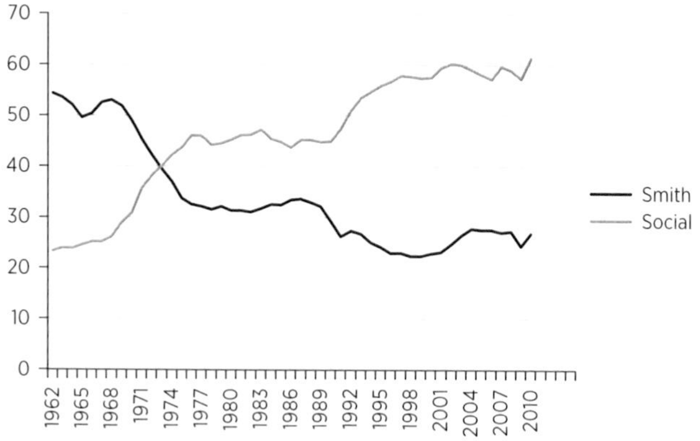

Source: Lipford and Slice 2007 with extensions by author to match up with Dudley and Warren 2011.

and has shown little sign of abating since. Figure 10.1 presents an extension of their findings.

Along with the influx of social spending has come expanded regulation in the areas of health, environment, housing, and other areas. Consider the data on constant dollar outlays for the two categories of regulation for selected years from 1960 to 2010, shown in table 10.1. The decade-over-decade growth of expenditures for social regulation outstripped economic regulation expenditures in all but one decade.

This trajectory could be chalked up to greater social awareness and/or popular appeal for social justice. But this is effect masquerading as cause when viewed from Yandle's framework. That the polity would allow government to exceed its traditional functions is a consequence of the warren of associations active in the body politic (see Yandle 1990). As social regulations have become more common, this has attracted greater lobbying efforts and campaign contributions, to the point where social regulation may even prove a more effective investment at the margin for lobbying dollars (see McLaughlin, Smith, and Sobel 2019). It may be that regulation in areas such as health, the environment, civil rights, and poverty fall more readily in the public interest than, say, financial market reforms. Who, after all, would not support making life easier for the poor or improving the environment? Opinions on systematically significant institutions in risk management are more nebulous. If there is less resistance to social policy positions, this would expand the capacity for

Table 10.1. Spending by Social and Economic Regulatory Agencies: Fiscal Years 1960–2010 in Millions of 2005 Constant Dollars

Real Outlays	1960	1970	1980	1990	2000	2010
Social regulatory agencies	$1,903	$4,511	$12,679	$15,424	$23,815	$39,503
Percent increase over prior decade		137%	181%	21.6%	54.4%	65.8%
Economic regulatory agencies	$962	$2,002	$2,585	$3,523	$4,944	$7,392
Percent increase over prior decade		108%	29.1%	36.3%	40.3%	49.5%

Source: Dudley and Warren 2011.

Bootlegger and Baptist groups to engage in rent-seeking through the political process.

THE RISE OF OBAMACARE

The Patient Protection and Affordable Care Act (ACA) is an example of a policy that brings enormous change to the market. It essentially reinvents one-sixth of the US economy through its bundle of regulations, fees, and grants. The episode brings to life Yandle's Bootleggers and Baptists framework by observing the behavior of affected parties, including consumers, hospitals, insurers, and pharmaceutical companies, who positioned themselves to interact with new models of healthcare delivery under the guiding influence of the executive branch and the Department of Health and Human Services (HHS) through implementation of the new law. In covering the law, the media focused more on the bureaucratic pitfalls coinciding with the launch of the department's healthcare exchange website (www.healthcare.gov) and less on how the government engaged throughout the process with industries directly impacted by the new law: hospitals, pharmaceutical companies, and insurers. These groups continue to undergo transformations as a result of HHS rules.

Placing health care at the forefront of his domestic agenda, President Obama publicized his vision. In his first State of the Union Address, the president claimed, "The cost of our health care has weighed down our economy and the conscience of our nation long enough. So let there be no doubt: healthcare reform cannot wait, it must not wait, and it will not wait another year" (Obama

2009). He followed up with a campaign to create support for his keystone legislation. Town hall forums and campaign-style appearances were part of a broader effort to convince the public that legislation was not only desirable but also mandatory for a modern democracy. In an address to Congress, Obama argued, "We are the only democracy—the only advanced democracy, the only wealthy nation—that allows such hardship for millions of its people" (*New York Times* 2009).

To avoid the failure of previous healthcare reform efforts, Obama began developing a coalition of special interest groups. One of the chief strategies of the White House was to "neutralize the opposition," an approach that reflected the shortcomings of the Clinton effort 15 years before (see Staff of the *Washington Post* 2010, 22). The president found many Baptists (and a few early bootleggers) willing to support his cause. For example, a joint statement in January 2009 from the American Cancer Society, American Medical Association, Families USA, Pharmaceutical Research and Manufacturers of America, Regence BlueCross BlueShield, and Service Employees International Union declared, "In order to fix the ailing economy, the nation needs healthcare reform that addresses the related problems of healthcare costs and people losing health coverage" (Reuters 2009).

But the president faced a hard sell with the public. A Gallup poll showed that half the country disapproved of new government interventions in the private healthcare system. Disapproval increased as debate continued on the issue: from a low of 28 percent disapproval in 2007 to a high of 50 percent in mid-2009 (*Gallup* 2010). A similar trend appeared when respondents were asked whether they favored preserving the current system or overhauling it through government intervention. In November 2007, 41 percent favored replacing the current system; by November 2009, this number had dropped to 32 percent. As debate continued and the rationally ignorant became more informed, Americans were less inclined to approve of government intervention in the private healthcare system (Newport 2009b).

One reason for voters' increasing wariness may have been a fear of higher costs under a public healthcare system. Even though the United States was spending the largest share of gross domestic product on health care across developed nations, the adjustment problem posed by the ACA remained (OECD 2012). Firms in the healthcare sector looked warily at the potential for rising costs as a result of new coverage requirements and restrictions on pricing. In 2009, Americans were just waking up from the 2008 financial crisis and suffering the effects of the global recession that followed. Unsurprisingly, 70 percent of Americans described economic issues as the nation's top problem; only 16 percent cited health care (Newport 2009a). In September 2009, 38 percent of those polled cited cost as the biggest problem. Only 15 percent saw too many uninsured persons as the biggest problem. In other words, more than twice as many respondents were chiefly concerned about cost as were concerned about lack of coverage (Saad 2009).

In response to the conversation in Washington, an unlikely alliance of bootleggers and Baptists emerged to guide the legislation. In March 2009, the president met with the elite of the bootlegger interests, including "leaders from organized labor and the American Medical Association, corporate executives, consumer advocates and officials from the U.S. Chamber of Commerce," and well-known lobbyists from pharmaceutical and insurance interests. These "strange bedfellows," as they called themselves, were not really strange at all, at least when considered within Yandle's framework. They had a common interest in ensuring the bill would benefit them. In addition, the veiled threat loomed that failure to get on board could put these interests in a difficult position should the bill pass without their help. As the US Chamber of Commerce President Thomas J. Donahue stated, "If you don't get in this game . . . you're on the menu" (see Staff of the *Washington Post* 2010, 22–23). Under the umbrella of coalitions such as Health Economy Now, these groups lobbied to shape healthcare policy in their favor.[6]

A consensus existed on the broad claims—expanding coverage, reducing costs, and improving the overall quality of the system. These goals were vague enough to allow ample room for bootleggers and Baptists to operate. The more imprecise the ends of a reform campaign were, the greater the opportunity would be for bootleggers to fill in the desired fine print when choosing the means. With 17 percent of the economy weighing in the balance, suitably designed healthcare legislation could pump billions of dollars in the direction of hard-working bootleggers.

Despite these warning signs, the ACA soon became national law. But the coordinated efforts among the three major bootlegger groups—insurers, hospitals, and pharmaceutical companies—did not end. In fact, HHS was just getting warmed up as chief televangelist (Cannon 2013).

REINING IN THE BOOTLEGGERS

Although passage of the law was itself enough for some to claim victory, the resulting implementation of the law still matters, as it provides crucial signals to Baptist groups that keep the public sympathetic to the overall goals of the law. By placating the public interest through making health insurance a "right"

(Wilson and Wiggins 2012), HHS can then impose a sometimes-cumbersome (even unworkable) structure on its somewhat reluctant bootlegger allies. So while the passage of ACA is a political outcome in the sense that it was a significant public victory for supporters,[7] it is also the vehicle for a significant rearrangement of the healthcare market. A vast entangled landscape attempts to redesign how health care is provided. For example, the law's proponents claim the reason costs are rising in the health sector is that doctors are not being held accountable for the services they recommend, passing off their fees to insurers and ultimately generating higher premiums for consumers. The law champions a systemic move away from the so-called fee-for-service payment method to one where users pay for a bundled set of service providers, located within a newly formed "accountable care organization" (Sebelius 2013).

As explained below, the ACO is less a new model for the provision of health care than an attempt to manage the bootlegger groups who stand to benefit most from the new market process generated by the law. In this sense, the ACO legislates the broad outline of a healthcare providers' cartel, leaving it to the interested parties to build, perhaps spontaneously, resulting management processes that fit time and place considerations. That is, the ACO does not provide for a single national healthcare provider cartel but makes it possible for multiple regional cartels that allow for large differences in state law and regulation.

The Medicare program, for example, was expected to benefit enormously from the arrangement in that it could now exert more leverage over the healthcare industry. At the time of the law's passage, Medicare ACOs were serving approximately 2.4 million people across 40 states and the District of Columbia, according to the Department of Human and Health Services (Vestal 2012). As Capretta (2017, 1) explains, "the nation's vast network of hospitals, clinics, physician practices, labs, hospices, and other providers take their cues heavily from the financial incentives embedded in Medicare's complex payment rules and regulations. Those promoting Medicare ACOs want to change the signals being sent by the Medicare program to promote more efficient models of care delivery." While the ACO model potentially offers benefits to consumers, it is implemented under significant bureaucratic influence that manipulates the underlying market process and invites bootlegger action.

The primitive ACO concept was developed at the Dartmouth Institute for Health Policy and Clinical Practice (see Goldsmith 2011, 33).[8] ACOs attempt to create a network of coordinated healthcare providers that share financial responsibility for patient services (Gold 2015). With the financial responsibility distributed across doctors and healthcare providers, the intended result is less expensive health care for consumers. An ACO network can be developed by any number of health service providers taking on many forms. Providers can include physicians, specialty care, hospitals, or any other organization involved with patient care. As Frech et al. (2015, 170) explain, "ACOs are a type of joint venture that encompasses existing health care providers. There is a vertical element: the combination of complementary providers, such as hospitals and physicians of various specialties. There is also a horizontal aspect, since they combine otherwise competing providers, such as physicians. They are expected to incentivize coordination of health care, improve quality, and lower costs."

The propagation of ACOs coincides with (and likely accelerated) the consolidation of hospital systems. While this angle may seem tangential, it illustrates how ACOs emerge within previously nested bootlegger relationships between hospitals, insurers, and independent specialists. Grauman and Tam (2012) review hospital merger activity from 2001 to 2011, showing that hospital mergers were "nearing historic lows" in 2009, with only 52 mergers, but increased to 75 in 2010, and 86 in 2011. They note that the downgrading of hospital bonds by Standard & Poor's from 2007 to 2009 also likely contributed to the increasing number of hospital mergers. The S&P ratings as of June 2011 showed that hospital systems were much more likely to have higher bond ratings than stand-alone hospitals. That is, hospitals operating within previously integrated networks were likely to have greater investment potential.

The call to align within integrated networks from ACA has created tremendous pressure on hospitals seeking to remain independently operated. Grauman and Tam contend that hospitals must consider their alignment with the targeted goals of healthcare policy, noting that "Even hospitals and health systems that are in a reasonable financial position may consider affiliation with a larger hospital or system in the community, solely to position themselves for strategic or financial success" (Grauman and Tam 2012, 5). Indeed, 87 percent of hospital administrators polled said that participation in an ACO was at least somewhat likely by 2016. In identifying the relationship between greater market power and the formation of ACOs, Berenson (2015, 720) explains that "An essential element of health plan–provider negotiations over price and other contractual terms and conditions is the willingness of consumers to accept narrow or tiered network products that effectively limit their choice of provider to those willing to accept the health plan's pricing." Berenson argues that elevating the status of ACOs effectively raises the market power of what he terms "must-have" provider organizations such as local hospitals.

Local hospitals are the principal bootleggers in this new market process created by the law. Goldsmith et al. (2015, 2) maintain that, "From the *societal* perspective, there is little evidence that integrating hospital and physician care has helped to promote quality or reduce costs. Indeed, there is growing evidence that hospital–physician integration has raised physician costs, hospital prices and per capita medical care spending."[9] Burns et al. (2015) use empirical data from 4,000 hospitals from 1998 to 2010 to test the relationships of different hospital systems to costs. They find no evidence that system members exhibit lower costs relative to non-system members in pricing their services, noting that more centralized systems may extract rents from the network. The authors discuss the implications of these findings on ACOs, arguing that "these systems' ability to contribute to lower cost health care is nonexistent or limited at best" (Burns et al. 2015, 266).

Doctors, physicians, and other providers have scrambled to form networks that appeal to the contours created by the law. The benchmarks that ACOs follow are controlled by HHS, which has led the charge in changing distribution networks, pushing providers to group into ACOs, and working with insurers to form a more inclusive, network-driven delivery model. Moreover, due to the oversight of premium increases established by ACA, insurance companies have a mandate to rigorously impose cost controls on hospitals and doctors (US Department of Health and Human Services 2015). Because insurance companies want to limit premium increases, they increasingly rely on previously specified networks of providers (Martin 2013). The relationship between the agency and industry has become so entangled that it amounts to cartelization of the industry.

How ACOs apply for government funding helps illustrate this. Recall that ACOs bundle healthcare service providers within a common network in a way that ostensibly cuts down on the number and cost of procedures. It accomplishes this by passing any savings back to the service providers. If conducted using Medicare payments, this savings is matched by subsidies originating from provisions in ACA. Once an ACO is established, it must apply to the Medicare Shared Savings Program (MSSP). The MSSP was created by section 3022 of the ACA. This shared savings plan is the driving factor for healthcare providers to join to create a network of providers as an ACO. It provides financial incentives to the healthcare providers to reduce Medicare spending per capita. From there, savings from reduced Medicare spending will be redistributed to the doctors and physicians participating in the network as a form of gain-sharing under the MSSP (Goldsmith 2011).

The general requirements for an ACO to enroll in the MSSP and receive the monetary benefits of saved Medicare dollars are based on a variety of quality metrics (Frech et al. 2015, 172).[10] Stone and Hoffman (2010, 33) explain that generally, "an eligible ACO is defined as a group of providers and suppliers who have an established mechanism for joint decision making, and are required to participate in the shared savings program for a minimum of three years, among other requirements." Geilfuss and Vernaglia (2013) note that the application requires specific and accurate information regarding the "legal structure of the ACO, the eligibility of those forming the ACO, governance, leadership and management structure, contracted participants, providers, and suppliers, documentation of policies and clinical processes, and ability to report on quality and cost metrics." Once the Center for Medicare and Medicaid Services (CMS) receives the application, it determines if the applicant ACO is adequate to enroll in the MSSP.[11] By assuming the risk of losses, the ACO is then eligible for a higher percentage of shared savings if Medicare spending is reduced.

Once enrolled in the MSSP, the ACO has the ability to choose from two tracks of participation. They differ based on the amount of risk the ACO wishes to accept during the three-year enrollment period. DeLia, Hoover, and Cantor (2012) explain that the first track, called the one-sided model, allows the ACO to accept minimal risk so that it is not held responsible or financially accountable for Medicare spending increases. With this track, the ACO will only benefit if Medicare spending is decreased to where there are savings to be distributed. If the ACO agrees to enroll in the second track, the two-sided model, it would assume the risk of losses created by increased Medicare spending. The core concept is that healthcare providers share insurance risk by being held accountable for costs that exceed previously established benchmarks, though only in the first track is risk truly pooled between the participating parties, as the second track puts the downside risk fully on the ACO organization.

Even if the ACO chooses the less risky track, the expectation is that benefits accrue in the long term through the compilation of short-term savings through the MSSP. The broader goal of the savings plan is to exert downward cost pressure on the ACO, which in turn enhances coordination of physicians and healthcare providers. This is thought to lead to further efficiency and saved Medicare dollars through the elimination of duplicative services across different providers (*Healthcare Financial Management* 2015), though as Schoonveld and colleagues claim, "In reality, the program seems to mainly entice a quest for short-term savings opportunities; an open question is whether there will be any longer term cost and quality impact" (Schoonveld, Coyle, and Markham 2015, 740).

A NEW MARKET PROCESS UNFOLDS

If ACOs were the panacea their proponents hoped for, allowing the healthcare industry to manage them into workable shape through conventional market channels would seem straightforward. Yet upon learning that this process entails limitations on who can participate in the newly constituted networks, the Obama administration reacted by calling for greater regulation rather than considering the limitations of the ACO model (Pear 2014). This ongoing relationship between private and public entities resembles the entangled political economy model presented by Wagner (2007). As public and private entities become increasingly entangled, the incentives and other managing directives become lost or obscured in the greater complexity created by additional network connections between private and public enterprises.

To wit, the ACA was delivered on the Baptist promise of greater coverage and lower costs. The reality has strayed far from these lofty goals. Moreover, the Trump tax reforms and ongoing judicial challenges have thrown much of this into limbo. As Dudley documents (see chapter 7), administrative changes have enormous impact on bootleggers and Baptists relationships (see also Goodman 2018). The change to the underlying market process is key in determining whether this monumental piece of bill-making will have a positive or negative influence on health outcomes in practice. While ACOs changed how health services are delivered, they have done little to relieve cost pressure. By favoring local hospitals, they have instead increased the market power for a subset of bootleggers in determining prices for consumers.

Schoonveld and colleagues (2015, 741) summarize this new mode of entanglement as a "dinner-for-three" in which Bob orders, Betty eats, and Ben pays. The authors explain how, within the new entangled landscape created by the law, "Payers face unprecedented budget pressures, as employers and patients criticize the cost of private insurance plans, and political pressure is exerted with respect to government-funded plans." While insurance companies may potentially see a long-run boon from the newly minted federal health exchanges, it is unclear at present whether this is realistic.[12] In the meantime, "payers" must increasingly scrutinize the cost of services while keeping in the good graces of locally favored ACOs. As Pope (2014, 3) explains, "Because third-party-payment systems insulate patients from the true costs of care, hospitals without nearby competitors are able to leverage the strong patient preference for geographic convenience to demand a premium from insurers."

Handel (2015, 707) explains this further, noting that "In the typical ACO-insurer relationship in the private market, the insurer has to negotiate both low prices and efficient payment incentive schemes with providers; if providers have substantial market power as an organization, they will extract more of the rents in this scheme because they are not worried about competing with other insurers and reducing costs." He claims that "formation of Medicare ACOs under the [MSSP] could facilitate formation of ACOs for the private market, where insurers do not have the same inherently strong bargaining position. Additionally, it is worth pointing out that realizing efficiencies in ACOs requires payers to appropriately set incentives for the ACO to control costs. This occurs via the MSSP for Medicare ACOs, but private insurers should be able to provide stronger incentives to ACOs and, ultimately, realize greater efficiencies as a result" (Handel 2015, 709).

Handel also argues that policies restricting the formation of narrow networks will decrease the likelihood of an ACO realizing efficiencies, while relaxed regulations would be more likely to result in efficient ACOs. By prohibiting narrow networks and requiring particular providers or services to be included, state and federal regulations increase the holdout power of providers and the market power and concentration of ACOs. Conversely, if insurers are allowed to credibly threaten the exclusion of an ACO, they are more likely to be able to keep costs down. If state and federal regulations significantly restrict provider networks, then this complements and enhances the ability of the ACOs to extract higher prices. Regulations that restrict insurers' ability to form narrow networks include (1) those that require certain types of "essential" providers to be covered and (2) those that require some providers of a given type to be available within a certain distance radius for all consumers enrolled in an insurance plan (Handel 2015, 706).

The healthcare "provider" is subject to new cost-controlling pressures, though these are driven more by other restrictions on pricing practices under the ACA than implementation of the ACO model. As Schoonveld and colleagues (2015, 742) explain, "Although this can free providers from administrative burdens associated with running their own practice, it tends to mean that they must more actively consider group policies and protocols, thus limiting their autonomy. For those that remain in private practice, maintaining the practice's financial health will require more attention than ever."

Pope (2014, 16) explains further how, "Rather than checking the revenues of dominant hospitals, the development of ACOs is likely to reduce their exposure to competitive threats, limit the number of independent competing providers, and facilitate collusion among incumbents. Hospitals that integrate and take up insurance services to form the basis for ACOs are unlikely to push patients towards low-cost outpatient care. Indeed, doctors may be forced to participate in ACOs if they want to be reimbursed for treating Medicare patients." Integrating within local hospital systems means conforming to a set network that will help comply with the ACA restrictions on pricing practices. But as Frech et al. (2015, 188) maintain, hospital systems may discourage ACO entry if these cost considerations overwhelm the gains from participating in the MSSP. That hospitals would be so readily receptive to a program designed to decrease hospital visits is especially telling. Clearly, any reduction in visits fostered by the ACO will be offset in payments from the MSSP along with anticipated premium increases generated by the greater market power created by network integration.

Moreover, the fact that the ACO model is propagated out of nested bootlegger relationships reduces the political transaction costs of adopting the delivery model preferred by bureaucratic fiat. The trouble on the horizon for hospital bootleggers is that the benefits used to attract providers to the model are likely to be transient. Tullock (1975) originally introduced the concept of the "transitional gains trap" to encapsulate this notion that pecuniary benefit made through political processes tend to run into diminishing returns until gains fall to competitive levels, as additional entities enroll in hopes of gaining from government largesse. In the case of ACOs, these gains are likely to accrue to the local wielder of market power, be it physician groups or hospitals.

Finally, the healthcare "patient" is finding an increasingly complex set of choices in the new landscape, especially with respect to different insurance outcomes (e.g., co-pays, deductibles, participating physician networks). This comes as "physicians continue to evolve from being an autocratic decision maker toward becoming a health consultant" (Schoonveld, Coyle, and Markham 2015, 742). This increasing participatory role of the patient could be considered beneficial, but only if it makes underlying healthcare costs more apparent. Healthcare consumers are limited by their understanding of the healthcare system and pricing, limitations that have become more salient with the complexity introduced by ACA, but also by the restructured availability of choices. If ACO networks inadvertently constrain the overall set of choices open to the healthcare consumer by reducing the choices open to consumers in favor of offering the lowest-cost package, then "choice" has dubious meaning.

Moreover, as Capretta (2017, 3) argues, "The fundamental problem with the ACO model, both as constituted in the ACA's MSSP and as established through CMS's [Centers for Medicare and Medicaid Services] demonstration authority, is that it tries to avoid direct engagement with the beneficiaries." While the concept of the ACO is understood by providers and the recently created healthcare networks, consumers have not received clear information about what ACO models mean for them, especially those not enrolled in Medicare. Goldsmith (2011) notes that consumers enrolled in Medicare programs are encouraged to visit healthcare providers and physicians within the ACO network, though they still have the choice to be seen by providers outside of the network. Analysis by Wyman shows that over 40 percent of Americans live in an area served by two or more ACOs, providing consumers with the choice of what ACO, if any, they wish to be served by (Marsh & McLennan Companies 2014). Healthcare consumers who are enrolled in Medicare often do not even know if they are receiving the service of an ACO. This has caused many Medicare patients to question the transparency of the ACO model, especially when the MSSP is partly based on the quality of care that is provided (Sullivan 2010).

Trade-offs between cost and choice are nothing new; only the fact that they are encouraged by the new law is novel. This has already generated negative feedback from consumers who complain of the limited set of choices of the new networks and lack of access to desired providers. This has also caused existing plan holders to resist changing to new, "more affordable" plans as guaranteed by the new law (Pear 2015). In addition, preliminary evidence indicates that these models do not reduce costs in the manner conceived by its original proponents (see Burns and Pauly 2018), and may instead increase the profitability of hospitals, particularly government hospitals (see Duggan, Gupta, and Jackson 2019). In the end, Baptist cries ultimately favor bureaucratic management of market decisions.

CONCLUSION

The ACA has been a game-changer for the health industry. The most significant change is the set of newly integrated ties among government agencies, insurers, pharmaceutical companies, and hospitals. As Oberlander (2010, 1114–15) said, "Arguably the most consequential decision that reformers made in 2009 was to work with, rather than against, health system stakeholders. . . . The administration negotiated deals with health industry groups to support reform in exchange for the promise of having millions of newly insured patients to treat."

President Obama presided over a conference of his health secretary and insurance executives in April 2013 in which he said, "We're all in this together," noting that business and government were now "joined at the hip" (Calmes 2013). President Obama might as well have said "For the first time, we have enabled the organization of multiple healthcare provider cartels that will be operated by highly visible and more accountable bootlegger and Baptist interest groups."

This episode could be considered just another instance of powerful special interest groups corrupting the purity of progressive reform. But the Bootleggers and Baptists narrative provides another story. By co-opting these groups early in the process, the administration ensured that they would be entangled with government decision makers such as HHS. Thompson and Gusmano note that the law represents the further extension and discretion of the executive branch of government. The law endows administrators with "vast latitude to shape who gets what, when, and how from the ACA" (Thompson and Gusmano 2014). Administrators are using this latitude to rein in bootlegger and Baptist groups toward their collective goals. Whether these goals are in the public interest is a moot point. The more salient factor is how the underlying market process has changed, as this will determine whose preferences are being considered at public and private levels.

Political decision-making is difficult to stop when it replaces market decision-making. Hagel and Grinder (2006) explain how transferring decisions into the political domain tends to lead to more of the same. They argue that the difficulties in information accumulation and instability caused by political interference only exacerbate the need for bureaucrats to further consolidate power. In the case of the ACA, this circumstance is already apparent in how the law has unfolded. As elements of the law become unworkable within the new market process—such as the Community Living Assistance Services and Supports (CLASS) Act (Wayne and Armstrong 2011), employer mandates (Kliff 2013c), and small business health exchanges (Kliff 2013b)—these legislative pieces were jettisoned in favor of greater consolidation within the bureaucratic apparatus.

Ikeda (2005) further outlines the incremental process by which bureaucratic management replaces market process. He explains how a number of factors support incremental intervention once started. Part of his explanation rests on persistent error, in which bureaucrats fail to correct their behavior even when given countervailing evidence. For example, insurers' protestations that the ACA would lead to rate hikes were blamed on greed rather than taken at face value as evidence of the law placing additional costs on insurers. Ikeda also shows how ideology plays a role in increasing intervention. As society becomes accustomed to government controlling the service, further intervention is easier to justify. The Bootleggers and Baptists framework buttresses this observation in that interest groups brought into the fold by a political coordinator such as HHS will adjust their operations to the point where incremental intervention becomes easier to manage. Reversion to the older market process would be more difficult. Indeed, when these groups are fully entrenched within the political apparatus, they often become the loudest supporters of greater government intervention in market processes (see Yandle 1983).

NOTES

1. The individual mandate has since been partly repealed as part of the Trump administration's tax reforms (see Mukherjee 2017). Also, a Texas federal judge notably called the entire law into question over the individual mandate, claiming that it "can no longer be sustained as an exercise of Congress's tax power" (see Goodnough and Pear 2018).
2. Note that this moral framework is itself a product of evolutionary selection that reflects a number of non-moral factors. As Hoffman, McCabe, and Smith (1998, 337) explain, "A capacity for the natural learning of strategies that induce cooperation in social exchange has fitness value. But the implementational form of what is learned varies widely, depending upon the environment, accidents of nature, and how parental, familial, and societal units organize exchange processes."
3. It is only when laboratory subjects are prevented from sending signals of reciprocity that cooperation breaks down altogether (see Hoffman, McCabe, and Smith 1996).
4. Though Hoffman, McCabe, and Smith (1998, 338) argue that "mutual recognition and defense of informal property right systems need not require the pre-existence of a Leviathan."
5. Solyndra was an energy company that received over $500 million in federal funding to produce solar panels that failed to return a market profit (see Stephens and Leonnig 2011).
6. This particular coalition included the Pharmaceutical Research and Manufacturers of America, the AARP, the American Medical Association, Business Roundtable, Families USA, and the Service Employees International Union, among others (*Fox.news.com* 2009).
7. A Texas judge has since challenged the law through a ruling in a federal district court in Fort Worth (see Goodnough and Pear 2018).
8. The initial proposal was designed to create an incentive for hospitals and other providers to reduce Medicare spending per capita. The savings from reduced spending of Medicare dollars would then be equally distributed across the physicians and doctors participating in the network, once they are enrolled in the Medicare Shared Savings Program, as a form of gainsharing (Goldsmith 2011). Adopting this form of the proposal would put power in the hands of healthcare providers in regard to the amount and quality of care that was provided.
9. Berenson (2015, 717) also points this out, remarking that ACOs are able to extract 250 percent of the Medicare price tag for health services.
10. For example, quality standards must be met in the following areas: patient and caregiver care experiences, coordination of care, patient safety, engagement in preventive health care, and the at-risk population that is being served. Satisfactory performance in these areas will result in an "upfront, fixed payment of $250,000 in the first month, an upfront, fixed payment of $36 per beneficiary assigned to the ACO in the first month, and a monthly payment of $8 per beneficiary assigned to the ACO."
11. Withdrawals by major insurance groups suggest that profit opportunities on the exchanges remain elusive. See Johnson (2016).
12. Gruber and McKnight (2016) observe a related tension between primary care and specialist care. After examining enrollment behavior in limited networks from the Massachusetts GIC, the insurance plan for state employees, they find that "primary care office visits increase, with a statistically significant 3% rise in spending in the reduced form, implying a roughly 28% rise in spending on primary care for those who move into narrow networks. At the same time, visits to specialists fall significantly, with a large 5% decline in

spending in the reduced form implying a roughly 45% reduction in specialist spending" (Gruber and McKnight 2016, 21). They note that these results suggest a move away from specialist care in favor of the primary care physician, with cost per visit potentially rising for the latter as well.

REFERENCES

American College of Physicians. n.d. "Accountable Care Organizations." https://www.acponline.org/advocacy/where_we_stand/assets/aco.pdf.

Becker, G. S. 1983. "A Theory of Competition among Pressure Groups for Political Influence." *Quarterly Journal of Economics* 98, no. 3: 371–400.

——. 1985. "Human Capital, Effort, and the Sexual Division of Labor." *Journal of Labor Economics* 3, no. 1: S33–S58.

Berenson, R. 2015. "Addressing Pricing Power in Integrated Delivery: The Limits of Antitrust." *Journal of Health Politics, Policy, and Law* 40, no. 4: 711–44.

Buchanan, J. M. 1975. "The Samaritan's Dilemma." In *Altruism, Morality, and Economic Theory*, edited by E. S. Phelps, 71–86. New York: Russell Sage Foundation.

Burke, T. 2011. "Accountable Care Organizations." *Public Health Reports* 126, no. 6: 875–78. http://www.ncbi.nlm.nih.gov/pmc/articles/PMC3185325/.

Burns, L. R., J. S. McCullough, D. R. Wholey, G. Kruse, P. Kralovec, and R. Muller. 2015. "Is the System Really the Solution? Operating Costs in Hospital Systems." *Medical Care Research and Review* 72, no. 3: 247–72.

Burns, L. R., and M. V. Pauly. 2018. "Transformation of the Health Care Industry: Curb Your Enthusiasm?" *Milbank Quarterly* 96, no. 1: 57–109.

Calmes, J. 2013. "Obama Sees Insurers; Health Law Is Subject." *New York Times*, April 12. https://www.nytimes.com/2013/04/13/us/politics/obama-and-insurance-executives-discuss-health-care-exchanges.html, accessed December 30, 2018.

Cannon, M. 2013. "Sebelius Shakes Down Companies She Regulates for Cash to Implement ObamaCare." *Cato Institute*, May 13. http://www.cato.org/blog/sebelius-shakes-down-regulated-industries-cash-implement-obamacare.

Capretta, J. C. 2017. "Replacing Medicare ACOs with a Better Integrated Care Option." *Mercatus on Policy*, May. https://www.mercatus.org/system/files/capretta-replacing-medicare-acos-mop-v1.pdf.

Crosson, F. J. 2011. "The Accountable Care Organization: Whatever Its Growing Pains, the Concept is Too Vitally Important to Fail." *Health Affairs* 30, no. 7: 1250–55.

Dafny, L., M. Duggan, and S. Ramanarayanan. 2012. "Paying a Premium on Your Premium? Consolidation in the US Health Insurance Industry." *American Economic Review* 102, no. 2: 1161–85.

DeLia, D., D. Hoover, and J. Cantor. 2012. "Statistical Uncertainty in the Medicare Shared Savings Program." *Medicare & Medicaid Research Review* 2, no. 4. https://www.cms.gov/mmrr/Downloads/MMRR2012_002_04_a04.pdf.

Dudley, S. 2019. "Bootleggers & Baptists: The Experience of Another Regulatory Economist." In *Advanced Studies in Political Economy*, edited by V. H. Storr and S. Haeffele. Arlington, VA: Mercatus Center.

Dudley, S., and M. Warren. 2011. "Fiscal Stalemate Reflected in Regulators' Budget: An Analysis of the US Budget for Fiscal Years 2011 and 2012." Murray Weidenbaum Center on the Economy, Government, and Public Policy at Washington University in St. Louis and George Washington University Regulatory Studies Center.

Duggan, M., A. Gupta, and E. Jackson. 2019. "The Impact of the Affordable Care Act: Evidence from California's Hospital Sector." Stanford Institute for Economic Policy Research, Working Paper no. 18-026.

The Economist. 2010a. "The Health-Scare Squeeze." March 25. https://www.economist.com/business/2010/03/25/the-health-care-squeeze.

——. 2010b. "Now What?" March 25. https://www.economist.com/leaders/2010/03/25/now-what.

——. 2017. "Lobbyists Go Underground." August 31. https://www.economist.com/united-states/2017/08/31/lobbyists-go-underground.

——. 2018. "Which Firms Profit Most from America's Health-Care System." March 15. https://www.economist.com/business/2018/03/15/which-firms-profit-most-from-americas-health-care-system.

Epstein, A., A. E. J. Jha, Orav, D. Liebman, A. Audet, M. Zezza, and S. Guterman. 2014. "Analysis of Early Accountable Care Organizations Defines Patient, Structural, Cost, and Quality-of-Care Characteristics." *Health Affairs* 33, no. 1: 95–102.

Foxnews.com. 2009. "Strange Bedfellows? Industry Groups Join in Effort to Push Health Care Reform." August 12. https://www.foxnews.com/story/strange-bedfellows-form-advocacy-group-to-push-health-care-reforms.

Frech, H. E., C. Whaley, B. R. Handel, L. Bowers, C. J. Simon, and R. M. Scheffler. 2015. "Market Power, Transactions Costs, and the Entry of Accountable Care Organizations in Health Care." *Review of Industrial Organization* 47, no. 2: 167–93.

Gallup. 2010. "Healthcare System." June 8. http://www.gallup.com/poll/4708/Healthcare-System.aspx.

Geilfuss, C. F., and L.W. Vernaglia. 2013. "ACOs in the Medicare Shared Savings Program: Issues for Compliance Officers." *Journal of Health Care Compliance* 15, no. 6: 5–77.

Glaeser, E. L., and A. Shleifer. 2001. "Not-for-Profit Entrepreneurs." *Journal of Public Economics* 81, no. 1: 99–115.

Gold, J. 2015. "Accountable Care Organizations, Explained." *Kaiser Health News*, September 14. http://khn.org/news/aco-accountable-care-organization-faq/.

Goldsmith, J. 2011. "Accountable Care Organizations: The Case for Flexible Partnerships between Health Plans and Providers." *Health Affairs* 30, no. 1: 32–40.

Goldsmith, J., L. Burns, A. Sen, and T. Goldsmith. 2015. "Integrated Delivery Networks: In Search of Benefits and Market Effects." National Academy of Social Insurance, February 15. https://www.nasi.org/research/2015/integrated-delivery-networks-search-benefits-market-effects.

Goodman, J. 2018. "How Donald Trump Is Radically Reforming Obamacare." *Forbes*, December 5. https://www.forbes.com/sites/johngoodman/2018/12/05/how-donald-trump-is-radically-reforming-obamacare/#18b028cf3b2b.

Goodnough, A., and R. Pear. 2018. "Texas Judge Strikes Down Obama's Affordable Care Act as Unconstitutional." *New York Times*, December 14. https://www.nytimes.com/2018/12/14/health/obamacare-unconstitutional-texas-judge.html.

Gould, B. 2014. "How the Countervailing Power of Insurers Can Resolve the Tradeoff between Market Power and Health Care Integration in Accountable Care Organizations." *George Mason Law Review* 22: 159–72.

Grauman, D. M., and M. P. Tam 2012. "The Urge to Merge." *Healthcare Financial Management* 66, no. 11: 76–86.

Gruber, J., and R. McKnight. 2016. "Controlling Health Care Costs through Limited Network Insurance Plans: Evidence from Massachusetts State Employees." *American Economic Journal: Economic Policy* 8, no. 2: 219–50.

Hagel, J., and W. E. Grinder. 2006. "From Laissez-Faire to Zwangswirtschaft." In *The Dynamics of Intervention: Regulation and Redistribution in the Mixed Economy*, edited by P. Kurrild-Klitgaard, 59–86. Bingley, UK: Emerald Group.

Handel, B. 2015. "Commentary—Accountable Care Organizations and Narrow Network Insurance Plans." *Journal of Health Politics, Policy and Law* 40, no. 4: 705–10.

Healthcare Financial Management. 2015. "HFMA Submits Comments on Changes to the Medicare Shared Savings Program." 69, no. 3: 16.

Hoffman, E., K. McCabe, and V. L. Smith. 1996. "Social Distance and Other-Regarding Behavior in Dictator Games." *American Economic Review* 86, no. 3: 653–60.

——. 1998. "Behavioral Foundations of Reciprocity: Experimental Economics and Evolutionary Psychology." *Economic Inquiry* 36, no. 3: 335–52.

Ikeda, S. 2005. "The Dynamics of Interventionism." In *The Dynamics of Intervention: Regulation and Redistribution in the Mixed Economy*, edited by P. Kurrild-Klitgaard, 21–57. Bingley, UK: Emerald Group.

Johnson, C. 2016. "UnitedHealth Group to Exit Obamacare Exchanges in All but a 'Handful' of States." *Washington Post*, April 19. https://www.washingtonpost.com/news/wonk/wp/2016/04/19/unitedhealth-group-to-exit-obamacare-exchanges-in-all-but-a-handful-of-states/.

Kliff, S. 2013a. "Budget Request Denied, Sebelius Turns to Health Executives to Finance Obamacare." *Washington Post*, May 10. https://www.washingtonpost.com/news/wonk/wp/2013/05/10/budget-request-denied-sebelius-turns-to-health-executives-to-finance-obamacare/?utm_term=.6ebf4a981dc1.

——. 2013b. "Obamacare's Online SHOP Enrollment Delayed by One Year." *Washington Post*, November 27. https://www.washingtonpost.com/news/wonk/wp/2013/11/27/obamacares-online-exchange-for-small-businesses-is-delayed-by-one-year/?utm_term=.f13025400f43.

——. 2013c. "White House Delays Employer Mandate Requirement until 2015." *Washington Post*, July 2. https://www.washingtonpost.com/news/wonk/wp/2013/07/02/white-house-delays-employer-mandate-requirement-until-2015/?utm_term=.e9d988d5a30d.

Lewis, V. A., C. H. Cola, K. L. Carluzzo, S. E. Kler, and E. S. Fisher. 2013. "Accountable Care Organizations in the United States: Market and Demographic Factors Associated with Formation." *Health Services Research* 48, no. 6.

Lipford, J. W., and J. Slice. 2007. "Adam Smith's Roles for Government and Contemporary US Government Roles: Is the Welfare State Crowding Out Government's Basic Functions?" *Independent Review* 11, no. 4: 485–501.

Lowell, K., and J. Bertko. 2010. "The Accountable Care Organization (ACO) Model: Building Blocks for Success." *Journal of Ambulatory Care Management* 33, no. 1: 81–88.

Marsh & McLennan Companies. 2014. "ACO Update: Accountable Care at a Tipping Point." April. https://www.oliverwyman.com/content/dam/oliver-wyman/global/en/files/insights/health-life-sciences/2014/April/NYC-MKT08001-034%20(4).pdf.

Martin, T. 2013. "Shrinking Hospital Networks Greet Health-Care Shoppers on Exchanges." *Wall Street Journal*, December 13. https://www.wsj.com/articles/no-headline-available-1386970905.

McLaughlin, P., A. Smith, and R. Sobel. 2019. "The Risk of Rent Seeking." Working Paper.

Mukherjee, S. 2017. "The GOP Tax Bill Repeals Obamacare's Individual Mandate. Here's What That Means for You." *Fortune*, December 20. http://fortune.com/2017/12/20/tax-bill-individual-mandate-obamacare/.

National Public Radio. 2012. "Clean-Tech Industry Facing Lean Times after Solyndra." *Fresh Air*, February 2. https://www.npr.org/2012/02/02/146280685/clean-tech-industry-facing-lean-times-after-solyndra.

Newport, F. 2009a. "Americans on Healthcare Reform: Top 10 Takeaways." *Gallup*, July 13. http://www.gallup.com/poll/121997/Americans-Healthcare-Reform-Top-Takeaways.aspx.

——. 2009b. "More in U.S. Say Health Coverage Is Not Gov't. Responsibility." *Gallup*, November 13. http://www.gallup.com/poll/124253/Say-Health-Coverage-Not-Gov-Responsibility.aspx.

New York Times. 2009. "Obama's Health Care Address to Congress." September 10. http://www.nytimes.com/interactive/2009/09/10/us/politics/20090910-obama-health.html.

Obama, B. 2009. "Remarks of President Barack Obama—As Prepared for Delivery Address to Joint Session of Congress." Office of the Press Secretary, White House. http://www.whitehouse.gov/the_press_office/Remarks-of-President-Barack-Obama-Address-to-Joint-Session-of-Congress.

Oberlander, J. 2010. "Long Time Coming: Why Health Reform Finally Passed." *Health Affairs* 29, no. 6: 1112–16.

Organisation for Economic Development and Co-Operation. 2012. "How Does the US Compare?" Briefing Note, OECD, Paris.

Pear, R. 2014. "White House Tightens Health Plan's Standards after Consumers Complain." *New York Times*, March 14. See https://www.nytimes.com/2014/03/15/us/white-house-tightens-health-insurance-standards-in-response-to-complaints.html.

——. 2015. "Health Insurance Companies Seek Big Rate Increases for 2016." *New York Times*, July 3. http://www.nytimes.com/2015/07/04/us/health-insurance-companies-seek-big-rate-increases-for-2016.html?smprod=nytcore-ipad&smid=nytcore-ipad-share&_r=3.

Peltzman, S. 1976. "Toward a More General Theory of Regulation." National Bureau of Economic Research, Working Paper no. 133. https://www.nber.org/papers/w0133.pdf.

Polanyi, M. 1958. *Personal Knowledge: Towards a Post-Critical Philosophy*. Chicago: University of Chicago Press.

Pope, C. 2014. "How the Affordable Care Act Fuels Health Care Market Consolidation." Heritage Foundation, August 1. http://www.heritage.org/research/reports/2014/08/how-the-affordable-care-act-fuels-health-care-market-consolidation.

Reuters. 2009. "Obama Health Reform Drive Gets Diverse Backing." January 8. http://www.reuters.com/article/2009/01/08/us-usa-obama-healthcare-groups-s-idUSTRE50766N20090108.

Saad, L. 2009. "Cost Is Foremost Healthcare Issue for Americans." *Gallup*, September 23. http://www.gallup.com/poll/123149/Cost-Is-Foremost-Healthcare-Issue-for-Americans.aspx.

Schoonveld, E., B. Coyle, and J. Markham. 2015. "Impact of ACA on the Dinner-for-Three Dynamic." *Clinical Therapeutics* 37, no. 4: 733–46.

Sebelius, K. 2013. "Affordable Care Act at 3: Paying for Quality Saves Health Care Dollars." US Department of Health and Human Services. http://www.hhs.gov/healthcare/facts/blog/2013/03/anniversary-quality.html.

Smith, A. [1759] 1982. *The Theory of Moral Sentiments*. Indianapolis, IN: Liberty Fund.

——. [1776] 1982. *An Inquiry into the Nature and Causes of the Wealth of Nations*. Indianapolis, IN: Liberty Fund.

Smith, A. C., R. E. Wagner, and B. Yandle. 2011. "A Theory of Entangled Political Economy, with Application to TARP and NRA." *Public Choice* 148, nos. 1–2: 45–66.

Smith, V. L. 2003. "Constructivist and Ecological Rationality in Economics." *American Economic Review* 93, no. 3: 465–508.

Staff of the *Washington Post*. 2010. *Landmark: The Inside Story of America's New Health-Care Law—The Affordable Care Act—and What It Means for Us All*. New York: PublicAffairs.

Stephens, J., and C. Leonnig. 2011. "Documents Show Politics Infused Obama 'Green' Programs." *Washington Post*, December 25. https://www.washingtonpost.com/politics/specialreports/solyndra-scandal/?noredirect=on.

Stone, J., and G. Hoffman. 2010. "Medicare Hospital Readmissions: Issues, Policy Options and PPACA." Congressional Research Service, September 21. http://www.ncsl.org/documents/health/medicare_hospital_readmissions_and_ppaca.pdf.

Sullivan, K. 2010. "The History and Definition of the 'Accountable Care Organization.'" Physicians for a National Health Program. http://pnhpcalifornia.org/2010/10/the-history-and-definition-of-the-%E2%80%9Caccountable-care-organization%E2%9D/.

Thompson, F. J., and M. K. Gusmano. 2014. "The Administrative Presidency and Fractious Federalism: The Case of Obamacare." *Publius: The Journal of Federalism* 44 no. 3: 426–50.

Tullock, G. 1975. "The Transitional Gains Trap." *Bell Journal of Economics* 6, no. 2: 671–78.

US Center for Medicaid and Medicare Services. 2017. "National Health Expenditures 2017 Highlights." https://www.cms.gov/Research-Statistics-Data-and-Systems/Statistics-Trends-and-Reports/NationalHealthExpendData/downloads/highlights.pdf.

US Department of Health and Human Services. 2015. "Rate Review." http://www.hhs.gov/healthcare/insurance/premiums/rate-review.html.

Vestal, C. 2012. "Accountable Care Explained: An Experiment in State Health Policy." *Kaiser Heath News*, October 18. http://khn.org/news/aco-accountable-care-organization-states-medicaid/.

Wagner, R. E. 2007. *Fiscal Sociology and the Theory of Public Finance: An Exploratory Essay*. Northampton, MA: Edward Elgar.

——. 2016. "The Peculiar Business of Politics." *Cato Journal* 36: 535–56.

Wall Street Journal. 2012. "ObamaCare's Secret History." June 11. http://online.wsj.com/article/SB10001424052702303830204577446470015843822.html.

Wayne, A., and D. Armstrong. 2011. "Kennedy-Backed Long-Term Care Program Scrapped by Sebelius." *Bloomberg*, October15. https://www.bloomberg.com/news/articles/2011-10-15/obama-scraps-kennedy-backed-long-term-care-plan-as-too-costly.

Wilson, S., and O. Wiggins. 2012. "Obama Defends Health-Care Law, Calling Health Insurance a 'Right.'" *Washington Post*, September 26. https://www.washingtonpost.com/politics/obama-defends-health-care-law-calling-health-insurance-a-right/2013/09/26/9e1d946e-26b8-11e3-b75d-5b7f66349852_story.html?utm_term=.3d87a266d698.

Yandle, B. 1983. "Bootleggers and Baptists: The Education of a Regulatory Economist." *Regulation* 7, no. 3: 12–15.

——. 1990. "The Decline and Rise of Political Economy." *European Journal of Political Economy* 6, no. 2: 165–79.

——. 1999. "Bootleggers and Baptists in Retrospect." *Regulation* 22, no. 3: 5–7.

CHAPTER 11
Corporate Social Responsibility and Corporate Welfare
A Stronger Case than Friedman Realized and the Shortage of Yandle Baptists

DWIGHT R. LEE

Almost 50 years ago, Milton Friedman (1970) wrote a famous article on corporate social responsibility (CSR) that most economists found more convincing than did most academics in other business and social science disciplines. In a nutshell, Friedman argued that the only responsibility of corporations is to make as much profit as possible subject to obeying the laws of honesty and fair dealing. My initial intention was to mention Friedman's argument only to introduce CSR for the purpose of making a connection between it and corporate welfare, and to use that connection to develop yet another example of the richness of Yandle's "Bootleggers and Baptists" model at providing insights into the politics of rent-seeking (Yandle 1983).[1] Yet, as is so often the case when writing a paper, I found the road map I had in mind when I started to be different from the road map the paper decided to follow.

In particular, it occurred to me as I wrote that Friedman's argument against CSR was stronger than he realized because of the connection between CSR and corporate welfare that I intended to make. As writing continued, I also discovered that the straightforward Bootleggers and Baptists model didn't perfectly apply to the rent-seeking implications of the connection between CSR and corporate welfare I had in mind. So instead of standing on both of Yandle's shoulders as I anticipated, I ended up standing mostly on his bootleggers' shoulder. Yet without the Bootleggers and Baptists model, this paper would never have been written. I can only hope it is worthy of Bruce Yandle and his contributions to economics and public choice.

In the next section, I discuss why I went from thinking Friedman's argument against CSR is slightly weaker than he thought, to being stronger than he realized. In section 3, I present evidence that CSR is a mouse compared to the elephant of corporate welfare. Yet, in the context of discussions and debate about CSR, there is little, if any, mention of the elephant even though the connection between the two should be obvious. In section 4, the "seen and unseen" insight of Bastiat (2016) is used to explain why the public notices the social benefits of the mouse and ignores the social costs of the elephant, and illustrate that bias with a hypothetical comparison. That bias is illustrated again in section 5 with examples of two actual corporations. I give reasons in section 6 for the existence of a mutually reinforcing connection between CSR and corporate welfare and consider the corporate welfare implications in the case of tax-funded sports stadiums. I conclude in section 7 by highlighting important differences between corporate rent-seeking as I discuss it taking place, and the way it takes place in Yandle's Bootleggers and Baptists settings. I argue there can be shortages of Yandle Baptists that can increase the value of CSR as a useful complement to them by supporting rent-seeking efforts in ways that Baptists do not. I also circle back briefly to section 2 to reemphasize that the connection between a corporation's CSR and corporate welfare increases the strength of Freidman's argument against CSR in a way he never considered.

FRIEDMAN'S ARGUMENT IS STRONGER THAN HE THOUGHT

Friedman wasn't against CSR; he was for firms maximizing shareholders' profits. He recognized that up to some point CSR increased goodwill and could increase shareholder returns. In excess of that point, CSR infringed upon the shareholders' right to spend their money as they preferred and reduced a firm's ability to produce goods and services as productively as possible. The debate over Friedman's attack on CSR continues today, though mostly in college management courses, with little evidence that Friedman's argument has changed many minds or reduced the willingness of corporations to make significant community contributions at the expense of their shareholders.

Richard McKenzie and I entered the debate by arguing that corporations can be justified in making "contributions to charities and communities beyond the point that maximizes shareholder profits" (McKenzie and Lee 1998, 261). We recognized that even though shareholders have different views on how contributions should be distributed, they can still benefit from corporate managers distributing some of their money. For example, many charitable contributions generate general benefits for the entire community, which create free-rider problems. Friedman (1962, 191) recognized this when he stated, "I am benefited by its [poverty's] alleviation; but I am benefited equally whether I or someone else pays for its alleviation; the benefits of other people's charity therefore partly accrue to me. . . . [W]e might all of us be willing to contribute to the relief of poverty, *provided* everyone else did. We might not be willing to contribute the same amount without such assurance" (emphasis in original).

Of course, this statement by Friedman isn't enough to claim he would agree with letting corporate managers usurp the charitable decisions of their shareholders, and I doubt he would have. Obviously, the strength of the argument McKenzie and I make is weak unless the corporation's shareholders make up a fairly large percentage of the community's population. Yet, as we also argued, one can also justify this usurpation if shareholders appreciate shifting some of the responsibility for their charitable responsibilities to corporations in which they have invested and are willing to pay for this service with somewhat lower profits.

John Mackey, the founder and former CEO of Whole Foods, pointed out in a debate with Milton Friedman and J. D. Rogers (*Reason* 2005) that seven years before its initial public offering, Whole Foods' mission statement made clear that 5 percent of the net profits would be donated to philanthropy.[2] He then asked, "[h]ow can Whole Foods' philanthropy be 'theft' from the current investors if the original owners of the company unanimously approved the policy and all subsequent investors made their investments after the policy was in effect and well publicized?" Mackey continued, "shareholders of a public company own their stock voluntarily. If they don't agree with the philosophy of the business, they can always sell their investment, just as the customers and employees can exit their relationships with the company if they don't like the terms of trade." While not explicitly agreeing with Mackey, Friedman said that by staying in business, "Whole Foods behaves in accordance with the principles I spelled out in my 1970 *New York Times Magazine* article." In effect, Friedman gave Mackey credit for increasing Whole Foods' shareholder profits with its CSR contributions by at least as much as the cost of making them.

Of course, no one knows for sure if a corporation's CSR contributions increase profits enough to pay for themselves. The answer to the general question regarding the effect of CSR contributions on profits remains elusive despite the many academic studies that have considered it. But what these studies, as well as the debates and Friedman's 1970 paper, don't consider is that possibly quite a lot of the extra profits come from the corporate welfare a firm's CSR contributions allow it to capture. This positive connection between CSR and corporate welfare doesn't seem to interest advocates of CSR, but it should concern economists who recognize the efficiency losses from CSR. Even if the additional profits more than cover the cost of the CSR contribution creating them, those contributions can still be inefficient if some of the additional profits are the result of corporate welfare. A positive connection between a firm's CSR contribution and its receipt of corporate welfare clearly increases the power of Friedman's argument against CSR.

APPRECIATING THE MOUSE WHILE IGNORING THE ELEPHANT

American corporations contribute a large amount of money to their communities, and those contributions provide real benefits to, and are appreciated by, those in the communities receiving them. In 2016, corporations made $18.6 billion in charitable contributions, according to the *Chronical of Philanthropy*.[3] Obviously, not all this giving is motivated by generosity since up to some point corporate giving can more than pay for itself with higher profits from the goodwill created. Yet, from the corporation's perspective, it is hoped that people see it as generosity. Surely many do, and not just recipients. Many people look at measures of CSR to help them make what they hope are more socially responsible investment decisions.[4] What these measures invariably ignore, however, is the fact that the net amount American corporations contribute to society, as measured by CSR, is decisively *negative*.[5] Even if all corporate giving was motivated by generosity, we would have to conclude that corporate managements are more enthusiastic about taking than giving. A Cato Institute study (DeHaven 2012) found that the federal government budgeted $98 billion dollars to corporate welfare in fiscal year 2012.[6]

These expenditures "include direct and indirect subsidies to small businesses, large corporations, and industry organizations" (DeHaven 2012, 2). Corporate welfare has surely increased since 2012, and the $98 billion figure greatly understates the cost of corporate welfare in 2012 for at least three reasons. First, it doesn't include tax breaks and protections against competition provided by import restrictions and other regulations that benefit corporations but don't show up in the federal budgets. Second, it doesn't include the "corporate welfare" received from state and local governments. Finally, it doesn't include the loss from the socially unproductive rent-seeking by corporations to capture government benefits.

One would think those interested in determining the social responsibility of different corporations would consider not only the CSR mouse but also the corporate welfare elephant by which corporations are profiting at the expense of the entire country. Yet few seem bothered by the fact that measures of CSR consider the former and ignore the social cost of corporate welfare. This is partly explained by that welfare being depicted as public-spirited partnerships dedicated to such noble objectives as protecting American jobs (import restrictions), lowering consumer prices (third-party payments), helping the poor (subsidizing products they produce), or protecting the environment. Another reason people tend to notice a corporation's CSR activities while ignoring the social cost of corporate welfare is that it is easier to see the former than the latter.

WHAT IS SEEN AND WHAT IS NOT SEEN[7]

Imagine two hypothetical corporations, A and B, both operating within the law. Assume they are initially equal in terms of the net value they contribute to society by producing and selling their products in open markets, with neither contributing to CSR.

Assume that the CEO of corporation A decides to start playing the political game. First, he decides it would improve his standing in the communities in which A operates if he began making noticeable charitable contributions out of A's profits in the communities in which A operates. Of course, he claims to be motivated by his love of the communities and the desire to "give back" rather than any personal benefit for himself. But he makes sure corporation A's generosity, and his, is well publicized. This experience soon suggests to him the potential corporate benefits from taking corporation A's improved CSR reputation to the next level. He hires a lobbying firm at the local or state level (and in cases of large corporations, Washington, DC) and starts befriending influential politicians and contributing to their campaigns, all paid for by corporation A and its shareholders. In return, the corporation receives subsidies and regulations that artificially increase its competitiveness. The additional revenues are expected to more than cover the rent-seeking costs, the CSR contributions, and the losses that would result without the subsidies from such ventures as green-energy projects.

Turning to corporation B, its CEO continues her refusal to make charitable contributions or to lobby for, or accept, protections, subsidies, or special interest privileges of any kind from government (this is the seriously hypothetical part). She concentrates her efforts, and the money she could be spending on CSR contributions and rent-seeking, on producing better products at lower costs, resulting in B expanding its market share.

Obviously, corporation A is less socially responsible than corporation B, but the superiority of B will go unnoticed. To explain why, consider first what is easily seen about the two corporations. Corporation A's public relations department will make sure that A's CEO is seen being honored by grateful community leaders and direct beneficiaries of his and corporation A's contributions to the community. Even if few people benefit directly from any particular contribution of A, many will know about and appreciate the frequent contributions A is making to their communities. On the other hand, corporation B's refusal to contribute anything to the betterment of any community is also easily seen, in stark contrast with corporation's A's munificence, and remarked upon as evidence of corporation B's lack of social responsibility.

Next consider what is not easily seen. The social cost that results from A producing lower-quality goods and services is not easily seen because of the subsidies that allow their prices to be lower. And the slightly less productive economy, and slightly higher taxes, are spread so thinly over so many millions that it goes unnoticed by most of those being harmed.

The social benefits that corporation B creates are the result of not accepting corporate welfare and thus not creating the social costs that corporation A creates by doing so. But, for the same reason the social cost created by A goes largely unseen, so do the social benefits B provides. No one can see how much wealth would not have been destroyed if corporation A had not taken corporate welfare. Similarly, no one can see how much additional wealth is being produced because corporation B did not take corporate welfare.

So the value of the mouse, as measured by corporation A's CSR, is seen as positive, while corporation B's zero CSR is seen as well. On the other hand, the social cost of A's corporate-welfare elephant is unnoticed, as is the social benefit of B's refusal to lobby for, or accept, such an elephant. This seen versus unseen problem could be reduced if those constructing CSR measures were serious about providing a reasonable measure of both the giving and taking of corporations. No one would argue that such measures would be infallible, but they would provide better information for making serious comparisons of the social responsibility of corporations than current CSR measures provide.

TWO ACTUAL EXAMPLES

Corporation A is hypothetical but is unfortunately representative of many actual American corporations. Yet, as just discussed, individual corporations are more likely to be lauded for their seemingly benevolent CSR than shamed for the social harm caused by the corporate welfare they receive. Still, at some point a corporation's behavior can become so egregious that the public appreciation for its CSR is overwhelmed by the harm it is doing. My first example concerns a corporation that continues to receive public plaudits for its social responsibility despite benefiting from corporate welfare at great expense to consumers, taxpayers, and probably the environment. In my second example, the corporation was disgraced despite its impressive CSR record because of the harm it imposed. The difference between the examples isn't found in the size of the social cost of the corporate welfare received. Instead, the second corporation imposed a social cost that was far more focused than the social cost of the large amount of corporate welfare it received.

I start with Archer Daniels Midland (ADM), a large processor of agricultural commodities such as oilseeds, corn, wheat, and cocoa. As such it has benefited for years (the company was founded in 1923), both directly and indirectly, from US Department of Agriculture subsidies and environmental regulations. Economists did not start focusing criticism on ADM until late in the 20th century with the controversy over corn-based ethanol and ADM's aggressive lobbying of the federal government to subsidize its production, and then to mandate increasing percentages of ethanol be added to gasoline. An estimate by Holcombe (2015) of the annual cost of ethanol to the American consumer is $31.95 billion, which includes the higher price of food because of the diversion of agricultural land and corn into ethanol production. Of course, some of this cost goes to (mostly wealthy) farmers and large farming companies, to ADM and a few other food processors, and to lawyers and lobbyists. Some of these transfers can be dismissed as not being a social cost, but even with transfers, real social cost remains from deadweight losses from economic distortions that destroy wealth by directing resources out of more valuable and into less valuable uses. Recognizing the difficulty of accurately measuring social costs, and for the sake of argument, I assume that the annual social cost of ethanol to Americans is not $31 billion (which seems high to me, even including transfers), but $9 billion. Also, since ADM's share of the ethanol sold in America is approximately one-third, I attribute $3 billion dollars in social cost to ADM (Koplow 2006). I am ignoring corporate welfare that ADM receives from government programs unrelated to ethanol.

One can find people still arguing that putting corn-based ethanol into gasoline diminishes carbon emissions and helps reduce the problem of global warming. But there are several reasons for doubting there are any appreciable environmental benefits, as explained by Eaves and Eaves (2007) and by Naik (2008). It is also worth noting that even Al Gore has admitted that "I shouldn't have supported corn-based ethanol" (Kolawole 2010). If carbon emissions are considered a serious negative externality, then the most cost-effective way to reduce them is with a carbon tax (which should be accompanied by reductions in taxes that are currently being imposed on, and reducing, socially desirable activities). This would eliminate any rationale for politicians to subsidize ethanol of any kind. If ethanol is the least-cost way to reduce carbon emissions, ADM would be able to profit from selling it without government forcing taxpayers to subsidize it and consumers to buy it.

Economists are so focused on the cost ADM is imposing on Americans that they haven't given much consideration to what a socially responsible reputation it has. ADM has an active community giving program (ADM CARES), which gives significant amounts of money to worthy causes in numerous communities.[8] The only evidence I have found on the amount of recent contributions is from a 2013 website (which is no longer available) that gave a figure of a little more than $15 million that ADM and its employees had recently given (I assumed it was an annual figure) to a variety of causes.[9] However much ADM gives to worthy causes, it is enough for it to be admired for its social responsibility, among other attributes. For example, in 2016 *Fortune* magazine ranked ADM the world's most admired company in the food production industry for the second year in a row.[10] Not knowing how much ADM contributed to CSR causes in recent years, I assume those contributions were $30 million a year. That would count as an impressive social contribution until compared against $3 billion dollars in social cost, a cost that goes unmentioned in the ADM news release on the *Fortune* award. In addition to its social responsibility, the news release mentioned that ADM was also being admired for its financial soundness. There is no reason to doubt that the corporate welfare ADM receives contributed to that financial soundness. No doubt ADM will continue to receive admiration for its social responsibility even though that is being swamped by the social cost of its corporate welfare, since the former is seen and the latter is largely unseen.

Enron is another company that was lauded for its CSR while using its political influence to take far more from the public than it gave to worthy causes. Enron may seem like a poor example since no one today remembers Enron as a socially responsible corporation. Before 2001, however, when it collapsed from losses that had been obscured by accounting fraud, Enron was widely appreciated as socially responsible because of its generous charitable contributions. Sims and Brinkmann (2003, 243) state, "[n]ow, when most people hear the word 'Enron' they think of corruption on a colossal scale. . . . Not long ago, the same company had been heralded as a paragon of corporate responsibility and ethics—successful, driven, focused, philanthropic and environmentally responsible." As long as Enron appeared to remain profitable, the large benefits it was receiving from corporate welfare never made the news. Even after Enron collapsed, few pointed out that corporate welfare helped it survive longer than it otherwise would have by making it possible for the corporate managers to obscure the losses longer, which increased the cost of the collapse when it happened. It was the sudden and concentrated losses suffered by Enron shareholders that made the news, not the widely dispersed, but surely greater, cost of the corporate welfare Enron had received for numerous years. Bradley (2008) discusses the corporate welfare Enron received, and McChesney (2002) comments on the perils and lessons that should have been learned from the Enron experience.

Without discussing other examples of firms receiving more credit for social responsibility than they deserve, it is worth pointing to an interesting example of a firm receiving a high ranking for both its CSR and for the corporate welfare it received. Within a two-year period, Intel, the well-known producer of semiconductor microchips, received high marks for both. Based on an analysis of 170,000 companies in 15 countries, Intel was number six in 2017 on a top ten list for CSR compiled by Reputation Institute, a Boston-based reputation-management consulting company, and posted on a Forbes website (Strauss 2017). Yet Intel was number three, with a take of $3.87 billion, on a 2015 list of the eight American companies receiving the most corporate welfare from all levels of government. The list was compiled from data gathered by Good Jobs First, a group that tracks subsidies (Becker 2015). It is a safe bet that most, probably all, of the eight companies on this corporate welfare list receive lots of accolades for their CSR.

One would expect including measures of both CSR and corporate welfare would be considered important information to those thinking about limiting their investments to socially responsible corporations. Yet, looking over dozens of socially responsible investing websites, I found no mention of corporate welfare.[11]

Nothing is mentioned about taxpayers, or the social cost of benefiting from wasteful special interest government benefits, or regulations that reduce competition and economic efficiency.

FORGING A CONNECTION

Critics of both CSR and corporate welfare have never, as far I as I can find, considered how the two mutually reinforce each other, with corporations using the political goodwill from the former to profit from the latter, and then using some of those profits to increase their image as socially responsible.

It is widely recognized that by developing an image of social responsibility a corporation can increase its profits by increasing the goodwill of the community and, in particular, consumers. There is good evidence that consumers respond favorably to the products of firms they believe are socially responsible (Sullivan 2014). I have been able to find little, however, indicating that corporations use CSR activities to increase the effectiveness of their lobbying for special interest political advantages. A couple of articles I found seemed to be moving in that direction but didn't get there.

An article by Kitzmueller and Shimshack (2012) looked promising initially, but never got close. They cite Friedman (1970) as contributing to the question of whether CSR should or shouldn't exist but claim that most scholars now agree that CSR can be justified as socially desirable in some cases, but not all. Their paper investigates conditions under which social welfare can be improved more by CSR than by other means. They do mention a possible political advantage to be realized by firms from CSR, but that advantage comes from hedging against risks from activist campaigns harming their reputations or from avoiding government regulatory action. There is no mention of corporate welfare or rent-seeking. Lobbying is mentioned, but only in terms of CSR discouraging activist groups from securing government policies that are socially harmful, which they point out assumes the possibility of government failure. One would think they would acknowledge government failure instead of assuming it. So the implication is that CSR makes it possible to avoid the inefficiency of government failure, assuming it exists.

An article by Carroll (2015), who supports CSR, is concerned that corporate giving is motivated increasingly by the desire for political influence. His article, however, is not about giving to community charities, but giving directly to politicians and charitable foundations established by influential politicians (or former politicians)—in particular, the Clinton Foundation—in expectation of profitable political advantages. His last sentence concludes that "CSR is primarily about improving society not augmenting business's influence. To do otherwise is to invite further government regulations, and who wants this? Certainly not the business community." Again, an advantage business supposedly receives from CSR that improves society is that it wards off government regulation. Carroll ignores the logic of bootleggers and Baptists and the possibility that corporations often embrace regulation because it allows them to benefit at public expense.

As opposed to Carroll's article, however, I don't see CSR contributions being given to those who are able to return direct political favors. That would be direct lobbying. Instead, I see CSR primarily as providing support to desirable causes and activities with little expectation of direct returns from the beneficiaries. This does not rule out a connection between CSR contributions and the expectation of corporate welfare, but the connection is subtler and less direct than the process normally associated with lobbying for corporate welfare. This subtlety and indirectness, along with what I believe is the largely local influence of CSR giving on political decisions, provides an explanation for why the connection between CSR and corporate welfare remains below the radar screens, even of economists.[12]

Decisions on CSR and corporate welfare at all levels are made largely by people in the same social class, whose members have high levels of education, wealth, and professional success. At the local as well as the state (particularly in small states) levels, these "movers and shakers" tend to belong to the same social organizations, have mutual friends, associates, and neighbors, and, within a couple of degrees of separation, are on a first-name basis with a large number of socially and politically influential people, including state, local, and federal representatives. Such a social network is a valuable political asset for corporate CEOs (or heads of businesses or organizations making CSR contributions) and influences the CSR decisions they make.[13] For those decisions to be profitable, they don't have to generate reciprocity directly, just support causes and activities that make people, particularly those in the upper class, feel good about the contributions and their source.

Such contributions commonly support activities that benefit the socially influential directly and/or that they believe enhance the community for others. Contributions to the arts (the symphony, opera, ballet, and theater) clearly satisfy this condition. The arts appeal to the upper class because many of them genuinely enjoy artistic performances and exhibits. In addition, for many successful people, appreciating the arts is seen as a way of signaling their sophistication and refinement to others considered to be sophisticated and refined. Also, the arts are seen as elevating the status of the entire community by offering opportunities for residents to enrich their lives through exposure to artistic expression. For very similar reasons, contributions to universities, museums, aquariums, and historical preservation are also popular objects of

CSR contributions. One can question how much the poor benefit from some of these contributions, but community leaders also donate, and respond favorably to CSR contributions, to help the poor and homeless. Also, contributions to protect the environment are seen with great favor. And though I am interested primarily in CSR contributions, members of society's upper echelon make their own individual contributions to a wide range of good causes.

The main point, however, is that the response of the general community, and particularly of the community's social and political elite, to a corporation's CSR can do a lot to increase its ability to achieve political favor and harvest corporate welfare. There are large numbers of businesses and other organizations in small and large communities that contribute to the betterment of their communities, and obviously not all these contributions are motivated entirely by the expectation of political favors. But just as obviously, many are, to one degree or another. Consider the connection between CSR and the public financing of football stadiums owned by wealthy owners of professional football teams.[14]

The NFL Foundation is a nonprofit organization that represents the 32 NFL teams. According to NFL Commissioner Roger Goodell, the foundation committed $45 million in 2014 to its program "USA Football" to support health and safety efforts through "Heads Up Football," youth and high school football programs, and community health initiatives.[15] Also on the website one can discover that the NFL Foundation has a tradition known as "NFL Tuesdays" when, during the football season, players volunteer to help at local schools, shelters, and hospitals. Each team's website is also available, with some of them providing information on their charitable contributions. For example, the Green Bay Packers organization has given $7.2 million for charitable purposes since 1966. I couldn't find information on contributions on some of the other teams' websites, but no doubt they also make them. Although not on the NFL website, the team owners surely donate to their local communities through their own foundations, and in many cases through the CSR contributions of the businesses many of them own. These owners are wealthy, well-known, and influential members of their local communities and states. No one can doubt that the NFL and the owners of professional football teams "give back" to their communities. But in this case, there is more meaning to the well-worn term "give back" than they would like to admit. The problem is that they don't give back as much as they take.[16] Football owners, and their teams, no doubt benefit from several types of corporate welfare, including some provided by the federal government. Yet, in the case of professional football teams, as well as professional teams in other sports, the most obvious examples of corporate welfare are the government subsidies to build and refurbish sport stadiums belonging to the team owners.

According to Heller (2015), "Over the past 15 years, $12 billion in public money has been spent on privately owned football stadiums." These deals transfer such large sums of money from local taxpayers to wealthy owners of sports teams that, as opposed to most examples of corporate welfare, they *are* noticed by taxpayers. But even when opposition to these transfers to the rich arises, it often doesn't succeed, even when it is voted down. Indeed, demands for a vote on such deals are often ignored. As Heller describes it, the intense support for these deals comes from "local plutocrats" who prefer "quiet, behind-the-scenes" meetings, with the less public involvement the better. There is little reason to doubt, despite Heller's pejorative description, that many of these "local plutocrats" are often very public in their charitable activities. As Heller (2015) recognizes, "publicly funded stadiums face the least opposition in cities [where the public funding is favored by] strong growth coalitions, [that] can claim to represent the interests of a community—not an outrageous claim on its face, since it comprises the powerful and prominent local leaders." Heller suggests that these "powerful and prominent local leaders" are also strongly influenced by the team owners.

This section suggests that rent-seeking forges a connection between CSR and corporate welfare, particularly at local levels, that hasn't been considered, at least as far as I know, by either those advocating the former or those criticizing the latter. It is not surprising that advocates of CSR haven't seen a connection between the charitable activities of corporations and their ability to grab special interest political privileges at public expense. It is surprising that economists, especially public choice economists who are skeptical of CSR and see corporate welfare as a serious problem, haven't made, and emphasized, a connection between the two.

CONCLUSION

I believe the best way to conclude the story I have told about CSR and corporate welfare is by considering the differences between it and the stories Yandle has told about bootleggers and Baptists. My story is about how corporations, in the role of bootleggers, could use CSR contributions to generate political support to obtain corporate welfare. As indicated in the introduction, I anticipated that a group would be identified who, motivated by CSR contributions, would serve as Baptists in corporation rent-seeking for corporate welfare. As the writing reached section 6 and I needed to make the identification, I had to admit that there was no group that I thought qualified as Yandle Baptists. Yandle Baptists have the ability to provide critically important political support to the bootleggers' desired political purpose, and a strong motivation to provide it even though they are opposed to the bootleggers' general motivation. In other words, we are talking about two groups that make strange bedfellows, more political enemies than political allies in general. This is the counterintuitive feature of Yandle's bootleggers and Baptists stories that makes them so interesting and lacking in my story.

A community that contains lots of people who are mildly appreciative of a corporation for its CSR activities can be an asset in its rent-seeking activities, but it is unlikely a good substitute for Yandle Baptists. Yet there are cases where the political desires of a corporation would be served by legislative victory that would appeal to few, if any, groups of Yandle Baptists. Corporations in, for example, the soft-drink, petroleum, or payday loan industries are examples of bootleggers facing a shortage of Baptists. Of course, even the tobacco industry found helpful Baptists in the form of anti-smoking groups, as explained by Smith and Yandle (2014, 87–89). But Smith and Yandle (2014, 129) also have a chapter dealing with "a bootlegger without a Baptist" in which they say that when there are no Baptists for political endeavors, those "endeavors typically fail."

When Yandle Baptists are unavailable, however, a rent-seeking corporation can benefit from having cultivated a reputation for CSR in the relevant community as a second-best alternative.[17] It is worth recognizing that both have strengths that complement each other. Yandle Baptists provide strong and direct political support that is focused on a narrow facet of a corporation's political agenda, while the political support derived from a corporation's CSR activities is weaker but not limited to any particular reason for the support. So, even when a corporation has Baptists willing to focus their support for one of its political wishes, it can still find its CSR activities helpful in motivating support for a broader array of its political agenda, including many that no group of Baptists would support.[18]

As opposed to what I anticipated when starting this paper, I cannot claim I have extended the applications of the standard bootleggers and Baptists insight. At most I have shown how the connection between a firm's CSR and its ability to capture corporate welfare reinforce each other. A firm's CSR increases its profits from rent-seeking, which in turn can be used to finance more CSR activities. Of course, this process doesn't increase indefinitely because of diminishing marginal effectiveness of CSR on rent-seeking and diminishing marginal effectiveness of rent-seeking on profits.

The stronger the positive connection between CSR and corporate welfare, the more it strengthens the argument that CSR reduces social welfare in ways not discussed by Friedman, or anyone else of whom I am aware. But I regret to say that the connection between CSR and corporate welfare might also be used by some CSR enthusiasts to argue that it is even more beneficial than they had previously thought. They might claim that not only does CSR increase profits by creating more consumer goodwill, it also creates more political goodwill and thus fosters more private- and public-sector cooperation that benefits us all. Who would bet against the existence of a large number of otherwise sensible people who would applaud this claim as a brilliant insight?[19] What an ironic and unintended result this would be of an argument meant to honor Bruce Yandle.

NOTES

1. Many have used and expanded on Yandle's initial paper, including myself. Also, the book by Smith and Yandle (2014) has greatly expanded and updated the applications of the Bootleggers and Baptists model and deserves serious attention.
2. Also in a speech Mackay gave at the 2006 Mont Pelerin meeting held in Guatemala.
3. See Sandoval (2017). Even though I am referring to corporations because of the popularity of the term "corporate social responsibility," not all these contributions are made by incorporated businesses, and indeed many are small businesses. Also, a relatively small amount of charitable contributions by businesses take the form of what Sandoval refers to as sponsorships, something called "cause marketing," and volunteer activities by employees, which aren't captured in the reported data. In keeping with custom, however, I continue to use the term corporations, and the acronym CSR, when referring to businesses more generally.
4. For information on CSR measures, google "measuring corporate responsibility." Not surprisingly, corporations are not bashful about measuring their own social responsibility.
5. Not counting their contribution from the production of goods and services for profit.
6. Just as unincorporated businesses make charitable contributions, so do they receive benefits from government commonly called corporate welfare. So again, in keeping with custom, I shall continue to refer to corporate welfare.
7. This subtitle is taken from Bastiat (2016).
8. For more details, ADM CARES can be searched to find some of its individual contributions.
9. These causes included research on improving agricultural technology, improvements in getting food distributed to poor countries, United Way, and natural disaster aid.
10. The *Fortune* rankings are based on several considerations, including social responsibility.
11. See Bank of America (n.d.) or search Google for US Trust's Socially Innovative Investing Strategy. For a look at other socially responsible investing websites, google "socially responsible investing." If anyone finds a website recommending socially responsible investing that lists corporate welfare as a negative, I would be happy, but surprised, to hear about it.
12. Most discussions of lobbying for political advantage focus more on the federal level than the local level or even the state level. For example, Smith and Yandle (2014) devote more attention to federal issues such as TARP (and financial legislation), Obamacare, global warming, and federal regulation of automobile mileage. Their discussion of sin taxes considers

lobbying at the state level, but also discusses the federal role in reaching the 1998 Master Settlement Agreement with tobacco companies. This is not a criticism, since lobbying, like bank-robbing, is strongly influenced by where the money is. But there is also a lot of money distributed at the state and local level. It is also interesting to note that the political activity of the historical bootleggers and Baptists took place at the local level.

13. When considering CSR, particularly at the local level, it is important to recall that I am using the word corporations broadly to consider businesses that are not incorporated; professional associations of occupations such as lawyers, dentists, medical doctors; and owners of professional sports franchises, among others.

14. The standard argument for public financing of professional sports stadiums is that they increase local economic growth enough to pay for themselves. Studies have consistently failed to support this claim. See Siegfried and Zimbalist (2000) for an explanation of why this economic growth fails to materialize. They also show that sports stadiums were until rather recently privately financed.

15. This is in a letter available on the NFL community website at http://www.nfl.com/community, under "Read more about the NFL's commitment to the community."

16. This isn't the most serious problem. Taking in corporate welfare and giving it all back in CSR contributions would not be nearly as good as not taking it at all.

17. It is easy to find examples online of the charitable activities of corporations in the soft-drink and petroleum industries. But I could find nothing for a payday loan company, although a few of them probably sponsor little league baseball teams. This is not to imply, of course, that corporations benefiting from the support of Yandle Baptists will ignore the benefits from a favorable reputation based on CSR contributions. The more moral gloss the better when seeking corporate welfare.

18. In chapter 9 in this volume, Morriss (190) argues that bootleggers can find advantage in adding complexity to their policies as a way "to make policy objectives opaque to public scrutiny."

19. In an important paper, DeBow (1992) considers the question of whether rent-seeking is ethical from the perspective of corporate social responsibility. He does not, however, argue that establishing a reputation for CSR is a means of increasing the effectiveness of rent-seeking.

REFERENCES

Bank of America. n.d. "Understanding Socially Innovative Investing." https://www.privatebank.bankofamerica.com/articles/understanding-socially-innovative-investing.html.

Bastiat, F. 2016. "Economic Sophisms and 'What Is Seen and What Is Not Seen.'" In *The Collected Works of Frederic Bastiat*, edited by Jacques de Guenin. Indianapolis, IN: Liberty Fund.

Becker, S. 2015. "The 8 Biggest Corporate Welfare Recipients in America." *Cheat Sheet*, May 7. https://www.cheatsheet.com/business/high-on-the-hog-the-top-8-corporate-welfare-recipients.html/?a=viewall.

Bradley, R. L. 2008. "Enron: The Perils of Interventionism." *Library of Economics and Liberty*, September 3. http://www.econlib.org/library/Columns/y2012/Bradleyenron.html.

Carroll, A. 2015. "Political CSR: Why Companies and Foreign Governments Give to Foundations Like Clinton's." *The Conversation*, February 27. https://theconversation.com/political-csr-why-companies-and-foreign-governments-give-to-foundations-like-clintons-37876.

DeBow, M. E. 1992. "The Ethics of Rent-Seeking? A New Perspective on Corporate Social Responsibility." *Journal of Law & Commerce* 12, no. 2: 1–21.

DeHaven, T. 2012. "Corporate Welfare in the Federal Budget." *Policy Analysis* 703. Cato Institute, July 25. https://object.cato.org/sites/cato.org/files/pubs/pdf/PA703.pdf.

Eaves, J., and S. Eaves. 2007. "Neither Renewable nor Reliable." *Regulation* (Fall): 24–27. https://object.cato.org/sites/cato.org/files/serials/files/regulation/2007/10/v30n3-1.pdf.

Friedman, M. 1962. *Capitalism and Freedom*. Chicago: University of Chicago Press.

——. 1970. "The Social Responsibility of Business Is to Increase Its Profits." *New York Times Magazine*, September 13.

Heller, C. 2015. "The Impossible Fight against America's Stadiums." *Psmag.com*, September 2. https://psmag.com/economics/the-shady-money-behind-americas-sports-stadiums.

Holcombe, R. G. 2015. "The Costs and Benefits of Ethanol." *Mises Wire*, March 18. https://mises.org/blog/costs-and-benefits-ethanol.

Kitzmueller, M., and J. Shimshack. 2012. "Economic Perspectives on Corporate Social Responsibility." *Journal of Economic Literature* 50, no. 1: 51–84.

Kolawole, E. 2010. "Al Gore: I Shouldn't Have Supported Corn-Based Ethanol." *Washington Post*, November 22. http://voices.washingtonpost.com/44/2010/11/al-gore-i-shouldnt-have-suppor.html.

Koplow, D. 2006. "Biofuels—At What Cost? Government Support for Ethanol and Biodiesel in the United States." Earthtrack, Inc., October. http://www.iisd.org/gsi/sites/default/files/brochure_-_us_report.pdf.

Lee, D. R. 2013. "Socially Responsible Corporations: The Seen and the Unseen." *Library of Economics and Liberty*, February 4. http://www.econlib.org/library/Columns/y2013/Leecorporations.html.

McChesney, F. S. 2002. "Enron's True Lesson: Political Opportunism." *Library of Economics and Liberty*, March 11. http://www.econlib.org/library/Columns/Mcchesneyenron.html.

McKenzie, R. B., and D. R. Lee. 1998. *Managing through Incentives: How to Develop a More Collaborative, Productive, and Profitable Organization*. Oxford: Oxford University Press.

Naik, G. 2008. "Biofuels May Hinder Antiglobal-Warming Efforts." *Wall Street Journal*, February 9. https://www.wsj.com/articles/SB120241324358751455.

Reason. 2005. "Rethinking the Social Responsibility of Business." http://reason.com/archives/2005/10/01/rethinking-the-social-responsi/1.

Sandoval, T. 2017. "Giving USA." *Chronical of Philanthropy*, June 13. https://www.philanthropy.com/article/Donations-Grew-14-to-390/240319.

Siegfried, J., and A. Zimbalist. 2000. "The Economics of Sports Facilities and Their Communities." *Journal of Economic Perspectives* 14, no. 3: 95–113.

Sims, R. R., and J. Brinkmann. 2003. "Enron Ethics: Culture Matters More than Codes." *Journal of Business Ethics* 45, no. 3: 243–56.

Smith, A., and B. Yandle. 2014. *Bootleggers and Baptists: How Economic Forces and Moral Persuasion Interact to Shape Regulatory Politics*. Washington, DC: Cato Institute.

Strauss, K. 2017. "The 10 Companies with the Best CSR Reputations in 2017." *Forbes*, September 13. https://www.forbes.com/sites/karstenstrauss/2017/09/13/the-10-companies-with-the-best-csr-reputations-in-2017/#74b0f630546b.

Sullivan, P. 2014. "Consumers Will Pay More for Corporate Social Responsibility." *NonProfit Times*, June 17. http://www.thenonprofittimes.com/news-articles/corporate-social-responsibility/.

Yandle, B. 1983. "Bootleggers and Baptists: The Education of a Regulatory Economist." *Regulation* 7, no. 3: 12–15.

CHAPTER 12

What Has Happened to Economics?

Some Thoughts on Economics and Policymakers

BRUCE YANDLE

This much-appreciated, not so well deserved, opportunity to participate in a generously supported Festschrift brings to mind Mark Twain's marvelous account of Tom Sawyer's experience when he, Huck Finn, and Joe returned home from a long-lost adventure only to find that the home folks had given them up for dead and were in the midst of conducting their funeral:

> As the service proceeded, the clergyman drew such pictures of the graces, the winning ways, and the rare promise of the lost lads that every soul there, thinking he recognized these pictures, felt a pang in remembering that he had persistently blinded himself to them always before, and had as persistently seen only faults and flaws in the poor boys. The minister related many a touching incident in the lives of the departed, too, which illustrated their sweet, generous natures, and the people could easily see, now, how noble and beautiful those episodes were, and remembered with grief that at the time they occurred they had seemed rank rascalities, well deserving of the cowhide.

> The congregation became more and more moved, as the pathetic tale went on, till at last the whole company broke down and joined the weeping mourners in a chorus of anguished sobs, the preacher himself giving way to his feelings, and crying in the pulpit. (Twain 1876, chap. 17)

It was at that point that the three missing lads, having entered the rear of the church, walked down the center aisle, much to the amazement of the preacher and everyone else in the assembled congregation. So here I am, grateful to the contributors to this volume and for the overly generous thoughts that emerged in the discussion of the drafts of the papers.

The Festschrift highlights the importance of institutions, economic incentives, regulation, and the interplay of economic agents in the nation's political economy. These concepts characterize my work and interests, so here I consider these same notions in the context of economics itself. What about economics, broadly considered? How has the subject matter changed over my career? How might we assess the process that brings new economic learning to bear on public policy? Can we find some Bootleggers/Baptists influence in the process?

In this paper, to illustrate how economics has changed, I first offer some thoughts on the content of economics I encountered as an undergraduate college student. The struggle over how economics becomes applied to public policy follows this discussion. I then share some thoughts on the production of economic knowledge and how that has been influenced by the rise of high-powered computing. This discussion is followed by a section that examines the tournament of ideas that can cause older conventional wisdom to be dislodged and perhaps replaced by newer, more robust theories. Throughout the discussion that follows, I suggest how Bootleggers/Baptists activity affects which theories—new or old—will be used politically to justify action.

EARLY ENCOUNTERS WITH ECONOMICS AND THE PRODUCTION OF IDEAS

Word about the Festschrift caused me to think about my first formal encounter with economics in 1951, when I took principles of economics at Young Harris College, a small school located in the northern Georgia mountains. I retrieved the textbook we used that semester. It was Paul F. Gemmill's *Fundamentals of Economics*, 5th ed. (New York: Harper and Brothers, 1949). The contents included strong micro coverage, lots of supply and demand, and heavy treatment of the firm. There was also a surprisingly strong discussion of monetary theory and the equation of exchange, but there were no chapters on macroeconomics and nothing on GDP and national income accounting. Remember, those measurements were first provided routinely in 1947 (Bureau of Economic Analysis 2017). There was also no discussion of public-sector economics, and nothing on antitrust, government regulation, and what might be called legal foundations that affect market transactions.

Of course, and as might be expected, Gemmill's book held no treatment of natural resources and external effects, and it contained no discussion of rent-seeking behavior. Indeed, there was hardly any comment on political economy, because, in truth and relative to now, there wasn't much political economy at the time. Not only that, there was little in the way of abstract analytical engines other than the equation of exchange, and only limited use of data that might relate to a theoretical topic. At the time, the cost of doing empirical work was extraordinarily high. After all, this was 67 years ago. The typical economist was working with a manual typewriter and a 10-key calculator. Economic debate rested heavily on anecdotes and hardheaded theoretical reasoning.

What economists do, and perhaps economics itself, changed dramatically over the intervening years for two important reasons. First, government policy making and activity, the traditional object of economic analysis, grew rapidly; the public sector itself became a larger entangled part of the economy. Second, because of the rapidly falling costs of information retrieval and data processing, economics became an empirical science. Both the scale and scope of economic research expanded.

Continuing this journey into the past, I recalled the wonderful course I had as a senior at Mercer University in 1954 when Professor Victor Heck assembled five of us students around a table to discuss Robert Heilbroner's gracefully written *The Worldly Philosophers* (New York: Simon & Schuster), just published in 1952. By the way, the book is now counted as the second most popular book in economics; Samuelson's *Principles* is number one, at least according to Wikipedia. The course was history of economic thought. The stories in the book were so inspiring that they caused me to make several rare visits to the university library to read some economic treatises. I became smitten. At least the seeds of interest were planted then; it took a while for them to germinate and blossom.

MR. KEYNES ENTERS THE DISCUSSION

Heilbroner's introduction contained a quotation from John Maynard Keynes that is often partially repeated by those who wish to flatter themselves about the importance of economic ideas. The expanded quotation, with the less familiar part shown in boldface, offers a theory of idea germination and perhaps explains why even today in 2019, when arguing about the possible harmful environmental effects of expanding industrialization, economists, more often than not, resort to recommendations based on thinking that prevailed in the 1930s. Yes, the policy proposals of A. C. Pigou still seem to hold sway (Pigou 1920).

> The ideas of economists and political philosophers, both when they are right and when they are wrong, are more powerful than is commonly understood. Indeed the world is ruled by little else. Practical men, who believe themselves to be quite exempt from any intellectual influences, are usually the slaves of some defunct economist. Madmen in authority, who hear voices in the air, are distilling their frenzy from some academic scribbler of a few years back. **I am sure that the power of vested interests is vastly exaggerated compared with the gradual encroachment of ideas. Not, indeed, immediately, but after a certain interval; for in the field of economic and political philosophy there are not many who are influenced by new theories after they are twenty-five or thirty years of age, so that the ideas which civil servants and politicians and even agitators apply to current events are not likely to be the newest. But, soon or late, it is ideas, not vested interests, which are dangerous for good or evil.** (Keynes 1936, 383–84, emphasis added)

Put differently, we should expect to find a lag between newly hatched theories and their acceptance in the policy-making arena. Perhaps fascinated by the development and gradual transmission of ideas, Keynes addressed the topic in the introduction to *The General Theory*: "The difficulty lies, not in the new ideas, but in escaping from the old ones, which ramify, for those brought up as most of us have been, into every corner of our minds" (Keynes 1936, vii).

We might put this yet another way: there are rents associated with the possession and use of specialized knowledge by practitioners as well as lobbyists for government favors. New theory can be rent disruptive and therefore resisted. Eventually, however, new interpretations of how the world works, if superior to the old, can break through; at least we want to think that is the case.

But there is more to story. For example, current White House occupants—and some of their economic advisers—have proven once again that what some may have thought to be obsolete and costly theories of mercantilism can rise full blown from the grave and become the basis for regulating the economy. Interestingly enough (at least to me), the fact that popular fallacies from the past can become prevalent in a future period—in spite of what bright and articulate economists might say—indicates the power of Bootleggers/Baptists forces that play through the political economy. Yes, there is a choice process at play when politicians select theoretical justifications for their actions, and some theories serve their purposes better than others.

When industry bootleggers who find protectionism to be rewarding combine effectively with Baptist nationalists who are inspired by America First slogans, discarded policy tools from the past can become the toast of the town. And let us not stop here. Bootlegger/Baptist logic helps explain outcomes for environmental policy, health care, and education, to mention just three policy topics. Even though known to be costly and less effective than market-based regulation, Bootleggers/Baptists–preferred command-and-control, technology-based regulation tends to prevail.

THE PRODUCTION OF IDEAS

Imagine a production process—an economics workshop—where scholars seek to discover and measure economic relationships. They hope to add to the stock of knowledge. To simplify, we might think of the workshop's products as reports on various aspects of the national economy and political decision-making. Researchers in the workshop produce competing papers. The technology they apply, their capital, includes machinery for retrieving knowledge and for organizing data and doing statistical modeling as well. At various times—from early to recent times—the technology applied includes books, pen and paper, chalk and blackboards, then libraries, journals, guides to literature, computers, and ultimately digital retrieval methods and instantly available statistical treatment capabilities for almost unlimited amounts of data.

As we think about the production relationship, we picture isoquants that denote levels of output associated with combinations of labor and capital. We can imagine changing relative prices of labor and capital and how capital becomes substituted for labor when the cost of using digital computing capabilities falls. In early stages, when technology is crude, researchers apply lots of labor and not so much capital. There is theory without much data and statistical modeling. With technical progress, statistical testing becomes commonplace, and as larger, seemingly almost unlimited datasets become available, substitution of capital for labor becomes so pronounced that data analysis tends to overwhelm theorizing. Meanwhile, output expands markedly and specialization flourishes.

Along these lines, we may forecast that soon, workshop scholars will be able to voice questions to smart technology and almost instantly receive highly technical answers. For example, one might ask the smart cloud's Alexa to provide a multivariate estimate of the demand for SUVs, using 20 years' cross-sectional data, taking account of price, weight of vehicle, fuel efficiency, consumer age, gender, income, educational attainment, and the price of energy and competing modes of transportation, accompanied by appropriate statistical diagnostics and treatments.

If we were to visit the research workshop today, we might find three kinds of specialized labor. There would be some idea people—theorizers and storytellers—who specify models. There would be other specialists who translate the first group's more general models into sophisticated mathematical statements that are ready for statistical testing. And there would be a third group who access big data and use the data to estimate statistical relationships. Lower-cost retrieval mechanisms and data access lead to relatively more second and third category workers and fewer storytellers and theorizers. But as the substitution occurs, the theorizers, at the margin, become more valuable. Imagine what it will feel like to be the last storyteller standing. Meanwhile, the workshop produces new ideas and empirically based research products. Whether and how those ideas are used in the policy-making process is another matter.

TRANSMITTING OUTPUT TO POLICYMAKERS

We now return to Keynes and the larger all-encompassing world economics workshop. As Keynes pointed out, there is resistance to acceptance of the flow of new economic knowledge in the marketplace for ideas. There are also political elements that influence the pace of change. The new ideas can be disruptive to expert purveyors of existing knowledge, which includes public-sector agents. Some ideas accommodate rent-seekers; others erode rents. There are differential effects. Keynes, however, did not address the extent to which data and empirical work might accelerate acceptance of disruptive ideas. Nor, as discussed earlier, did he consider how political demand for policy ideas might be affected by coalitions of interest groups that influence the political process and policy shops engaged in that process. In a way, Keynes's brief theory of idea generation was like his theory of the macroeconomy. The government sector was exogenous to the economy; it was in a box by itself, not an integral part of the whole. The theoretical and actual outcome changes when government becomes endogenous.

To illustrate these points, let us now consider a few idea tournaments where champion placeholders were dislodged or at least influenced by competitors in idea dominance.

CHAMPION AND CONTENDER TOURNAMENTS FOR ECONOMIC THEORIES

In this section, I discuss four idea tournaments where an idea champion, what might be called the conventional wisdom, was dislodged by a contender. There are others that I might mention, but these four will suffice to illustrate how I see the noted idea competition occurring. I note that when I indicate that a previously prevailing idea has been dislodged, I do not mean that the former champion disappears from the scene entirely. Quite the contrary, the former champion sticks around and may, depending on the forces of political demand and supply, which is to say Bootleggers/Baptists activity, reemerge and may again become dominant. I note that some of the tournaments that led to changed dominance were driven by empirical analysis; others rested on historical or anecdotal analysis.

Here are my four examples of champions and contenders, where the contender won the intellectual tournament but perhaps failed to win the political battle. I list the champion that was nudged away first and give the names of leading scholars involved. For most items, I note the dominant form of argument, whether theoretical, anecdotal, or empirical, and I also offer a cryptic identification of an associated shock or crisis. I leave some less identified and in doing so appeal to others for their interpretations:

1. Keynesian (Heller) versus Monetarist (Friedman) explanations of the macroeconomy (Friedman and Heller 1968). This was an empirical contest that occurred in the mid to late 1960s. Slow growth and inflation were conditions that encouraged the scholarly debate. The accumulation of large amounts of empirical work facilitated the discussion. The result: the role of money in the economy could no longer be disregarded. However, rent-seeking bankers and populist politicians place pressure on the Fed to minimize the role of money in policy making and to emphasize Keynesian ideas and regulation.
2. Normative Public Finance (Musgrave) versus Public Choice (Buchanan and Tullock).[1] This intellectual struggle also took place in the 1960s; it was

initially a theoretical and anecdotal debate, supported later by extensive empirical work. Public Choice took a positive approach when analyzing public-sector behavior as opposed to the public interest—normative—approach previously applied. High public debt and low public-sector performance put a spotlight on the problem addressed by the contender. Result: Public decision-making is now understood using the same economic logic as private decision-making. However, Bootleggers/Baptists coalitions still emphasize a public interest argument for political actions that in turn favor organized private rent-seekers.

3. Externalities (Pigou) versus Property Rights (Coase).[2] This is largely a theoretical and anecdotal debate that started in 1960 and continues to this day. The environmental saga and misinterpretations of Pigou's remedy inspired the debate. Result: institutions and incentives were seen to be important for those who wish to understand public-sector institution building. It must be emphasized that Pigou's externality theory continues to command the attention of environmentalist-Baptists and industrialist-bootleggers who both prefer the Pigovian remedy to Coase's property rights, common law, remedy.

4. Antitrust Concentration Doctrine (everyone else) versus Market Behavior Model (Demsetz and Bork).[3] This debate emerged in the 1970s and relied on theoretical, anecdotal, and empirical analyses. Growing global competition in US markets provided a market-based remedy to domestic monopolization. Threat of entry brought competitive-like behavior to firms that appeared to hold a monopoly position. Only government-sanctioned monopolies should be of concern. However, populist special interest groups who still show deep concern about bigness or what may actually be the result of earlier successful rent-seeking are joined by industrialists who prefer regulation to antitrust breakup and international antitrust actions. Bootleggers and Baptists continue to ride the antitrust trail.

These four policy tournaments may illustrate how new thinking and insights can push aside or at least influence the treatment of older and more established theories in the process of developing an improved understanding of how the world works. As noted, however, policy actions, which can be justified on the basis of theories, are driven by politics, and purposeful politicians, who like other normal people, predictably seek success and good fortune in their work. That being the case, institutional change that may be justified by newly developed theories does not occur smoothly or permanently. Indeed, it is possible for the old to become new, and the new, old. Actions taken by bootleggers/Baptists in the political arena affect public policy production.

FINAL THOUGHTS

Let us now return to Mark Twain's account of the funeral:

> There was a rustle in the gallery, which nobody noticed; a moment later the church door creaked; the minister raised his streaming eyes above his handkerchief, and stood transfixed! First one and then another pair of eyes followed the minister's, and then almost with one impulse the congregation rose and stared while the three dead boys came marching up the aisle, Tom in the lead, Joe next, and Huck, a ruin of drooping rags, sneaking sheepishly in the rear! They had been hid in the unused gallery listening to their own funeral sermon!
>
> Aunt Polly, Mary, and the Harpers threw themselves upon their restored ones, smothered them with kisses and poured out thanksgivings, while poor Huck stood abashed and uncomfortable, not knowing exactly what to do or where to hide from so many unwelcoming eyes. He wavered, and started to slink away, but Tom seized him and said: "Aunt Polly, it ain't fair. Somebody's got to be glad to see Huck." "And so they shall. I'm glad to see him, poor motherless thing!" And the loving attentions Aunt Polly lavished upon him were the one thing capable of making him more uncomfortable than he was before. Suddenly the minister shouted at the top of his voice: "Praise God from whom all blessings flow—SING!—and put your hearts in it!"
>
> And they did. Old Hundred swelled up with a triumphant burst, and while it shook the rafters Tom Sawyer the Pirate looked around upon the envying juveniles about him and confessed in his heart that this was the proudest moment of his life. (Twain 1876, chap. 17)

Yes, this Festschrift and the reunion it generated has made this one of the happiest moments in my life.

NOTES

1. I select Musgrave (1959) as representing the conventional wisdom and Buchanan and Tullock (1962) as the challenging document.
2. This contest is typically framed by referring to Pigou (1920) and to Coase (1960).
3. I oversimplify here by saying "everyone else." My point is that antirust action was triggered on the basis of relative bigness, market concentration, and this was the prevailing doctrine. Two key contenders are Demsetz (1973) and Bork (1978).

REFERENCES

Buchanan, J. M., and G. Tullock. 1962. *The Calculus of Consent*. Ann Arbor: University of Michigan Press.

Bureau of Economic Analysis. 2017. "NIPA Handbook: Concepts and Methods of the U.S. National Income and Product Accounts." https://www.bea.gov/resources/methodologies/nipa-handbook.

Bork, R. H. 1978. *The Antitrust Paradox*. New York: Basic Books.

Coase, R. H. 1960. "The Problem of Social Cost." *Journal of Law & Economics* 3: 1–44.

Demsetz, H. A. 1973. *The Market Concentration Doctrine: An Examination of Evidence and Discussion of Policy*. Washington, DC: American Enterprise Institute.

Friedman, M., and W. W. Heller. 1968. *Monetary versus Fiscal Policy*. New York: W. W. Norton.

Gemmill, P. F. 1949. *Fundamentals of Economics*, 5th ed. New York: Harper and Brothers.

Heilbroner, R. 1952. *The Worldly Philosophers*. New York: Simon & Schuster.

Keynes, J. M. 1936. *The General Theory of Employment, Interest and Money*. London: MacMillan.

Musgrave, R. A. 1959. *Theory of Public Finance: A Study in Public Economy.* New York: McGraw-Hill.

Pigou, A. C. 1920. *The Economics of Welfare*. London: Macmillan.

Twain, M. 1876. *The Adventures of Tom Sawyer*. Hartford, CT: American Publishing Co.

ABOUT THE CONTRIBUTORS

Bruce Yandle, co-founder, Clemson Institute for the Study of Capitalism; dean emeritus, College of Business; Alumni Distinguished Professor Emeritus, Department of Economics, Clemson University; and Distinguished Adjunct Fellow, Mercatus Center at George Mason University

Terry L. Anderson, John and Jean DeNault Senior Fellow, Hoover Institution

Peter J. Boettke, University Professor of Economics and Philosophy, George Mason University, and director, F. A. Hayek Program of Advance Study in Philosophy, Politics and Economics, Mercatus Center at George Mason University

Donald J. Boudreaux, professor of economics, George Mason University, and senior fellow, F. A. Hayek Program of Advanced Study in Philosophy, Politics, and Economics, Mercatus Center at George Mason University

J. R. Clark, Probasco Distinguished Chair, The University of Tennessee at Chattanooga

Susan E. Dudley, director, The George Washington University Regulatory Studies Center

Dwight R. Lee, affiliated visiting faculty fellow, Institute for the Study of Political Economy, Miller College of Business, Ball State University

Jody W. Lipford, professor of economics, Presbyterian College

Richard B. McKenzie, Walter B. Gerken Professor, Paul Merage School of Business, University of California, Irvine

Roger Meiners, Goolsby-Rosenthal Chair in Economics and Law, and chairman, Department of Economics, University of Texas–Arlington

Andrew P. Morriss, dean, School of Innovation; vice president, Entrepreneurship and Economic Development; and professor, The Bush School, Texas A&M University

Sean E. Mulholland, professor of economics, Western Carolina University

Randy T. Simmons, professor of political economy, Utah State University

Adam C. Smith, assistant professor of economics, Johnson & Wales University

Todd J. Zywicki, George Mason University Foundation Professor of Law, Antonin Scalia School of Law, George Mason University

INDEX

Page references for figures and tables are italicized. Page references with *n* and *nn* refer to note and notes.